THE WISE WOMEN COUNCIL

Uniting Hearts, Helping Hands, Igniting Hope

"Where no counsel is, the people fall: but in the multitude of counsellors there is safety." Proverbs 11:14

The Wise Women Council © Copyright September 11, 2021

Excerpts from *The Laborers Are Few* 2018
Used with permission of author, Barbara Taylor Sanders

ISBN: 9798498404387

Each chapter is a true account, but some names were changed to protect the privacy of my friends experiencing sensitive situations in life.

Cover featuring the **Peace** Statue
North of the Statehouse stands a winged female figure clad in flowing garments holding aloft the universal symbol of peace, an olive branch. This is the **Peace** statue. Erected just after the end of WWI, the monument was intended to honor those who serving in the Civil War.

The Women's Relief Corps, the auxiliary of the largest and most influential Civil War veterans organization, the Grand Army of the Republic (GAR), commissioned the statue from Bruce Wilder Saville, a faculty member at Ohio State University. The statue was unveiled in 1923, and honors those who served in war. Peace was also designed to recognize the contributions made by those folks left behind while they were away from home.

The inscription reads:

PEACE

Commemorating the heroic sacrifices of Ohio's Soldiers of the Civil War 1861 - 65 and

the loyal women of that period

Erected by the Woman's Relief Corps Department of Ohio in 1923

THE WISE WOMEN COUNCIL

Uniting Hearts, Helping Hands, Igniting Hope

"Where no counsel is, the people fall: but in the multitude of counsellors there is safety." Proverbs 11:14

We are older and wiser women refusing to fade into the woodwork. Instead, we are using our life experiences and valuable wisdom to create a better life for our offspring, as well as shining our Lights within community service agencies in great need of mentors and volunteers.

The word wisdom reflects someone who has experience, knowledge and good judgement. A wise woman is authentic; one who trusts her intuition by learning from past mistakes. She is dependent on God and honors the Lord in all daily affairs, especially concerning family.

Through Biblical principles, a wise woman is guided, instructed and open to learning new things. She works for the common good rather than self-interest or worldly gain. When times are difficult, she chooses the path of compassion and mercy rather than resentment. She seeks ways to serve others by giving generously without regret.

By utilizing treasured talents, practical skills, and offering wise counsel to build up those less fortunate, she is *"storing her treasures in heaven where neither moth nor rust destroys and where thieves do not break in and steal"* (Matthew 6:19-21).

After feeling compassion for the crowds who were harassed and helpless, Jesus compared them to sheep without a shepherd. He said to his disciples, *"The harvest is plentiful, but the laborers are few; therefore, pray earnestly to the Lord of the harvest to send out laborers into His harvest"* (Matthew 9:35-38).

Wise Women Council welcomes new participants to make a difference in every community across America. Weekly Bible studies with prayer meetings are encouraged, along with monthly luncheons to hear inspiring guest speakers promoting volunteerism.

We are a coalition of Christian women of worth, mature in the Lord, grounded in the Word, apt to teach, exhort and challenge younger women to grow and blossom by adhering to the principles of God.

The Wise Women Council is comprised of mature women, rich in faith towards God, favor with man and committed to prayer. Women concerned with the needs of others, reaching out to the poor and disadvantaged in united community effort. Their desire is to rescue the lost and dying, especially women trapped in sinful lifestyles such as drug and alcohol abuse, domestic violence and the adult entertainment industry.

The Wise Women Council is interested in supporting and bringing unity among other ministries such as local churches, faith-based non-profits and evangelistic outreach.

The Wise Women Council is a potential round table discussion of current affairs and concerns, especially atrocities being committed in the nations. (The New View)

The Wise Women Council is comprised of women leaders desiring significant social change, willing to sacrifice time to pray and research ways to implement peaceful solutions or recommendations for community problems, especially racial tensions.

The Wise Women Council remain up to date in current affairs, legislation and politics especially anything concerning pro-life and the loss of religious freedoms.

The Wise Women Council take joy in giving to charities supporting needy families in third world countries and those in our own urban communities. Special events, conferences and other worthwhile seminars will help champion the cause and establish The Wise Women Council as a powerful coalition to reckon with in this community.

Arise, shine, for your light has come, and the glory of the Lord rises upon you.
Isaiah 60:1

But when Jesus saw the multitudes, He was moved with compassion for them because they were weary and scattered like sheep having no shepherd. Then He said to His disciples, *The Harvest truly is plentiful, But the laborers are few.*

Therefore, pray the Lord of the harvest to send out laborers from His harvest.
Matthew 9:36-39 (NKJV)

Dedicated to eleven very anointed ladies who have inspired my heart by their faithful ministry to women in need. These mighty Christian warriors are the epitome of Wise Women expressing Godly Counsel from heavenly places.

Jacqueline Ayemperoumal, *New Creation Illumination Ministries*

Vernistine Lias, *Jesus House International Ministries*

Millie McCarty, *Light House Counseling Services, Center Point Life Planning*

Susan Ridley, *RAAH House of Recovery*

Christie Sawyer, *River Dwellers*

Tina L. (Smith) Young, *Redemption Doors Outreach*

Jennifer Tabora &
Kimberly Receveur *Two Girls & A Bible, Inc*

Jeannie Turner, *One Way Out*

Connie Weizel, *Living from the Life of Christ*

Cheryl Williams, *Fit for a King Mentoring Camp*

Table of Contents

Wise Women Council		Page 3
Introduction by WWC founder Barbara Taylor Sanders		Page 8
Practical Ways to Help the Poor	Chapter One	Page 11
Fear Hath Torment	Chapter Two	Page 15
Let Your Light Shine	Chapter Three	Page 25
The Poor You Will Have with You Always	Chapter Four	Page 29
True Warriors of Faith	Chapter Five	Page 33
Faith to Follow Where He Leads	Chapter Six	Page 37
Faith for Missionary Service	Chapter Seven	Page 43
Building Bridges Through Faith	Chapter Eight	Page 47
Life in the Inner-City	Chapter Nine	Page 51
Mentoring Spiritual Daughters Past Poverty	Chapter Ten	Page 59
Women Empowering Women	Chapter Eleven	Page 63
Faith Overcome Fear	Chapter Twelve	Page 67
The Mountain Man & The Mountain Mover	Chapter Thirteen	Page 75
Our Reason for Hope	Chapter Fourteen	Page 81
A Burglary Gone Right	Chapter Fifteen	Page 89
Miracle Fundraiser Connection	Chapter Sixteen	Page 93
Laborers Beware!	Chapter Seventeen	Page 99
Out of the Miry Clay	Chapter Eighteen	Page 103
Inner City Gangs	Chapter Nineteen	Page 109

Forsaking all to Follow Jesus	Chapter Twenty	Page 115
Foster Care for Families in Crisis	Chapter Twenty-One	Page 121
Faith is an Adventurous Journey	Chapter Twenty-Two	Page 127
Heavenly Songs of Deliverance	Chapter Twenty-Three	Page 135
The Fires of Revival are Still Burning	Chapter Twenty-Four	Page 139
The Power of Prayer	Chapter Twenty-Five	Page 147
Tolerance and True Hospitality	Chapter Twenty-Six	Page 153
In the Face of Death	Chapter Twenty-Seven	Page 159
Take Me to the Nations	Chapter Twenty-Nine	Page 163
Perfecting Godly Character	Chapter Thirty	Page 173
Faith is a Journey Forward	Chapter Thirty-0ne	Page 189
Discovering Your Motivations Gifts		Page 190
Harriet Beecher Stowe Legacy		Page 197
Special Exhortation from Barbara		Page 201
National Directory of Agencies		Page 203
About the author, Barbara Taylor Sanders		Page 211

Introduction

We humans are happiest when we find a cause to support and set out to change the world. Sometimes such lofty and noble notions lead to disappointing complications and frustrations, but, nonetheless, we were created to help others and live a self-sacrificing life.

"By this we know love, because He laid down His life for us. And we also ought to lay down our lives for the brethren. But whoever has this world's goods, and sees his brother in need, and shuts up his heart from him, how does the love of God abide in him? My little children, let us not love in word or in tongue, but indeed and in truth." 1 John 3:16-18 (NKJV).

Life doesn't seem fair when considering the immense human suffering in the world. I've often thought: *There go I, but by the grace of God.* Throughout my Christian journey and numerous mission trips abroad, I've been down many eye-opening paths. This rugged road has jarred my senses and challenged my faith because there is so much misery out there. Life really isn't fair. As a wife and mother, I can't imagine scrounging around for food to feed my family. Or not having access to running water.

Whenever I returned home from a mission trip to a third world country I'd feel guilty for several weeks. Each morning that I made my beautiful, solid-brass, king-size bed with its coordinated comforter and bed skirt, my life felt decadent compared to the meager living conditions I had just witnessed on a goodwill trip to an impoverished nation. I have learned to count my blessings.

Thankfully, our Bible believing churches reach out to help the homeless and usually support foreign missionaries. As Christians, most of us tithe and give additional offerings to help the poor and disadvantaged. Consequently, Christians are granted numerous opportunities to share the love of Jesus Christ by extending hands of mercy to those in need right within our own sphere of influence.

Within our own families and throughout our local communities there are countless men and women who struggle, suffer, and wonder where God is within their messed up lives. If we're able and willing, God will place needy people within our reach to help. We never have to hunt for trouble. Problems will usually show up just when we are feeling content and self-satisfied with life. Just when I have an extra chunk of change to put away in savings, God puts a struggling Christian with a financial need in my path. It never fails. God tests my heart through the purse strings. When I die I might not have a hefty bank account, but I'll have no regrets. Beginning in high school, I have spent my entire adult life helping others. My hospitable and generous parents were my early role models.

As an earthen vessel and in my own unique way, I've served and sacrificed by going the extra mile. It is rewarding to see others succeed by my life being laid down for the sake of Christ. Through His grace I've done my little part for the betterment of society, and by sharing some of my life-changing testimonies I now hope to inspire and challenge you to reach out and make a difference in the life of another. You can do it, too.

Get involved. Be ready to travel next door, downtown, or to the nations with the might of the Lord. Or within your sphere of influence, mentor a young man or young woman by reproducing your gift, whatever it might be, in the life of someone worth dying for. Yes, indeed – dying for. It is your death that God requires. Death-to-self. Death-to-fear. Death to that new pair of shoes you really don't need. On a daily basis develop a willingness to take up your cross to help those in need. Look around you. You won't have to wait long. If you are willing to reproduce your gifts and talents in the life of another, then get ready for the adventure of a lifetime. It will be God's doing. He will orchestrate your time, talents, temperament, and resources with the need of another through divine appointments and unusual circumstances. Just say yes. You'll be glad you did.

I'm convinced that so many don't get involved in mission outreach because of fear. My ability to be a light for Jesus Christ began with a profound deliverance. The power of love conquered a fearful and debilitating stranglehold in my life, which has enabled me to move forward with God. That dramatic deliverance gave me faith to conquer other spiritual snakes in my life as my journey with Christ continued. This book is my journey. As the Lord leads, may it inspire your own unique steps of faith.

This book covers every problem under the sun because we are a fallen generation in need of a Savior.

Throughout the pages you'll encounter stories about Christians who courageously reached out with the love of God.

You'll understand the importance of mentoring through the remarkable story of Ruth. You'll meet a 13-year-old Russian lad who came to America and later helped evangelize Russia through radio broadcasts without knowing he was actually being heard throughout a very dark nation. You'll encounter a successful young physician who took his wife and two youngsters to live in poverty to help evangelize a village in India. You'll come face-to-face with racism, domestic violence, inner-city gangs and the death of a drug lord. You'll understand the epidemic of sexual abuse and how one brave teacher cracked down on it by opening a Christ-centered mental health clinic for abuse victims. You'll hear the heart of a pastor who opened a community center but came face-to-face with the jealous older brother syndrome in his congregation. Two ladies who opened their hearts to foster children will inspire you. A former nurse who uses her hospital training for in home medically fragile babies addicted to crack cocaine will amaze you. You'll witness true miracles within a dedicated family that adopts discarded children with severe handicaps. You'll meet a single mother who was spared from death by the power of prayer.

Ultimately, you'll gain inspiration and insight into the lives of those who use their power of influence to impact a city, a nation and our world.

Barbara Taylor Sanders, B.A.
Author/Advocate/Artist
Cape Coral, Florida

Email: expressimagepublications@gmail.com
www.barbarataylorsanders.com

The true stories shared in this study guide are borrowed from my previously published book,
The Laborers Are Few

Chapter One

Practical Ways to Help the Poor

Helping the disadvantaged is a privilege. In the process, the beneficial life-lessons gained certainly outweigh any hardship endured. That might sound trite, but it's true. Christians have numerous opportunities to help because desperate needs surround us like the air we breathe. When the heart is ready, God sends someone with troubles your way. If it's a test of obedience, how will you score on Judgment Day?

Before attempting to share the Gospel of Jesus Christ with the poor and disadvantaged, it is important to study the culture. Our middle-class values often become hindrances to teach core principles to those with lower standards. To gain access to the hearts of those we are attempting to transform into the image of Christ, we must see this class of society as a "people group," just as a Christian missionary must respect foreign culture in other countries. Be prepared for exposure to different values and parenting styles. It is not up to you to point out problems or give unsolicited advice. Trust must be established before guidance will ever be received. Wise counsel should be given in small doses with love as the motivation to bring correction.

For the most part, the key to an effective outreach ministry is consistency and daily help. Obviously, one must be willing to meet the need of another on a practical level. Perhaps teaching one to read or tutoring a child struggling in math would be one way. Someone might need help composing a resume to find decent work. However, before you start organizing someone's cupboards or cleaning out a refrigerator, it is best to first establish an ongoing, stable relationship with that individual. Obviously, good hygiene and a clean house are vital to overall success, but addressing those issues would be too personal to point out in the early stages of your developing friendship. Be sensitive to the timing of everything. Respect, coupled with common sense, will aid you in your ministry. A person will appreciate you more if don't come on too strong.

We must always teach by example. Not on a classroom blackboard, but coming alongside someone in need. Successful guidance is accomplished by a close relationship with an attitude of respect for the person you're mentoring.

Change doesn't happen overnight. Be patient and allow the Holy Spirit to give you wisdom to speak correction before you open your mouth. Become a coach who challenges with inspirational words of *encouragement.* "A word aptly spoken is like apples of gold in settings of silver," (Proverbs 25:11). Good advice is usually accepted if a person is teachable. But, chances are, the reason a person is in a terrible situation is because of his or her unwise choices in life. Stubbornness originates from a stronghold of pride or refusing to admit mistakes. It is true that some of the best lessons in life are learned the "hard way." But, don't sit back and say, "I told you so." A person caught with mud on the face will usually come to that conclusion without someone rubbing it in. Love covers a multitude of sins, which include dumb mistakes as well. Keep in mind your own personal failures and the loving mercy the Lord granted you as a new Christian. Remain humble because we *all* have a hallmark hall of shame. No one should come off as a know-it-all or someone with all the answers.

The greatest challenge I've faced is motivating a new convert to read the Bible on a consistent basis. The Word of God is our greatest source of truth and strength. Many people who come up on the streets are survivors. They've had to tough it out and fend from themselves. Reliance on God is often viewed as weakness.

Of course, church attendance is vital. Building relationships with other Christians is a formula for success. So often a person receiving your help likes the special attention, but they might continue to associate with friends who drink or do drugs. Sooner or later the corruption will take back over if a person hasn't developed a strong support group of praying Christian friends. Allow some grace time because breaking away is very difficult, especially if these negative influences include siblings or close family members.

Unconditional love leads a person to godly sorrow and true repentance. A person will mature faster in the ways of Christ through after-church fellowship and by establishing strong Christian friendship with other believers. I can't stress that enough. A phone call the night before becomes a gentle nudge to help a person remember the importance of church attendance. Open your home to food and fellowship often. Loneliness leads to depression and self-medicating with drugs. Single moms especially, need fellowship the most. Invite those who cannot repay you as part of the mix of church people. Your loving hospitality will teach other women how to creatively serve guests as a cheerful giver.

Aiding the less fortunate will accomplish several things in your character. For one thing, you will also become incredibly grateful for the privileged life you enjoy in the suburbs. Generosity will deliver you from boredom, depression, self-pity, self-hatred, and criticalness. Best of all, your newfound joy will inspire missions of goodwill in others. Needless personal spending will halt if you sincerely desire extra money to give to the less fortunate.

However, getting involved with the poor and disadvantaged is daunting because fear stops most Christians in their tracks. Vain imaginations and lofty thoughts often hinder an attempt to fulfill Christ's command: "Religion that God our Father accepts as pure and faultless is this: to look after orphans and widows in their distress and to keep oneself from being polluted by the world." James 1:27 (NIV)

Trepidation prevents personal involvement because the underprivileged usually live in unsafe neighborhoods. Don't attempt any inner-city ministry without the prayer support of your spouse and/or your pastor. Best of all, find a prayer partner who shares your ideals. Together, you might start a support group or Bible study for single moms who need your encouragement and friendship.

Love is patient and kind. Love is not jealous or boastful or proud or rude. It does not demand its own way. It is not irritable, and it keeps no record of being wronged. It does not rejoice about injustice but rejoices whenever the truth wins out. Love never gives up, never loses faith, is always hopeful, and endures through every circumstance. 1 Corinthians 13:4-9 (New Living Translation)

Discussion Questions

1. What special abilities or skills do you possess that might be a useful tool to support a struggling family in your neighborhood or church family? Some ideas might be English or Math skills to tutor a student struggling in school. One church offers free "haircuts" to kids of single mothers. If you own a car, you might offer to take a single mother (without transportation) to a doctor's appointment or grocery shopping.

2. What prevents you from getting involved with those less fortunate?

3. Are you willing to pray about getting involved with those in need?

4. Have you ever wondered why you were not born into poverty?

5. If you were raised in a lower-income household, what things can you share about the needs of your family growing up?

Notes

Chapter Two

Fear Hath Torment

The terror of snakes passed on to me from my dad. At the impressionable age of eight I watched my frightened father use a shovel to hack up a harmless garden snake in a woodpile behind my grandfather's house. My fear led to a transfer of a demonic stronghold, which nearly passed onto my son two decades later.

After Grandma died at age 49, we moved in with Grandpa to help rear my mother's younger sisters, who are close in age to me. As a child, after a hard rain my aunts, Claire and Bonnie, often tormented me by dangling earthworms in my face because I screamed at the sight of anything that slithered. Whenever it stormed I waited several days before venturing outside.

Unfortunately, those fears carried over into my adult life. One summer day, on top of a stepladder, I was attempting to hang a tree swing near a sandbox for my three-year old son. Home from college, my stepdaughter, Tammie, stood by helping me as my son Bo, age three, watched us. As I flung the roped rubber-tire over the large tree branch I spotted a black snake slithering along at the base of the tree. Without a word I leaped off the ladder's top rung and raced into the house without screaming, because I didn't want to scare my son and pass on my terror of snakes to him. Once I got inside the house I shook from head to toe. Later that day, per my request, my husband took our little boy out to locate and handle the non-poisonous snake to make sure Bo wasn't afraid.

The next morning, I washed dishes at the kitchen window while Bo ate his cereal at the table. Outside, our big goofy Newfoundland dog was near Bo's play area and tree swing, frantically scratching at the railroad ties that boxed in the sand. Without thinking I said, "Oh, that dumb dog is digging for that snake hiding in the sandbox."

"Mommy, why don't you like snakes?"

Caught off guard, I hesitated before answering his innocent question. How would I explain "fear" to a three-year-old?

"Well," I began with halted words, "you see Mommy is a little bit afraid of snakes. But you shouldn't be afraid because snakes don't scare Daddy. He's strong and brave like you."

Bo looked at me and boldly stated, "Fear ye not."

What do you say to a three-year old quoting scripture? Busted. A year or so later, I would discover that my father had indeed, passed on his fear of snakes to his grandson through me.

The next year Tammie transferred from The Ohio State University to Oral Roberts University in Tulsa. Her leadership maturity quickly manifested while being recruited to step into the position of Spirit-Life Director of her dormitory floor, which entitled her to free tuition. In her newly appointed position Tammie got involved with intercessory prayer with other ORU team leaders. Every Friday night fellow student Myles Munroe taught the principles of prayer to a group of dedicated prayer warriors. Tammie often quoted profound "spiritual tidbits" from Myles, who is now an outstanding bestselling international author and Christian leader.

Our country home was located near a correctional institute for teenage criminals who were too young for women's prison. The first year we moved to our waterfront home, two incarcerated teens

They ended up in our yard, but we weren't home. Sue, my next-door neighbor, rescued the bleeding and near frozen girls, who had been badly cut up from climbing jagged rocks. While they warmed up under blankets and drank hot coffee, Sue secretly called the police. As a social worker, the Good Samaritan was not frightened in that precarious situation. A few days after the ordeal, Sue telephoned me to report the news.

"Boy, it was a good thing you weren't home last weekend." She gave me a blow-by-blow account of what had happened. I became spellbound listening to her. She said, "The girls in that prison are really dangerous. Most of them are in there for murder. They'd just as soon kill you as look at you." As a social worker, I considered Sue a voice of authority on those matters. Her words fortified my dread about that place.

One day when Tammie was home on spring break, she and I drove by the correctional institute. We were accustomed to praying out loud with each other, so it was not unusual for spontaneous prayers to be lifted up.

"Lord, send a missionary into that prison to be a light to those girls," I pompously prayed while traveling past the ominous gates.

Tammie glanced over at me. She challenged me by stating, "Myles Munroe says, 'Unless you're willing to be that missionary, don't ask God to send someone else.'"

I felt convicted to the core of my being, but my cheeks flushed at the thought of going inside those prison walls. It seemed like such a dangerous place, shrouded with mystery, because whenever I drove by I never saw a single soul outside of the dormitory style cottages.

A few months after my enlightenment by Myles Munroe, our local newspaper featured a picture of a volunteer who taught sewing to some of the girls inside those prison gates. I studied the photograph intently. It was my first glimpse into the obscurity surrounding that state correctional institute. The smiling faces of the teenagers melted my heart. It caused me to realize that this institution was filled with eager young girls in need of mother figures to teach them basic homemaking skills. The Lord pulled on my heartstrings to get involved. The following week, I had an appointment with Karen, the Volunteer Coordinator.

On the morning of my late afternoon appointment with Karen, I took my son, now five, for a haircut in town. Next door to the barbershop was a pet store. I always took Bo inside to visit the puppies. I also made sure Bo viewed the reptile aquariums, while I secretly glanced in the opposite direction. That day, I noticed Bo rushed by the tanks, so we returned home without him looking at the reptiles.

My son loved to play Superman in the bright red and blue costume my mother had made for his fifth birthday. He told all his buddies in kindergarten, "Oh, my grandma will make you a Superman outfit, too." However, that day my darling little boy was decked out in a cowboy hat, boots, and holster with a gun. He was outside climbing on a dwarf size tree and the Lord spoke to my heart with this thought: *Take him with you tonight.*

My first thought was fear-based: *Oh, maybe he'll fall from a tree if I don't take him with me.* My stepson, Scott, age 19, worked a summer job while home from college, so I had a built-in babysitter arriving later. A presumptuous thought invaded my head: *Oh, this cute little cowboy is going to help the girls warm up to me.* However, both notions were false. The Lord had something profound planned for me, which forever changed my life.

My husband Daryl had traveled out of town on business, so, I fixed something kid-friendly to consume before my 7:00 p.m. appointment with the volunteer coordinator. While standing in the kitchen preparing food, I heard the front door slowly creak open. Seconds later, Bo appeared in the kitchen doorway. It was such an odd entry because Bo always barged through the door as a typical kid. It caused me to glance in his direction. His little face had become blanched with fear.

"Mommy, there is a *snake* outside in the grass."

"Oh, that's nice." I tried to sound nonchalant. "What's the snake's name? Did you talk to him?" I attempted to be cool, calm, and collected even though my knees felt like Jell-O.

"Oh no, Mommy. I *hate* snakes. I'm afraid of them," declared my son with a quivering voice.

My heart sank. Stark fear permeated the room like the smell of sulfur. In plain view stood the crippling fear that had paralyzed me all of my life. It was the same uncontrollable fear that kept me from flower gardening, camping, or strolling in a wooded park. I knew this identical fear would forever thwart my son, who loved playing army out in the woods with his little neighborhood buddy, Michael.

Oh, if only Daryl was home. He could march him right back out there to nip this thing in the bud, I thought, trying to think of another solution.

I lifted Bo into my arms and plunked him down on the kitchen counter to look him squarely in the face.

"Now Bo, look at Mommy. You are *not afraid* of snakes," I affirmed. "You and Daddy have picked up garden snakes before. So, you are *NOT afraid* of snakes!" I also pointed out that my little niece Bethany was terrified of our dog and used that example of irrational fear.

Bo kept declaring his fear and the more we argued, the more it reinforced the stronghold. This futile discussion continued several more minutes and neither side budged.

Exasperated, I said, "Okay, but will you pray with Mommy? If I pray about being afraid of snakes, will you pray with me, too?"

My sweet little boy nodded in agreement. For the first time I prayed about being delivered from a lifelong fear of snakes. When I ended the prayer, I started crying and so did Bo. I tenderly held him to my chest as we wept. Little did I know that within an hour, that prayer of deliverance would be put to the test with a 12-foot long boa constrictor. God doesn't mess around.

In his cowboy attire, Bo accompanied me to my appointment with Karen, a large, jolly woman who loved to talk. Her lively personality helped dissolve my apprehensions about becoming involved. But best of all, Karen had deep faith as a born-again Christian. Soon Bo grew weary of us yakking and fell asleep on her office sofa. Karen sat behind her desk in front of a large window with a partial view of the campus. A large group of girls were gathering outside so I jumped up to get a better look at them. Aside from the newspaper
photograph, it was my first real glimpse of the young women.

"What are so many girls doing outside?"

"Oh, Jack Hanna is out there with some exotic animals from the Columbus Zoo. Jungle Jack comes here often to put on shows for the girls."

I leaned into the window to see Jack Hanna holding a humongous *snake*.

"Oh, my gosh! Can my son go out there to watch? We just had a big discussion about him thinking he was afraid of snakes. I think this is an answer to prayer!" I fully intended to stay inside.

I gently awakened Bo with news of Jungle Jack Hanna outside. My little boy was delighted at the opportunity to see him and the zoo animals. However, he was not about to go out there among about fifty girls without tightly gripping my hand. Karen happily ushered us outside. I put up a brave front, but kept a very safe distance from the snake handler. In fact, I kept my eyes glued on the snake just in case it got loose. After running away, one hysterical girl was being dragged back by a large security officer and I thought: *You poor child, I completely share your sentiments about being forced to be that close to a snake.* Her screams caused me to slide up on the hood of a nearby-parked car so my feet didn't touch the ground.

Following the demonstration, Mr. Jack Hanna balled up the Boa constrictor to fit it into a large, white knapsack. He pulled the rope closed before placing the sack down on the grass.

He announced, "For any of you who want to touch the snake, I'll bring him out later." My eyes remained fixated on the bulging knapsack all the while Jack produced other exotic animals to wow the students and my son.

Moments later, Karen took Bo and me on a tour of the large campus overlooking the Scioto River. She pointed out large buildings that were landmarks from the mid-nineteenth century when a therapeutic Sulphur Spa thrived in the idyllic Scioto River Valley of Delaware County. It was a lovely setting covering hundreds of wooded acres.

As we rounded back toward her office, the crowd of students had narrowed to about three girls standing close to Jack Hanna and *the snake*.

"Hey! Look, Mom! Let's go touch the snake!" With excitement, Bo darted ahead of me. The emotional chains around my ankles made moving forward feel as if I was pulling a freight train.

Later, Karen chuckled when she said to me, "Your face turned completely green."

Jack had the boa constrictor stretched across his shoulders and the snake's belly was wrapped around his back and across his chest. Jack held the head of the snake over his right shoulder. As Karen and I approached, my eyes met the eyes of the snake. Standing about six feet away, I was completely mesmerized. As if mocking me, our eyes locked as his tongue flickered out at me.

"Okay, Mom, I just touched the snake. Now it's *your turn* to touch him."

Fear hath torment, but perfect love casts out fear.

It was a defining moment in my life. My feet felt like they were wedged in cement. I was stuck. My unconditional love for my son gave me supernatural courage to touch that snake. I knew I had to do it. I walked in front of Jack to contemplate touching the belly of this monster. A grace from God rose up within me to give me courage I have never known before. I slowly inched forward toward the snake. With one finger, I hesitantly extended my hand toward the smooth, light colored belly. I quickly touched it, as if testing a red-hot iron. But the second time, I boldly placed my entire hand on the belly of that mammoth snake and I held it there for a moment to conquer a Majar stronghold in my life. Considering my deathly fear of snakes, this became one of the greatest triumphs in my walk with Christ.

Afterward, I walked around to face the snake again. This time I stood triumphantly within one foot from its mocking eyes and flickering tongue. The Lord spoke to my inner spirit: *Now that you have conquered your physical fear of snakes, I am going to take you into this spiritual snake pit. You will never be afraid of anything that comes at you because I will be with you every step of the way.*

Karen welcomed me on as a new volunteer. The following years were some of the most exiting days of ministry I have ever experienced. I started out teaching calligraphy to a small class of interested teens. By listening to their tragic stories, I had many opportunities to pray and weep with them as I earned their trust.

Since this correctional facility was also a school, in one building there were two, side-by-side kitchenettes set up for home economic classes. I also taught cooking a few times a week to countless girls in various classroom settings.

One evening, one of my 13-year-old students was missing so I called the cottage attendant. I was informed that Takeesha was in a straightjacket because of a suicide attempt earlier that day. The officer informed me that Takeesha had fought with her cousin, another student in my class. I asked if Takeesha could come to class anyway. She was released and I purposely put Takeesha and her cousin together in the same kitchen to make Rice Krispy treats. During a fifteen-minute break I privately ministered to Takeesha about the power of forgiveness. She knew her Bible because she said, "I know Jesus said to forgive seventy times seven in one day." We prayed and she forgave her cousin. After the girls returned to their cottage the correctional officer called me.

"What did you do to this girl?" asked the same cottage officer. "Takeesha had been depressed all day. Yesterday, she tried to hang herself with her bra from a rafter in the ceiling. She was in a straightjacket when you called for her. Takeesha returned from your class smiling, and I hear her talking and laughing with her cousin right now."

Most of the girls came from destructive home situations: physical and sexual abuse, domestic violence, alcoholism, and rampant drug use. I expressed compassion and always spoke to them about the love of Jesus. I taught them catchy scripture songs so they could get the Word of God within their hearts. Many of them had never been to church or ever heard of the *Ten Commandments*. I had the privilege of leading many tender hearts to the Lord. I also opened my home, along with my heart and so did my entire family.

Many of the girls asked to go to church with me. I was granted permission to pick them up on Sunday morning and escort them to service with our family. With permission from Karen, we water baptized countless young women in our swimming pool throughout the summer months. Whenever four or five teenage girls came for dinner, I put out my best china and stemware to treat them with dignity and honor. And yes, it was true that many of them had committed murder in the second or third degree while strung out on drugs. Away from the corruptive influences and off of drugs, these girls were typical teenagers. My heart went out to them.

Soon I recruited my prayer partner, Shar Joyner, and together we converted a vacant storage room on campus into a volunteer center. This two-room facility had a kitchenette and a large living room. From our own personal resources and generous friends in business, we put together a large room with new carpeting, a sectional, custom draperies, fresh paint, and a stereo to play praise music. Within a few weeks the new volunteer center resembled a suite at the Hyatt! It was beautiful. Soon other church organizations began conducting Bible studies with the troubled teens there, too.

Throughout those few years, I led hundreds of incarcerated young women in singing praise choruses from my printed music sheets filled with scripture songs. When the girls showed up for Bible study, about fifteen at a time, there would be one or two girls who were stern and attempted to snarl at me. They were defiant. At first, they wouldn't join in the singing, but they'd show up the following week. Their hard demeanor would often make me want to avoid them. However, the Lord showed me that they were the ones who were the most desperate for His love. I'd go out of my way to extend kindness, even though they would glare at me. Within weeks, these same toughies were calling out requests of their favorite songs. When these tough nuts finally surrendered, their faith was genuine. Hearts were melted because God was in our midst. Shar provided hot cider, frosted cupcakes, and very big motherly hugs.

By recruiting local bands every few months, Shar organized Christian rock concerts in the large auditorium with the help of other Christian volunteers. Even though I couldn't hear the lyrics through the blaring rock music, many girls responded to the message and received Jesus Christ as their personal savior.

In addition, faithful Shar arrived early every Sunday morning to pick up about 10 or 12 teens for church. In her 15-passenger Chevy van, Shar drove the girls back to her large home for breakfast. They were treated to a closet filled with outfits and high heels of every size to dress up for church. More than anything, these lonely girls were seeking love and attention from a mother figure. Following church service, Shar brought them back to her home for Sunday supper. Shar was a dedicated soldier. She had been a victim of abuse and was no longer married. She operated a "safe home" for domestic violence victims. She is one of my true heroes in the faith, and she has been deeply missed since Shar went home to be with the Lord. Last year her daughter-in-law called me with the sad news that Shar had passed away peacefully in her sleep while visiting her only son and grandchildren. I cried for months mourning her death. She was a true champion for Jesus.

During that time period at the correctional institute, one bright 16-year old named Michelle, came to live with our family as a ward of the courts. We agreed to take Michelle to "90 Alcoholics Anonymous meetings in 90-days." Many times, Daryl accompanied Michelle to an AA meeting when I was unable to drive her into the city. As a recovering alcoholic, Michelle kept us on our toes at all times. We adored her, but she was a handful. We paid for her to attend a private Christian school with our son, Bo, so she could finish high school. She lived with us for almost two years and is still considered one of my true daughters. Through meeting me, her brother John received Jesus Christ as his savior. John went through the *Teen Challenge* rehabilitation program, and Dr. John is now a licensed psychologist at a Christian counseling center. You never know what the big picture is when God asks you to go where "angels fear to tread."

Today, Michelle is back in my life after many decades of wondering where she was and if she was okay. Of course, I prayed for her whenever the Lord brought her to mind and I stayed in contact with her mother for any possible updates. This year, Michelle surfaced after going through a Christian rehab center. Praise the Lord, she has been living a clean and sober productive life. We talk nearly every day and I am thankful the Lord protected her through every storm.

If I had been too fearful to move forward there would not have been a harvest of souls entering the Kingdom of God. Fear keeps us from moving mountains. Fear is a great enemy of faith. Conquer your snakes. Take a step of faith and see where the Lord leads you. God will never lead you unless you're willing to go.

There is no fear in love; but perfect love casts out fear, because fear involves torment. But he who fears has not been made perfect in love. 1John 4:18 (New King James Version)

When the Son of Man comes in His glory, and all the angels with Him, He will sit on His throne in heavenly glory. All the nations will be gathered before Him, and He will separate the people one from another as a shepherd separates the sheep from the goats. He will put the sheep on His right and the goats on His left. Then the King will say to those on His right, 'Come, you who are blessed by My Father; take your inheritance, the kingdom prepared for you since the creation of the world. For I was hungry and you gave Me something to eat, I was thirsty and you gave Me something to drink, I was a stranger and you invited Me in, I needed clothes and you clothed Me, I was sick and you looked after Me, I was in prison and you came to visit Me.'

Then the righteous will answer Him, 'Lord, when did we see You hungry and feed You, or thirsty and give You something to drink? When did we see You a stranger and invite You in, or needing clothes and clothe You? When did we see You sick or in prison and go to visit You?'

The King will reply, 'I tell you the truth, whatever you did for one of the least of these brothers of Mine, you did for Me.' Matthew 25:31-40 (NIV)

Go ye therefore, and teach all nations, baptizing them in the name of the Father, and of the Son, and of the Holy Ghost. Matthew 28:19 (KJV)

Discussion Questions

1. How do you personally define fear?

2. Has conscious or unconscious fear prevented you from doing something for the Lord?

3. How does a person overcome fear?

4. Do consider that irrational fear is a spirit?

5. Have you ever considered becoming part of a prison ministry? What about visiting a youth home with troubled teenagers?

Notes

Chapter Three

Let Your Light Shine

As soon as "Jimmy" hit the entryway, his booming voice began to resonate throughout the crowded AA meeting. He was decked out in a colorful rhinestone studded jacket wearing cowboy boots. He had a drawl and the charisma of Elvis in the early days of his music career. He greeted every fellow Alcoholics Anonymous member with a handshake and a burning question. "Hi, I'm Jimmy," he said in a fast talking, friendly manner. "Have you found it yet?" I was startled by this question, so I turned around in my seat to observe "Jimmy" weave his way in and out among the long tables to shake hands with at least 30 more people. He certainly had my attention.

Within a church congregation, I'd describe someone like Jimmy as a flaming evangelist. We certainly need more Jimmy's in the world. They make you feel welcome and seem genuinely glad to see you as you grace the door of church each Sunday morning. An evangelist also preaches the Word of God and cares about people's salvation. With outgoing personalities, they are natural born soul winners.

However, we weren't at church. It was a smoke-filled church basement where most AA meetings are held throughout every city in America. That night twenty-seven years ago most of the members were smoking cigarettes and drinking coffee from Styrofoam cups. It wasn't a church service and Jimmy sounded beleaguered. He was talking so fast and moving so quickly from person to person, that if you weren't paying attention, you would have missed what he said in passing.

As he reached across tables to shake hands, I heard him say, "I've been in this program for 3 ½ years and I haven't found it yet. Have you found it?" He kept moving through the crowd. "Hey, how ya doing? I'm Jimmy, glad to see you tonight. I'm going to commit suicide if I don't find it. Hey, I'm Jimmy, how are you?"

It seemed as if no one was paying attention to Jimmy. But I heard every word out of his mouth, and I knew God was up to something that evening.

Jimmy was seeking significance. He hadn't found "it" through the completion of a 12-step recovery program. Don't get me wrong. I certainly don't minimize the worth of AA because millions of alcoholics have successfully embraced sobriety through this fine program. Thankfully, in AA the "higher power" most people turn to for strength is our Lord Jesus Christ. But unfortunately, "it" can also be a banana or a radiator if that's what helps a struggling alcoholic through to the next step of this 12-step program. In other words, your personal "higher power" can be anything you need it to be as long as it works for you.

That evening I had accompanied two seventeen-year-olds, Christine and Michelle, who both had just completed a thirty-day stint in rehab. They became friends in the treatment center. Michelle was our foster child, and I'd made a commitment with her counselor to take her to "Ninety AA meetings in Ninety days." So, there I was, decked out in a fancy blue silk dress, my hair perfectly coiffed, wearing full make-up. After an earlier professional photo shoot for a family Christmas portrait, I was racing for time to squeeze in another nightly AA meeting with Michelle. I looked completely out of place for an AA meeting. I had forgotten to bring a change of casual clothing.

The only vacant seat was directly across from the three of us. Before Jimmy plunked down he reached across to shake the hands of Christine and Michelle. "Hey, have you found it?" The teenagers were bug-eyed and shrugged their shoulders at his bizarre question.

Jimmy glanced in my direction and did a double take. He was seated by the time he asked me, "Hi, have you found it?"

"Yes, I've found it," I said, smiling brightly. Leaning in his direction I began singing a happy tune, "His Name is Jesus . . . Jesus . . ."

At first, he probably thought I was joking because he snorted, "Oh, well not. . ." But he became instantly somber as he observed the sincerity in my eyes.

Without missing a beat, I said, "Jimmy, what you're looking for is going to require just one thing."

"What's that?" He seemed startled by my straightforwardness but genuinely interested in what I had to say to him.

"Your *death*," I said with calm assurance. "You need to *die* to Jimmy. You need to die to self. You must get off the throne and allow the Lord Jesus Christ take His rightful place in your heart. He needs to be the Lord and Master of your life. Jesus is *IT*. He's what you've been looking for all your life."

Tears welled up in his eyes. I'd struck an emotional chord because his casual comment about killing himself was no idle threat. He was longing for a spiritual connection with the Lord. Sadly, Jimmy represents the entire world of seekers. There are millions of love-starved people looking for "it." They usually seek *it* through shopping, gambling, eating, working too hard, drinking, or with drugs and free sex. Those substitutes will never produce true spiritual and emotional peace and contentment. All the money, power, and fame in the world will not fill the God-hole in every person's heart. Every month another famous Hollywood star dies of an overdose of drugs. It's just the tip of the iceberg. There is an epidemic of drug induced suicides and accidental deaths by nameless, faceless people who die without any fanfare or notoriety. But God knows every one of them by name.

We are losing our children to AIDS and STDs because premarital sex is a lure like drugs. Families are torn apart through divorce. I don't need to preview the mess our world is in.

That evening, after planting those seeds in Jimmy's heart, the AA meeting started up. Therefore, I couldn't continue my conversation with Jimmy. I had planted a kernel of truth in his spirit. His inner man was seeking a connection with God. I felt him observing me throughout the meeting. He witnessed the Light of Christ in me because there was genuine awe in his face. He looked at me as if I was Mother Theresa, and I appreciate that kind of admiration. Who wouldn't? All glory goes to the Lord Jesus Christ for the joy within my soul that others see.

I'm satisfied that had Jimmy finally discovered someone who found *it*. I never saw him again in the countless AA meetings I attended with Michelle. However, I found myself praying for his salvation until the Lord released me of the burden. My confidence is in the Lord. My delight is in Him because Jesus orchestrates divine appointments like the one I had with Jimmy that night. The Lord knows who is seeking Him. He allows our lights to shine for those who are sincerely endeavoring to know the one and only living God. The laborers are few.

Discussion Questions

1. Are you alert to those who are suicidal because of being hopeless?

2. Do you know how to help someone who might be suicidal?

3. Have you ever had thoughts of suicide?

4. Do you find comfort in the scriptures whenever you feel melancholy or "blue?"

Notes

Chapter Four

The Poor You Will Always Have with You

My ninety-two-old mother survived The Great Depression. My eyes widened when I learned that my grandparents, my mother, and her siblings were once recipients of a food basket at Christmas time. For a moment I felt the shame they must have felt being that poor.

I grew up in a working-class home on the fringe of upper crust in an affluent high school. I fit in because my friends adored me. This unconditional acceptance gave me confidence in myself. God gives everyone gifts and talents to use for His glory or for our own selfish gain. We have a free will. Throughout my life I continued using my outgoing personality, gifts and talents to inspire others, just as I did in high school. Developing a God-centered sphere of influence empowers women to change society for the better.

While visiting Sigrid, my dear childhood chum, in San Francisco not long ago, she shared a story during dinner with our husbands. I never classified myself in these terms, but my highly intelligent and analytical pal commented, "Barbara was a popular member of the 'A' crowd in high school." Laughing, she added, "And I was among the 'C' crowd." She explained that during study hall I had befriended a girl from the wrong side of the tracks and invited Patty to a pajama party in my home. Sigrid said, "Barbara told all of us, 'now this girl is different, but if you're not nice to Patty you won't be my friend anymore.'" That long forgotten story jarred my memory because I also remember giving Patty some better outfits from my closet to give her some dignity. I worked on weekends to earn money for those clothes, so they were mine to give away. My regard for the less fortunate has not changed, and as a Christian, I continue to reach out to the poor and disadvantaged whenever possible.

Jesus said, *"The poor you will always have with you,"* Mathew 26:11. Our Lord challenged believers not to ignore the poor, but to do something about their plight of poverty.

According to the dictionary, poverty is defined as *"hardship, distress, destitution and an overall state of neediness."* Poverty in an individual's life can be temporary or last a lifetime.

Poverty can also become a cycle affecting the offspring of families from generation after generation for centuries. Perhaps this is why the condition of poverty is sometimes thought of as a curse or disease. Consequently, sociologists and medical doctors have never found an actual cure for poverty. Great debate rages on because poverty is so complex and deeply rooted.

Today, our government and many non-profit organizations wage the battle against poverty because thousands of American children go to bed hungry, but that's not the only reason our government is concerned.

Poverty affects our overall society because crime rates are highest in impoverished communities. Poverty costs society in the long run because our taxes have to pay for government protection through the police force and undercover drug enforcement.

Unfortunately, poverty has many faces. Most of them are ugly and cause shame in those who are trapped in the cycle of poverty. Some, most likely, will place blame on those who struggle in an impoverished existence. It is easy to spout, "Why don't they just get a job?" Poverty is often equated with laziness, lack of motivation, or an unwillingness to prepare for a rainy day. But often drug addiction, alcoholism, and mental illness go hand in hand with poverty. Often, the breadwinner of a family, male or female, is unable to sustain a job due to these emotional problems, which then contributes to a cycle of ongoing need.

Poverty can remain a state of mind if that's all you've known. I once heard a single mother on welfare say, "Well, thank goodness, my children don't know we're poor. This is all they've known." However, once kids arrive in public school there are other children who aren't destitute and the picture changes quickly.

On the other hand, children raised in poverty are sometimes motivated to do better in school to escape the shameful effects of poverty. Nevertheless, the darkness of poverty can maim or handicap those from the slums because it causes people to feel hopeless. Without hope, it is impossible to see the light or a way out. Poverty is a prison without bars. Most people are rescued rather than escape on their own. Successful individuals who managed to escape poverty usually had a schoolteacher or other mentor who recognized their gifts and encouraged them to work hard to break out of the cycle. Sometimes it might be a parent or grandparent who spurs them on to make a better life.

The federal government offers countless programs to help the poor and disadvantaged in this country. These federally funded, direct-service agencies are set up to screen and actually qualify those who are in need. People who do not benefit from these programs might not have the documents necessary to prove their need. Someone living in a cardboard box under a bridge isn't likely to be carrying around a certified birth certificate, social security card, or proof of address.

Obviously, there is a lot of red tape to go through, but in the end, it can be life-saving. When a person ends up living in a tent or in their car it is because they have not accessed the help available for low-income housing, food stamps, and public assistance to help with utilities. Emergency shelters provide a bed and food on a short-term basis. Most shelters will help guide an individual to receive government assistance. Food pantries are also another way to receive food when food stamps run out. Sometimes a person has too much pride to accept a handout, but hunger is usually the motivating factor to seek assistance from the government or other resources.

Poverty is a grim stronghold. It is thought to be a spiritual condition of the soul. Many believe that poor people, with their countless problems, have a demonic curse over them. Through the Blood of Christ, every stronghold can only be broken through prayer. Countless people who have been delivered from the curse of poverty attribute the church or organizations like Alcoholics Anonymous for their deliverance. It is hard to argue with such life-changing testimonies. Jesus Christ has always been the cure, but not everyone in the poor house has embraced the Cross for deliverance.

Our government offers federally funded drug and alcohol recovery programs for addicts. There is aid for individuals on most levels of socioeconomic need. There are educational programs to help people obtain G.E.D.s and attend college or trade schools.

Poverty is a perpetual state of ignorance and a lack of education. However, you can be college educated, and still be poor, if alcoholism or any another mental or physical disease exists. This tentacle of poverty sucks energy. It robs people of their potential to succeed in life. Unfortunately, it takes money and the wherewithal to become educated or hospitalized.

Perhaps it is best to say that poverty, mental illness, and addictions go hand-in-hand, especially in urban cities where prostitution and drug or alcohol dependence is rampant. It is a vicious cycle that *can* be broken but it takes courage and a willingness to fight. However, most disadvantaged people are so beaten down that there is no stamina left for them to wage the war or win the battle against the decay of poverty. This is why most people need to be rescued by a dedicated mentor or a Good Samaritan who is willing to walk side-by-side with a poverty stricken individual until they can stand on their own two feet.

Unfortunately, the war on poverty continues. So far, no cure has been discovered. Our powerful government has helped combat poverty and so has the powerful church. But in the end, an individual has to make a choice to change. A person can escape poverty, but it is an act of their will. Willpower is something that cannot be harnessed or controlled by government agencies or religion, which is why the poor will always be with us.

I am certainly not defending anyone who has used or abused the system. Many Christians hesitate to get involved with the poor and disadvantaged because there is so much manipulation and corruption going on in our welfare system. It is not our place to judge or withhold love and mercy. My attitude has always been *"there go I but for the grace of God."*

In the parable of the Ten Virgins, five brides were lackadaisical in their attitude. However, five brides were considered wise by keeping their lamps filled with oil. Taking positive measures proved their expectancy. They were certainly filled with hope for the future. Our sphere of influence is developed by preparation, discipline, faith, attitude and vision for a brighter future with the help of God.

Throughout my years as a Christian, I've humbly used my socio-economic status to help those less fortunate. It's been my personal quest to motivate women and men to improve their lifestyles by attending church and accepting Jesus Christ as Savior.

It's also been my quest to challenge women to use their resources and time to make a difference in society. American women have so many advantages, so we are in a position of influence, regardless of income. Compared to other nations, we are among the richest women in the world. In terms of volunteer time in the community or with church membership, God commands us to not bury our talents. Everyone has at least one unique gift to multiply in the life of another. You'll discover that it's very fulfilling to strengthen the life of another human being of lesser ability or means.

Discussion Questions

1. Have you ever gone to bed hungry as a child? As an adult?

2. Do you know where emergency food pantries are located in your community?

3. Have you ever taken groceries or pre-pared food to a struggling single mom with kids?

Chapter Five

True Warriors of the Faith

Throughout my life I've been privileged to meet true warriors of the Christian faith. My long-time friend, Millie McCarty, is one of my heroes. She is a courageous Christian comrade who has learned to contend for the anointing like it's a matter of life and death because the devil is out to rob, kill, and destroy lives.

Millie is widely known in Ohio as a counselor and teacher, the founder and executive director of the first Christian counseling center in Central Ohio. Following the death of her husband, Millie retired at the age of 70 to write and teach. During that time, she became ordained as a pastor and served as pastor of a small Methodist church.

As a result of child sexual abuse in her own family, God used Millie's compassionate heart to search the depths of His word and to return to school to learn all she could to help and heal those suffering from childhood sexual trauma. Millie's forty plus years of service include ten years serving as a director of Christian education in a Presbyterian church, training and leadership in the field of human relations and group development, and her extensive training in prayer and service as an intercessor, as well as twenty years as a professional counselor – all of those years using her gift as teacher to instruct others.

Millie reports that in her master's program, she was advised that people with Dissociative Identity Disorder (formerly called Multiple Personality Disorder) were rare, so rare, that she may only encounter such a diagnosis once. To her amazement, God seemed to send dozens of women to her with this disorder as well as many mental and emotional and relational disorders that were rooted in sexual and physical abuse as well as satanic ritual abuse. Eventually other professional counselors referred their "difficult" clients to her. Her twenty years of counseling these clients laid the groundwork for her expertise in the areas of childhood sexual abuse, ritual abuse, and Dissociative Identity Disorder.

Her book, *Pathways to Hope and Healing*, has already ignited a torch that has been passed on to countless individuals who came under her training throughout the years. She founded

Lighthouse Christian Counseling in 1981 where for twenty years she ministered healing through prayer and biblical principles and professional wisdom to countless men and women who were victims of abuse. They experienced emotional and spiritual healing based on Christian principles

About twenty-five years ago, I invited Millie to speak at our church luncheon for the Bible study ladies. It was part of our monthly gatherings held at the Clintonville Woman's Club. It was a lovely, upper crust facility and we loved dressing up for the affair. I had heard Millie teach at a conference and felt our ladies should be "sitting at her feet to learn from this great lady of faith."

As the pastor's wife, that day I came to the luncheon hall early to greet our guest speaker and conduct pre-prayer with her and the planning-committee ladies. Millie came in, as scheduled, loaded down with a box full of handouts. Ever the teacher, she came equipped to inspire our ladies to higher ground. I greeted her with a hug and nervously asked what her topic was.

Earlier that year when I called Millie to book the engagement, I instructed her to ask the Lord what to teach our ladies. I didn't need to tell her that because she is a woman of prayer, so I gave her full liberty to teach whatever she wanted. When I called her a few weeks later to finalize the luncheon agenda, I asked her what the Lord put on her heart to "teach" our ladies. She said, "I'm going to present how the Lord can heal childhood sexual abuse."

"Oh, you don't have to do that topic …teach whatever you want," I responded with a knee-jerk reaction. "You have the freedom to change it." I was fearful that our ladies would recoil at such an icky topic for a formal luncheon.

"Well, Barbara, don't worry about having this topic presented. Statistics have proven that one out of four women have been victims of this kind of abuse. It's a national epidemic, and the church shouldn't close the door to those who need healing."

I hung up the phone secretly wishing Millie would change her mind. When she arrived for the luncheon that day, my heart lit up when I saw her carrying in a box of handouts. I thought she was going to do a safe 10-point teaching from the Bible. I was wrong. I reluctantly helped distribute the colorful pages of Bible-based information on sexual abuse at each of the linen-covered tables set up for about fifty women. Our church was located on the part of town of what would be considered the "higher echelons of society," so I didn't think this topic was a prevalent issue among wives of successful business men, attorneys, doctors, or airline pilots.

Millie's profound message turned out to be life changing for all of us. In addition, one out four women represented there that day had been sexually abused. It was also an eye-opener for those fortunate women who weren't affected by childhood sexual abuse. But sadly, it's in every family, so each of has encountered a victim along life's way. Millie's compassion for this problem in society made everyone feel the same sympathy. After her life-changing message, as Millie prayed, a holy hush fell upon the room as thirteen tearful women solemnly lined up for personal prayer from her. I actually felt the heavens open to these brave souls who were willing to admit they had been victims. The "one in four" ratio was correct, and I am forever grateful for the realization that this problem crosses all social and economic barriers.

Perhaps you are a victim and don't know where to turn for healing. I highly recommend Millie's book, *Pathways to Hope and Healing* as part of your recovery. Millie would be the first one to recommend you find a Christian counselor – a dedicated counselor who is trained in clinical and biblical principles of inner healing.

At the age of 47, Millie graduated Cum Laude from Defiance College, earning her B.A. degree in religious education. She went on to receive her M.A. degree in guidance and counseling from The Ohio State University in 1981, and became a licensed professional counselor in 1985. She returned to Ashland Seminary in 1992 to receive her Clinical Counselor endorsement. Millie is an avid learner, and has never stopped pursuing knowledge and wisdom regarding her life and the lives of those she helps. She has used her education to free others from the bondages of extreme trauma and as a result of her experience and research in the area of trauma, has developed a curriculum for survivors and those who work with survivors of trauma called *Why We Can't Just Get Over It: The Lasting effect of prolonged stress and trauma on our lives.* She is currently working with one of her most traumatized individuals to write a case study that will be used in conjunction with the trauma course. It is entitled RUTH, taken from the biblical story of Ruth and Naomi in the Bible.

Millie's training class is an excellent training tool for caregivers, agencies, professional counselors and social workers, chaplains, and pastors whose "high maintenance" patients, clientele, or parishioners are usually victims of abuse and trauma.

Since Millie is no longer doing private counseling, I asked her to recommend a counselor for a young friend who has been suffering from the emotional stress of childhood trauma. Without hesitation Millie pointed me to Renee Collon, a licensed therapist who operates Hope Counseling Services near Columbus.

For this chapter, I asked Renee to give me some thoughts about Millie. She said, "When I worked with Millie I was impressed with her ability to be *both* compassionate and clinical. She had an uncanny knack of combining her textbook training with God's heart for the women He brought before her. There was such tenderness in Millie with the utmost respect for her clients. She recognized the depth of wounding and its impact on them, but never failed to convey an eternal optimism and hope for recovery."

Renee aptly summed up the ideal therapist when she described Millie McCarty. Seek these character traits when you attempt to find help for yourself or a loved one.

If you're in a position of influence, please don't bury your head as I almost did as a pastor's wife. Allow the Lord to open your heart to those suffering in silence from this global epidemic. Become a warrior who exposes the lie and become brave enough to embrace the Millie McCarty's of this world. They're out there!

Contend for the faith and those who are in the trenches of God's mighty army of believers. Contend for an anointing that breaks the bands of wickedness and chains of bondage. Help liberate those in prison through the Blood of Jesus Christ, our Lord and Savior!

Dear friends, although I was very eager to write to you about the salvation we share, I felt I had to write and urge you to contend for the faith that was once for all entrusted to the saints. Jude 1:3

Is not this the kind of fasting I have chosen: to loose the chains of injustice and untie the cords of the yoke, to set the oppressed free and break every yoke? Isaiah 58:6

Discussion Questions

1. There are professional counseling centers based on the Word of God. Some take insurance plans or will charge counseling sessions based on a "sliding-scale" according to your income. Do you feel that most problems in life are spiritual in nature?

2. Can you share a time when your received counsel that helped you understand and overcome a problem?

3. Have you benefited from counseling? What did you learn about yourself that helped?

4. What would prevent you from seeking out spiritual counseling from your church or an agency?

Chapter Six

Faith to Follow Where He Leads

Ruth was a young Moabite widow driven by poverty to seek a better life. Considered a pagan, this young woman had a destiny with God in spite of her lowly place in society. Her story gives us hope, because Ruth found favor with the Lord. With great courage, she had left her parents and homeland to follow her mother-in-law, Naomi. Their spiritual mother/daughter relationship models what every Christian woman should consider doing with their talents and available time for the kingdom of God. Their bond and spiritual kinship is an example of what one-on-one mentoring is all about.

Hunger drove a Hebrew man named Elimelech ("God is my King") to take his wife Naomi and their two sons from Bethlehem to the pagan land of Moab to find bread, only eventually to die there, along with his two sons. Ruth married Elimelech's older son, Mahlon, whose name means "sickly."

Bethlehem is a city of Judah five miles southwest of Jebus (later Jerusalem). Moab is a land on the eastern shore of the Dead Sea, which oppressed Israel during the period of the judges, so there was hostility between them (Judges 3:12).

The Moabites descended from Lot through his son Moab, who was conceived by incest. Lot's two daughters feared dying alone with their father in a cave, so they got him drunk and each daughter conceived a son (Genesis 19:30-38).

One of the most grievous offenses committed by the nation of Moab occurred during Israel's wanderings. The King of Moab attempted to hire Balaam the seer to curse the Israelites, but Balaam blessed them instead. However, the soothsayer came up with a plan to seduce God's people into idolatry by sending Moabite women to entice them. The plan worked, and 24,000 people died as a result (Numbers 25:3).

Friendly relations with the Moabites were discouraged (Deuteronomy 23:3-6), but probably not forbidden, since the Moabites lived outside the Promised Land. Marrying a Canaanite (and all those living within the borders of the Promised Land) was against God's law (Deut. 7:1-4). Moabites were forbidden to worship in the tabernacle because they did not let the Israelites pass through their land during the exodus from Egypt.

The story of Ruth takes place when no king ruled over Israel. It was a period of disobedience, idolatry, and violence. But even during hard periods, there was always a remnant of people who followed after God.

Naomi was a woman of worth who believed in the one true God, despite the great hardships in her life. God achieves his purposes through those who are willing to pursue Him in the midst of great difficulty.

Naomi, whose name means "pleasant, my joy," lost her husband and two sons to death after living in Moab for ten years. She was left with two daughters-in-law, Orpah and Ruth. Naomi heard that the Lord had "come to the aid of his people by providing food for them" in her native land (Ruth 1:6).

Ruth must have perceived God's noble character in her mother-in-law because she refused to leave Naomi when the time came to depart from each other. Naomi and her daughters-in-law set out to follow the road back to Judah. Naomi wisely reconsidered taking them with her and admonished them "to each return to their own mother's home." (Ruth 1:7).

Naomi said, "May the Lord show kindness to you as you have shown to your dead and to me. May the Lord grant that each of you will find rest in the home of another husband." Then Naomi kissed them and they wept aloud and said to her, "We will go back with you to your people." By insisting on going to Bethlehem with Naomi, Ruth demonstrated her desire to reach out to the Hebrews' God, if He would have her. (Ruth 1:16-18).

The women clung to Naomi, but she refused to take them. "Return home, my daughters. Why would you come with me? Am I going to have any more sons, who could become your husbands? Return home, my daughters; I am too old to have another husband. Even if I thought there was still hope for me—even if I had a husband tonight and then gave birth to sons—would you wait until they grew up? Would you remain unmarried for them? No, my daughters, it is more bitter for me than for you, because the Lord's hand has gone out against me!" (Ruth 1:11-13). But what Naomi did have to offer was worth far more than gold or silver.

They wept again, and Orpah kissed Naomi good-bye, but Ruth continued to cling to her. "Look," said Naomi, "Your sister-in-law is going back to her people and her gods. Go back with her." Ruth's answer is profound and has been widely quoted throughout history.

"Entreat me not to leave you, or to turn back from following after you; For wherever you go,

I will go; and where ever you lodge, I will lodge. Your people shall be my people, and your God, my God. Where you die, I will die, and there will I be buried. The Lord do so to me, and more also if anything but death parts you and me." (Ruth 1:16-17)

Ruth's heart expressed her cry of faithfulness to her mother-in-law. She demonstrated courage and faith to follow Naomi. Ruth recognized Naomi's ability to lead and pledged loyalty and obedience to her even unto death. It takes this kind of commitment to follow the Lord, and Ruth's example of complete trust is honorable.

We know little of Ruth's background, but her words reveal sound character. Her name means "friendship or refreshment," which is what she offered to Naomi in exchange for the privilege to follow her to Bethlehem.

Since Ruth was a Moabite, she had no reason to think she would fare well in Israel. The laws stated that no Moabite could "enter the assembly of the Lord. .forever" (Deut. 23:3) because of what the Moabites had done to Israel during the wilderness journey. Moabites were so abhorred, Jews were forbidden even to "seek their peace (or) their prosperity" (Deut.23: 6).

As they enter into Bethlehem "all the city was excited because of them; and the women said, 'Is this Naomi?'"

Naomi's reply to her old-time acquaintances gives us an indication of her emotional state – she replied "Do not call me Naomi ("Pleasant") call me Mara ("bitter"), for the Almighty has dealt very bitterly with me. I went out full and the Lord brought me home again empty. Why do you call me Naomi, since the Lord has testified against me, and the Almighty has afflicted me?" (Ruth 1:19-21) Naomi gave an honest answer, but she was not rejecting God by openly expressing her pain. Her answers indicate she lost sight of her assets in Ruth and with the Lord. God welcomes honest prayers, but we should be careful not to overlook the love, strength, and resources that the Lord provides in our relationships.

Naomi admitted to her former townspeople that she was destitute and humbly accepted her bitter plight in life without any hope for the future.

Author Robert McGee says, "One reason we may think we deserve better is that we believe we know what is best for ourselves and for others. But we are not omniscient. We are not sovereign, gracious and good like God. Do we really deserve better than what the Sovereign, Almighty God has for us?"[1]

It was springtime. Ruth and Naomi had returned to this farming community in time for the barley harvest. There was plenty of leftover grain in the fields.

---

[1] *The Search for Significance* by Robert S. McGee, Word, Inc. and Rapha, Inc.

Naomi instructed Ruth to go behind the reapers and glean any leftover grain in the fields. Gleaning was a practice instituted by Levitical law to provide care for the poor and disadvantaged. This custom ensured assistance for the poor through work rather than handouts.

Naomi had a relative on her husband's side of the family from the clan of Elimelech, a man of great wealth whose name was Boaz. Coincidentally, Ruth picked the field belonging to Boaz. When he arrived from Bethlehem, Boaz stopped to greet the harvesters, "The Lord be with you!"

"The Lord bless you!" they called back. Boaz asked his harvester foreman "Whose young woman is that?" The foreman replied, "She is a Moabitess who came back from Moab with Naomi. She said, 'Please let me glean and gather among the sheaves behind the harvesters. She went into the field and has worked steadily from morning till now except for a short rest in the shelter'" (Ruth 2:4-6).

This also reveals Ruth's determination to provide for Naomi by working hard with little rest. This is another admirable character quality demonstrated by Ruth. Boaz told Ruth not to glean in any other fields and not to go from his land. Boaz also told her that he had instructed his men not to touch her and to allow her to drink from the water jars the men filled (Ruth 2:5-7).

Ruth bowed down with her face to the ground and exclaimed, "Why have I found such favor in your eyes that you notice me—a foreigner?" (Ruth 2:10)

Her humility proves that she feared the Lord. She was grateful that Boaz showed her kindness. Her graciousness allowed him to extend grace to Ruth despite her background.

Boaz revealed more about Ruth's character by answering, "I've been told all about what you have done for your mother-in-law since the death of your husband—how you left father and mother and your homeland and came to live with a people you did not know before. May the Lord repay you for what you've done. May you be richly rewarded by the Lord, the God of Israel, under whose wings you have come to take refuge."

This answer was prophetic because Ruth became the wife of Boaz, and their son, Obed, became the great-grandfather to David the future King of Israel, and the ancestor of Jesus, the Savior of all mankind.

When we choose to follow Jesus, we must have the same unselfish determination of Ruth. She left everything to follow God. It's not enough to want to serve the Lord; there must be a *place of death* associated with following Christ. Ruth saw a future in the Hebrew God, even though it seemed like He was frowning upon Naomi. Nothing was going right for Naomi, so that was not the basis on which Ruth chose to follow Naomi, a broken and bitter woman. There obviously was a beckoning from God within Ruth's heart that did not make sense in the natural realm.

It seemed a foolish thing to follow a forsaken old woman back to a homeland that was hostile toward her race. As a pagan, Ruth did not know if she would be accepted, so her faith in God was a true demonstration of courage. Naomi accepted Ruth as a beloved daughter. This acceptance gave Ruth honored status among Naomi's kinsman.

As Christian women, we give this same dignity and honor to the young women we adopt as spiritual daughters.

More importantly, Ruth's love and devotion for Naomi pleased God. The kindness and considerations Ruth extended to her mother-in-law were clear demonstrations of a heart that was right with God. Without right motives, God will not bless our journey. Despite her circumstances, Naomi's leadership and willingness to mentor Ruth is an excellent example of sacrifice.

Ministry outreach often leads to unpleasant circumstances. If you honor others in your quest to serve the Lord, then He will show you favor. The Lord will cause your plans to succeed, as He did in the life of Ruth.

Ruth's character became a shining light to the whole community. They admired her loving deeds to Naomi, the widow. Our deeds of kindness will often reveal the character of Christ to others. Often our actions speak louder than our words. By Ruth's noble example, we learn that treating others with honor and respect is a gateway to favor with God. We are most effective when we place the needs of others before our own wants and desires. Ruth became a servant of the Most High God by following Naomi to foreign soil. Ruth is one of the most significant women in the history of the world.

"When you came to Christ, you received more than salvation—you received love. That love is to be spread around with no strings attached. And when that happens, servitude begins. I read somewhere that some natives in a missionary country regularly traveled fifteen miles out of their way to go to a Christian hospital. Perplexed, the Christian doctor asked them, 'Why do you do it?' The government hospital is close to you, and the medicine is the same. Why don't you go there?' The natives answered, 'The medicine is the same but the hands are different.' The hands that made the difference were the hands made gentle by the love of Christ."[2]

May Ruth's zeal to follow after God be our passion too. May we commit to love others with the Spirit of Christ Jesus, our Lord. May our obedience be a powerful witness of our living God, who asks that we be salt and light to oppressed people and nations suffering from spiritual famine.

---

[2] Steve Brown, <u>Overcoming Setbacks</u> Colorado Springs: NavPress 1992

We have a nation of young women suffering from spiritual famine. They are desperate for role models and mentors who will take the interest and time to show them a better life. May the women in the church rise to the occasion and seek out those who need a Naomi to show them the way!

Perhaps the best example of this model is the story of Ruth. Her relationship with her mother-in-law, Naomi, gives us a glimpse into the spiritual significance of a teaching and mentoring rapport between women from two different cultures. These two women shaped history for all mankind.

By this we know that we love the children of God, when we love God and keep His commandments. For this is the love of God, that we keep His commandments. And His commandments are not burdensome. 1 John 5:2-3 (New King James Version)

Now by this we know that we know Him, if we keep His commandments. He who says, 'I know Him,' and does not keep His commandments, is a liar, and the truth is not in him. But whoever keeps His Word, truly the love of God is perfected in him. By this we know that we are in Him. He who says he abides in Him ought himself also to walk just as He walked. 1 John 2:3-6 (New King James Version)

Discussion Questions

1. Is there a time when you honored someone's lifestyle out of respect?

2. Have you had an influential mother-figure or church leader who influenced your life in a positive way?

3. How important do you feel that mentors are in our society?

4. Have you ever considered mentoring a young mother within your sphere of influence?

Chapter Seven

Faith for Missionary Service

A true missionary has a heart for the soul of an entire nation. I've been fortunate to meet dedicated men and women who serve on the mission field. Many have shaped my thinking and inspired me to cast my bread upon the waters.

Earlier in our marriage, our family moved to Trumbull, Connecticut to enter a new business endeavor. Our son was born during our eighteen-month sojourn in Connecticut. The year was 1974.

We became a part of a wonderful church called Calvary Evangelical Free Church. Pastor Paul and his wife, June Anderson, loved us into a deeper walk with the Lord. I am forever grateful for their kindness.

At a church missions weekend seminar, we had a divine opportunity to experience Alex Leonovich, God's humble servant to Russia and other remote parts of the world.

Alex was born in Belarus soon after the Bolshevik Revolution. Seven-year-old Alex and his family migrated to America just as The Great Depression struck. His parents honored their Russian heritage by insisting that the Leonovich children speak only their native Russian language while living at home. His parents were devout Christians who lived by faith, even though life in America was very difficult for them.

After graduation from a missionary training school in Nyack, New York, Alex was invited to South America by HCJB World Radio to expand its Russian programming. From Quito, Ecuador, Alex began broadcasting the gospel into the USSR in 1945 without certainty that anyone was able to hear him. Since the Iron Curtain blocked all communication with the West by jamming the airwaves, in blind faith Alex continued to produce Bible messages, entitled "New Life," through Trans World Radio.

Little did Alex know how massive the impact this simple act of obedience was becoming throughout the vast empire of the USSR. There are eleven time zones in Russia. Risking religious persecution and imprisonment, millions of Russian believers throughout this immense continent depended on these sacred, but secret radio broadcasts to keep hope alive. These gospel messages by Alex and other Christians helped to sustain them in an atheistic society.

In 1965, Alex was finally granted permission to visit his homeland and preach the gospel in several Majar cities. During this time, he was able to monitor the political and religious pulse of the USSR, noting that the forced closure of many churches, the convoluted regulations for registration, and the ban prohibiting young people under eighteen from attending services were driving wedges between believers. Unregistered church groups were fined, arrested, and imprisoned with increasing frequency.

Persecution drove the church to its knees in prayer for hours, days, and weeks. Every building was jammed with Christians, and hundreds waited outside for hours before the service began. If a building that held 450 people, 1,800 Christians managed to squeeze in to hear the Word of God preached. Whenever Alex was introduced to the congregation, they gasped. Many wept at the sound of his voice, which was synonymous with the gospel message being preached for two decades over the radio.[3]

By the time we heard Alex in the fall of 1975, he had just returned from key cities in Russia, his third missionary trip, to smuggle in Bibles and Christian literature. I was mesmerized by his passion for a people who did not fit my negative opinion of Russia. I thought the entire communist nation hated God and Americans. I had a lot to learn.

But what impressed me the most was hearing about their hunger for God's Word. Whenever Alex traveled by train or taxi in Russian cities, invariably his voice gave him away – just as many in America would easily recognize Billy Graham because he has preached in so many televised crusades during the past fifty years.

One story in particular caused me to weep. A young mother holding a baby came up to Alex in a crowded street. In the Russian language, she begged Alex for "bread" for her child. At first, he thought she wanted food, but she pointed to his Bible. "Please, give me just one page of the 'bread' to feed my children," she cried. Alex used her desperation to challenge the congregation. He asked, "How many of you have several translations of the Bible just lying around in your home? Think of how desperate she must have been to beg me to tear out just a single page of my Bible to give to her." Of course, Alex gave her the entire Bible, but the story left me limp.

At that time period in Russia, Christian literature was so rare that hundreds would gather in a building to hear a lone Christian magazine article being read. Men would take turns reading until

---

[3] Souder, Patricia, Alex Leonovich—A Heart for the Soul of Russia, 1999 Horizon Books

the entire article was finished. Alex said, "Prayer requests were written on pieces of paper that were dropped from the balcony. The bits of paper never reached the floor because Christians were jammed together like sardines in a can."

I could have listened to Alex Leonovich for days on end. I was sorry when the two-day missionary conference ended. His friendly face, twinkling blue eyes, and quick wit kept us spellbound by his testimonies. But it was his zeal for Russia that caused my heart to soar. God pierced my heart with compassion for a people I would someday meet in person. However, that would not take place for nearly twenty more years.

For a short period of time, in March 1976, we moved to Dearborn, Michigan, my hometown, before establishing a permanent residence here in Columbus, Ohio. During our stay in my mother's home, I recruited various family members to attend church with us each Sunday. I invited my Aunt Bonnie and her future husband Lenny to attend church the next week. Bonnie is three years older than me, so we are more like sisters. Leonard "Lenny" is a proud American whose parents were Russian immigrants. Since Lenny had never attended church, Bonnie was a bit apprehensive about the invitation. However, having his best foot forward during their dating relationship, Lenny was seated in the pew next to Bonnie the following Sunday.

After church we gathered back in my mother's home for brunch. I was in the kitchen pouring coffee listening to Daryl ask Lenny about attending "church" for the first time in his life. Lenny said, "I have an uncle who would be really proud of me for attending church. He is some kind of missionary to Russia. His name is Alex Leonovich."

I yelped and darted into the living room. Lenny was startled by our astonishment that he was related to Alex Leonovich. The next day I telephoned Alex at his home in New Jersey. Today, he is in his eighties, and he is still producing evangelistic broadcast programs for foreign countries. In 1976, Alex was delighted to learn that Lenny's mother, Anastasia ("Anna"), his first cousin, was still living because he had lost contact with her. He informed me that Anna was a born-again Christian, but her husband, Lenny's father, was not a believer in Jesus Christ. Since Anna was busy rearing her three sons, she did not learn to drive an automobile. Alex had lost touch with her throughout the years, so he was thankful to learn that she was doing very well.

The next week Bonnie and I invited Anna to attend a *Christian Women's Club* luncheon with us. Dear, sweet Anna was delighted to be in the company of fellow believers. She wept with tears of joy throughout the songs of praise during the music part of the program.

Although she spoke broken English, she communicated well with her beautiful smile and gracious spirit. Before we parted that day, I held Anna's sturdy hands and prayed with her. Looking into her large expressive eyes, I said, "Anna, God loves you very much. He has not forgotten you!"

We hugged each other, as tears streamed down our checks. Bonnie cried too. She later became Anna's daughter-in-law, an answer to Anna's prayers to have a Christian marry her son. That day, our sweet fellowship became the demonstration of mutual love for our Lord and Savior, Jesus Christ.

Sweet Anna is in Heaven now, rejoicing with the saints who were martyred, persecuted, and imprisoned for their faith. She was a loving and devoted mother to her three sons. Through her close-knit family and adoring sons, she lived a rich and fulfilling life. They all grew up to be successful, caring, and honorable men.

However, even though her husband and her three sons and grandchildren loved her very much, in many ways, Anna sacrificed for her faith. She must have been lonely for fellow Christians who spoke Russian. Before she died, Jesus let dear Anna know that the Lord had compassion for her loss of fellowship with fellow Russian believers in America. By orchestrating a chain of events, the Lord demonstrated His loving faithfulness. Before she died, Anna knew that Jesus still loved her, and He was waiting for her in Heaven with open arms.

We then who are strong ought to bear with the scruples of the weak, and not to please ourselves. Let each of us please his neighbor for his good, leading to edification. For even Christ did not please Himself; but as it is written, "The reproaches of those who reproached You fell on Me. Romans 15:1-3 (New King James Version)

Be imitators of God, therefore, as dearly loved children and live a life of love, just as Christ loved us and gave himself up for us as a fragrant offering and sacrifice to God. Ephesians 5:1-2 (New International Version)

Discussion Questions

1. Does your church support missionaries?

2. Do you pray for those on the mission field?

3. Have you ever considered going on a short-term mission trip to further your understanding of the Gospel Message?

Chapter Eight

Building Bridges Through Faith

My mother once told me that as a little girl my favorite playmate was a "colored" dolly. My dad was born and reared in the Deep South, but thankfully, he was not a racist. Before super highways were built, every summer our Michigan family of five traveled two days by car through the vast Blue Ridge and Smokey Mountains, finally, to reach South Carolina for a visit with grandmother and other family members. On one such family vacation, I experienced my first uneasy feeling over the differences of skin tone. I was five years old. We had stopped for a fill-up at a combined gas station and grocery. Skipping alongside my dad across the weathered wooden planks, a little bell over the doorway tinkled as we passed through. The clerk behind the counter was just about to accept money from a black man checking out with only one or two items sitting on the counter. But as soon as we entered the store, the clerk harshly rebuked the black man to "wait." His harsh and demeaning tone caught my attention.

My dad and I moseyed around the store selecting snacks. The same man was patiently waiting at the counter when we returned to pay for our purchases. It was obvious that the gentleman was forced to wait until we checked out. After my father was finished, the fellow was finally allowed to pay his money. Feeling a twinge of guilt for this injustice, I asked my dad to explain. My father simply said, "It's the South and colored people are considered less important than white people." He added, "But it is wrong." I still remember the incident as if it happened yesterday.

I grew up in Dearborn, Michigan. Believe it or not, the deed to my parents' house still reads: "No negroes allowed to buy this home." Orville Hubbard was the mayor of Dearborn, Michigan for thirty-six years from 1942-1978. Sometimes referred to as the "Dictator of Dearborn," Hubbard was the most outspoken segregationist north of the Mason-Dixon line. During his administration, non-whites were aggressively discouraged from residing in Dearborn, and Hubbard's longstanding campaign to "Keep Dearborn Clean" was widely understood to mean: "Keep Dearborn White." The civil rights movement was going on during my years at Dearborn High, but my teachers never mentioned it as a worthy cause to consider. Therefore, my initial cross culture encounters happened during college. I never saw an African-American my age until I entered college.

On the other hand, my husband grew up in the inner city as a minority white child. Daryl was bused out of the inner-city school system to suburban schools because teachers recognized his high I.Q. He developed as an athlete at the downtown Cleveland Y.M.C.A. Daryl's disabled father supported the family on a small pension. As a result, Daryl experienced poverty at an early age. By high school, his family had moved to a suburb with better opportunities; therefore, Daryl excelled in academics and sports.

At age 18, Daryl had married a pretty but troubled girl right out of high school. She was his very first love and being responsible, he married his pregnant 16-year-old girl friend. By the time Daryl finished college, he had two babies to support. He also worked a third job to pay for his wife's private psychiatric sessions. After ten years of a tumultuous marriage, life had become an emotional mess. Divorce was imminent. Daryl gained custody of his two children and moved on. We met two years later through a mutual friend.

When we eventually married Daryl was a successful businessman. I did not know him when he played for the NFL. Having those extremely contrasting experiences in life gave Daryl a balanced sense of values, especially regarding healing race relationships. As a leader in Columbus, Daryl set out to make social changes for the betterment of society. Sharing his ideals, I supported every effort to strengthen racial reform.

In 1990, Daryl started "The Churches . . . One Foundation." The title of this non-profit organization came from the famous hymn, "The Church's One Foundation," which of course, is Christ Jesus, our Lord. The board represented black, mainline, and white suburban churches.

These twelve honorable pastors worked in harmony for the
goal of the *One Foundation* mission statement: "Supporting Churches and Organizations That Help the Poor, the Disadvantaged or the Homeless in Central Ohio." The board adopted several inner-city ministries to assist financially through donations from their suburban church support.

In 1992, a One Foundation dinner was held at the King Arts Complex. Bank One sponsored this formal event for one hundred couples. As Daryl and I walked through the expansive King Arts Complex lobby, the Lord spoke to my heart. I heard the Holy Spirit say, "Stop. I want you to remember this moment." I stopped dead in my tracks. I looked down at the marble floor and waited for the Lord to speak further. But I heard nothing more from the Lord. It certainly was puzzling, so I hurried on to catch up to my husband. Daryl patiently waited for me at the elevator to reach the ballroom for the One Foundation gala event.

One year later, I crossed that same marble floor, personally accompanying Mrs. Coretta Scott King on a tour of a building dedicated to her late husband. It was April 3, 1993, the 25th anniversary of the death of Dr. Martin Luther King, Jr. Earlier that year I organized ongoing "race reconciliation" luncheons at the King Center. My goal was to bring black and white churches together for racial unity. During the planning stage the Lord spoke to my heart again. He said "Invite Mrs. King as your first guest speaker."

I offered her three dates, one each in March, April, and May. I was not connecting the sacred April date to Dr. King's death. I said to my husband, "Watch, she's probably going to pick the month of April because I have that Billy Graham women's event at World Harvest Church the night before."

It was a busy and productive time in our lives. Daryl and I both served on the executive and administrative committees for The 1993 Greater Columbus Billy Graham Crusade. I also served as co-chair of the women's committee.

By working with the 1,000 churches involved with the crusade, I helped recruit 4,000 women volunteers. The women's rally was on Friday, April 2. That night I returned home exhilarated, but exhausted. I had to get up early the next morning. As I pulled the covers up around my chin, the Lord said, "Go anoint that hanky for Mrs. King." I said, "Oh, Lord, I'll do it in the morning." But He said, "Do it now." So, I pulled myself out of bed and went down to the kitchen about 1:00 a.m. My alarm was set for 6 a.m. The hanky came from Bishop Timothy Clarke's "Martin Luther King, Jr. rally" in January. For sale in the church lobby was an array of tee shirts, plaques, hankies, posters, and artwork in honor of Dr. King. The soft cotton handkerchief had blue pansies embroidered on it with a scripture verse from the Psalms I planned to give it to Mrs. King. I retrieved the white handkerchief from my Bible. In obedience, I anointed it with a few drops of holy oil while dedicating the hanky to the Lord. I prayed that it would have special meaning to her. I tucked it back inside the cover of my Bible, which was sitting next to my camera and purse – lined up for my early morning dash.

Our good friend, Kevin Miles, was kind enough to donate a driver and Cadillac limousine from the company he owned and operated in Columbus. Kevin is also the executive director of Crime Stoppers in Columbus. Pastor Daryl and Pastor LaFayette Scales collected Mrs. King and her traveling companion at the airport in grand style. Along with a private reception in her honor, I waited with anticipation for her arrival at the King Arts Complex center. When Daryl introduced me to Mrs. King, the local news media stood close behind me, with several cameras focused on her face. I leaned over to embrace her and noticed a red lipstick smear on her beautiful white teeth.

It has happened to every woman at least one time in life. I whispered in her ear, "Mrs. King, you have lipstick on your teeth." As a typical female response, we both grabbed at the sides of our empty pockets for Kleenex and came up empty handed. Then I remembered the hanky in my Bible at a nearby table. I slipped away and quickly returned with the hanky as the cameras were still rolling. I slipped it in her hand and she quickly took care of the matter in one swipe. God anointed her mouth in a unique way because she was a voice to the nations. Her speech was eloquent. Many times, she departed from her printed notes and shared poignant things from her heart regarding her faith. It was a tribute I will never forget. The late Mrs. King was a gracious lady and her passionate speech touched every heart that gathered in her honor that day.

She sat next to me during our lunch and we privately shared a candid conversation. We chuckled about the lipstick smear. She took out the gift hanky and told me the scripture was her favorite Psalm. Unfortunately, I don't remember the exact Psalm imprinted on that hanky. It remains my one regret about that day.

Mrs. King loved the idea of *One Foundation*. As we traveled back to the airport she said to my husband, "I am going to tell my pastor all about this wonderful program!" After I hugged and kissed her cheek at the airport gate, she lovingly smiled. She looked into my eyes and spoke some final words to me. "Thank you for doing something important for race relations in your city. Keep this program going. I am very honored that you asked me to be a part of it."

Finally, all of you, live in harmony with one another; be sympathetic, love as brothers, be compassionate and humble. Do not repay evil with evil or insult with insult, but with blessing, because to this you were called so that you may inherit a blessing. 1 Peter 3:8-9 (NIV)

Discussion Questions

1. Did your parents teach you to respect people with a different skin color?

2. What can a church do about racial issues?

3. Do you understand the importance of evangelism?

Chapter Nine

Life in the Inner City

By the tremor in Tanesha's voice, I thought one of her children had died. I held my breath, fearing the worst. My 29-year-old friend, a struggling, single mother of four was calling from a hospital emergency room. She was being transferred to a trauma unit at a downtown hospital. Her older brother, Jamal, a drug lord, had physically attacked Tanesha for trying to intervene in a domestic quarrel with his live-in girlfriend, LaToya.

"Don't worry about anything. I'm leaving right now to take care of your children. I'll be praying for you, Tanesha. I am so sorry this happened to you."

My adult twin daughters came to the rescue, arriving at Tanesha's home as I pulled up with a large bucket of fried chicken for dinner. It was going to be a long night.

After getting Tanesha's four children fed and settled down, her oldest daughter, Keisha, age 13, begged to go with me to visit her mother. Seeing her grief-stricken face, I couldn't say no. Candy, another friend of Tanesha's, also rushed over after receiving my call. The three of us drove to the hospital in stunned silence with a sense of dread.

After passing through hospital security, we hurried down the long corridor to the trauma unit. A nurse warned "family members only." My clergy status allowed us to whiz through without further delay.

After what seemed like hours, an attendant led us back into a wide corridor, just as Tanesha was being wheeled through to surgery. Lying flat on the stretcher, her face was swollen beyond recognition. She peeked out at us through puffed-shut eyelids, like those of a bludgeoned prizefighter. I choked back tears while patting her arm. "I'm praying for you, Tanesha. I love you." A bloody tear trickled down her swollen cheek.

Through our own tears, Candy and I wrapped our arms around Keisha, who was sobbing.

The previous Christmas this family had withstood another emergency room drama. Tanesha's only brother, Jamal, had been shot. For several days, the entire family gathered for a bedside vigil, not expecting him to make it. During that stressful time, Tanesha's 9-year-old daughter experienced a severe asthma attack, requiring hospitalization, immediately followed by her 6-year-old son getting the flu, needing his mommy at home. Through it all, Tanesha remained a tower of strength, but she had to drop out of cosmetology school because of a financial penalty for such a prolonged absence. I was about to pay her $600 catch-up fee to the outside lending institution, but thought I better check on her return student status. The director told her that before Tanesha could return to school, she had to pay her $8,000 balance on her school loan! Thankfully, this criminal is now behind bars for fraudulent financial practices and the government closed down the school. Unfortunately, Tanesha was only one student out of hundreds who were also exploited.

Back in the surgery lounge, LaToya, Jamal's long-term girlfriend, explained what happened to her and Tanesha. She had a large bump on her forehead, but declined treatment. She also turned a deaf ear to my suggestion for domestic violence counseling.

Earlier that day, LaToya had telephoned Tanesha for help from a neighbor's house. After an argument, Jamal had smashed in the television, yanked the phone off the wall, and then struck LaToya's head with a sports trophy. He sped off, leaving her stranded without a car. The same neighbor had heard the commotion and called the police.

When Tanesha arrived, LaToya stood on the front porch holding the baby, motioning her in to survey the mess in the living room. LaToya had been with Tanesha's brother for eleven years and put up with the abuse. They had four children, including a nine-month-old baby.

Tanesha was recovering from a compound leg fracture and still needed support because the cast had just come off days earlier. She got out of the car and hobbled up the steps on two crutches. While sidestepping the broken glass all over the floor, the front door flung open. Like a raging bull, Jamal burst in the room, reappearing like a bad dream. This time, his mother was with him; in fact, Brenda had accompanied him back to the scene of the crime.

LaToya was holding their nine-month-old baby when Jamal knocked her down. From past experience, she stayed on the floor, curling up in a protective ball, shielding the baby with her body. Then Jamal punched Tanesha in the face with a cruel blow.

"Stay the F___ out of my business, you b____!" He screamed, while kicking his sister. Then he grabbed Tanesha's crutch to continue striking her in the face, using the crutch as a lethal weapon. Brenda remained mute in the doorway.

"Mommy, please, help me . . . Please, help me," Tanesha pleaded, looking up and over at her mother who was standing in the doorway watching. "Stop him!" she screamed, "Make him stop!"

Brenda carries a cell phone, but she drove off with Jamal without calling 911 for her daughter, whose battered face was bleeding profusely.

After Jamal's drug activities led to him getting shot the year before Tanesha kept her distance from him since she did not approve of his lifestyle. However, Brenda kept close to her son and, of course, the drug money.

A few months earlier, Tanesha broke her right leg at home. She had been working overtime on a new job. In a deep slumber from working a double shift, Tanesha heard a child scream from another room. Her two youngest had been squabbling. One child let out an exaggerated shriek, trying to get the other one in trouble. In a deep stupor, Tanesha shot out of bed like a cannon, slipping on the floor, splintering the femur bone in her right leg in several places. She nearly passed out from pain before calling 911.

During the assault, Tanesha's fragile right leg was re-fractured. While holding up her arm to protect her face, Tanesha's left forearm was also fractured. Her cheekbone was cracked and she required several stitches on her eyelid. The attending physician said that Tanesha would probably need surgery on her eyeball after the swelling went down. Her eye remained blood red for several months.

Tanesha's physical anguish was nothing in comparison to the emotional trauma she suffered. Later that evening, as we gathered around Tanesha's hospital bed, the atmosphere seemed more like a funeral wake following the burial of a loved one. Tanesha's rejection was extremely severe and the situation very grave. When I quietly prayed for her full recovery, she squeezed my hand. More death-like tears rolled down her cheeks.

Easter Sunday followed the day after Tanesha arrived home from her week in the hospital. Brenda came only once to see her daughter, all the while claiming that she had not seen Jamal beat Tanesha. LaToya had informed Jamal and Brenda that the police filled out a police report when she was admitted and that "Tanesha was intending to press charges." After that, the family, including LaToya, considered Tanesha an outcast.

During Tanesha's absence from home, the refrigerator had shut off and all the food perished. Tanesha had gone grocery shopping the day before she was hospitalized. She had no way of keeping additional food cold, nor could she prepare anything for her children. Brenda never came to help out with her grandchildren.

It was truly a time of trouble. But God is our refuge, a present help in time of trouble. Even though her family had forsaken her, God had not.

Following church, the Easter brunch in our home included a few World Harvest Bible College students. Afterward, I had planned to visit Tanesha and take her family some lavish food platters from our plentiful feast. With her permission, by telephone, two young evangelists accompanied me to Tanesha's home. These two young men eagerly shared the love of Jesus Christ with her, even though they had never met her. That evening, while bed-ridden, Tanesha rededicated her life to Christ, tearfully returning to the Lord after a two-year absence.

The weeks following the assault were the toughest. With great anguish, Tanesha made the difficult decision to press charges against her brother. LaToya would not cooperate and backed out, claiming that Tanesha was lying. Tanesha was left standing alone.

Behind massive wooden doors in the federal courthouse, Tanesha was ushered in on crutches to speak to the grand jury, already seated around a large conference table. I waited outside and prayed for her. While explaining what happened, Tanesha broke down and cried. With a cast on her arm and leg, and a blood red eye, she had no trouble convincing the grand jury that she was telling the truth.

Being with Tanesha throughout the entire ordeal was made easy because several professional victim-advocates helped her along the way. They encouraged and comforted her through the step-by-step process of reporting domestic violence and assault. I was very impressed with the sensitivity and kindness extended to her throughout each phase, on every level. Other victim advocate agencies rallied to her aid, including the Attorney General's office. She was reimbursed for her personal losses, which included the perished food and meat.

Jamal was arrested and released on bail. At Tanesha's request, in lieu of prison, Jamal was assigned to anger management classes and court-ordered to family counseling, an answer to Tanesha's prayers.

Eighteen months after the vicious attack, Tanesha's bones fully recovered, but not her heart. Her mother and brother did not apologize, acting as if nothing had ever happened. Disappointment in her mother was eating away at Tanesha's lonely spirit. She still had not attended church. Her unresolved conflicts and issues with her mother were blocking the Lord from working in her life.

Tanesha eventually found a church home, and her four children received Christ as their savior. She finally expressed her anguish in an open and honest dialogue with her mother, something she had been unable to do in the past. Her newfound freedom in Christ has led to a healthier relationship with her mother, who listened to her daughter with an open heart.

Through counseling Jamal had been getting to the root of his anger issues and childhood neglect. He was making strides to be a better parent to his four children with LaToya.

Tanesha hoped that her brother would be reunited with her as well. She had forgiven Jamal and released her sorrow to the Lord. Thankfully, during our darkest trials and tribulations, Jesus

Christ, our loving Savior, is in the midst of family discord.

However, tragedy struck again. A few years ago, on my birthday, another spiritual daughter of mine, Candy, invited me to lunch and a movie afterward. She arrived at the restaurant with Tanesha as a surprise. They had been friends in cosmetology school. We had a happy reunion over lunch then purchased tickets to see "Charlotte's Web" at 2:00 p.m. We all put our cell phones on vibrate mode to silence them for the movie. Throughout the early part of the movie Tanesha's phone kept humming. After about five or six consecutive calls she finally answered the phone. She got the horrible news that Jamal had been shot and killed earlier that day.

We rushed after Tanesha as she ran out of the theatre screaming. When we got in the main part of the mall she collapsed to the floor in a state of anguish. We'd walked a few yards and she collapsed again in hysterics. I've never felt so helpless in my life. There was nothing that Candy or I could say or do to console her. I quickly called Kevin Miles, my friend with Crime Stoppers. He directed me to a detective to look into the matter. After we finally got her to my car, we drove her to the hospital to meet the rest of the family. It had been a robbery gone badly. Within about six months an arrest was made. A thug associated with LaToya did the shooting. It was no surprise to anyone.

Although I never had the opportunity to meet Jamal to share my faith with him, I wrote the obituary for his funeral program. The family was deeply grateful, even though I was unable to attend the memorial service. We were out of town. Candy reported that a fight broke out in the vestibule of the funeral home between some thugs. Undercover cops were there to run plates of every vehicle in the parking lot. Tanesha and her mother will probably never recover from the loss of an only son and an only brother, despite the conflicts they experienced while Jamal was alive.

Life in the inner city is difficult and often tragic for men and women who live outside of Christ. A few years earlier, Jamal had been shot and almost didn't make it. His family surrounded his hospital bed during a four-day prayer vigil. God miraculously pulled him through. He got a second chance to get it right. Crime never pays and the consequences are often heartbreaking.

Last Sunday, Candy and I were coming up the aisle following church service. My husband had walked out of the sanctuary ahead of us. A woman stopped to greet Candy because she knew her from Columbus State Community College. As we talked to her, I discovered that this dear lady had stopped coming to church when her mother was shot and killed by her 16-year old son, twenty years ago.

Through tears she said, "I lost two people I dearly loved that day; my mother and my brother because he'll be in prison for the rest of his life."

The Sunday before last, I prayed with a mother who had accompanied her 38-year old daughter to our church altar. This young girl had been shot in the head when she was 19 years old. The doctors had given the mother no hope. Although her daughter can talk, she has severe brain damage.

This is the real world around us. There are so many tragic stories of families who have found life after death, through a church that extends love to those with tremendous emotional needs.

Thankfully, my friend Tanesha has journeyed forward with her life. She has a good job and works hard. I pray for her often. Years earlier, to help give her some dignity, I helped furnish her rented home with nice bedroom sets for her and each of her children's bedrooms through consignment shops or newspaper ads. I also bought matching bedspreads and curtains, dishes, and pots and pans. I've drilled holes to hang curtains for her and painted bedroom walls.

At a professional fundraiser luncheon, I sat next to my friend Sally who works in the Governor's office as the Executive Director of the AIDS Task Force. We were discussing the importance about helping those in need. I said, "I was more thrilled buying Tanesha her first dining room suit than if my husband had given me a diamond ring."

Sally said, "Oh, I know exactly how you feel. I've helped people out like that, too. It really is a joy to be able to provide for someone who cannot ever repay you."

As Christians we should give without expecting a payback. There is great joy in blessing those who are struggling to pay the rent or keep the electricity turned on. Women like Tanesha need mentoring and mature Christian women to guide them in practical matters such as managing a household budget or organizing closets. There are many simple ways to share the love of Jesus Christ. The Bible says that *"faith without works is dead."* James 2:20

We are members of World Harvest Church, which has a global evangelistic ministry. Five years ago, my dear pastor, Rod Parsley, started Metro Harvest, an inner-city outreach.

As a part of Metro Harvest, I'm just one of several hundred church volunteers who pray and minister at three recreation centers in the heart of the city. Each week Metro Harvest gives away food, clothing, and provides G.E.D classes, drug and alcohol counseling, and various anointed Bible studies.

In the last five years, close to 10,000 souls received Jesus Christ as Savior, and will go to Heaven. It has given me great hope to witness men and women getting saved and being delivered from drugs and alcohol. I am very sad that no one reached Jamal with the saving message of Jesus Christ before it was too late. Jamal represents hundreds of thousands of men and women who need Jesus. Let's unite in prayer for all the lost souls in our communities.

World Harvest Church also has a global evangelistic outreach through worldwide television. Another vital outreach is the *Center for Moral Clarity* and *Reformation Ohio*. Our church also sponsors *Bridge of Hope* that aids disaster victims in every part of the world.

Last year WHC opened *The Women's Clinic*, a pro-life organization located directly across the street from *Planned Parenthood*, a pro-choice agency. Our Christian clinic is staffed with professional nurses, counselors, and dedicated volunteers. A free ultrasound is provided to every mother in a crisis pregnancy along with loving Biblical counsel and encouragement not to abort her baby. We also provide a diaper bag, baby diapers, clothing, and other necessary nursery items for every new mother who decides to keep her baby. This ministry has already saved countless babies to the glory of God.

The opportunities to volunteer are vast.

The Lord is a refuge for the oppressed, a stronghold in times of trouble. (Psalm 9:9)

Discussion Questions

1. Have you ever experienced domestic violence in any form? Relationship? Parents? Family members?

2. Do you know how to find help someone trapped in a dysfunctional relationship?

3. Do you understand the term "co-dependency?"

Notes

Chapter Ten

Mentoring Spiritual Daughters Past Poverty

When my young friend telephoned me, Tina was screaming and crying so hard that I thought she'd failed her 1999 *Ohio State Board of Nursing* exam. But I was wrong. As a single mother of four young children on welfare, Tina had fulfilled her lifetime dream of becoming a nurse. What a thrill! I shared her joy because Tina was a spiritual daughter from church. I had been the one to encourage her to pursue the dream.

Our mother/daughter relationship began over thirty-years ago, when this young woman entered through the doors of our church with a newborn infant in her arms and a toddler in tow. At that time in Tina's life she was overweight and nearly homeless. We met each other on a Sunday evening after her car broke down on the way back to church for pre-service prayer. Thankfully, her two children weren't with her on the busy interstate highway. With perseverance, amazingly Tina made it to the church that night by getting a lift from a stranger.

Tina had a genuine hunger for God, but it was hard to recognize through all of her outward problems. So, when God spoke to my spirit about "mentoring Tina" I thought He was just testing my heart. As the pastor's wife, I had to gauge my time wisely because there were so many outstanding needs in our church. Since Tina was very desperate, it seemed as daunting as digging a hole through a tunnel with a teaspoon. I doubted if I had the time or energy to take on such a difficult task. But there was light at the end of that tunnel. In obedience, I took Tina under my wings and soon discovered why. Tina *taught me* some incredible lessons. Tina was Christ in action, ministering to the needs of the lowly downtrodden and social outcasts within her own realm of society. The more time I spent with her, the more I realized that Tina had a valid call from God on her life. God used me as a chisel because she was a diamond in the rough.

When Tina's brother-in-law hit a tree, driving under the influence of alcohol, she hardly left his side at the hospital. He died days later. During that prayerful ordeal, I witnessed the making of a genuine nurse at heart.

Tina has a rich spiritual heritage, but a tragic one. On the foreign mission field her Godly mother died of breast cancer when Tina was eleven. On her deathbed, Linda admonished Tina's father "to marry a nice woman from church to raise Tina and her younger sister, Rachel." He did. Within months he found a new wife.

Tina didn't accept her new mother. Troubled and feeling forsaken by God, Tina rebelled. She was an innocent fourteen-year-old virgin when an older man from her church took advantage of her loneliness and molested her, resulting in a baby at fifteen. Her father and stepmother have raised Tina's son as their own, putting a wall between them. In a homeless shelter at age eighteen, Tina somehow survived on the streets with a second son out of wedlock. Later she married, for the first time, to a cruel man who controlled and abused her. After briefly serving time in jail, Tina showed up at our church with her two babies seeking help. That was when I first met her.

During Tina's second marriage to an alcoholic, she bore two more sweet children. She made a decision *not* to be an enabler to his addiction, divorcing someone she deeply cared about. As a single mother without many options, her faith in God never wavered.

Those years following divorce were extremely difficult. When Tina finally got reliable transportation, an elderly woman hit her broadside while her children were in the back seat. Thankfully, no one was hurt. Tina lost her car, but she never lost faith.

Without a strong male figure and no second income, Tina experienced many trials with rambunctious teenagers. It would've been easier to place them in temporary foster care and be free from financial burden, but she never gave up. My commitment to her never wavered, but together we went through many years of severe testing. God never failed, and our faith grew as the goodness of God prevailed in every circumstance.

God wanted me reaching out to this desperate young girl in need of a mother and a friend. Mentoring is the role of the older women in the church. However, it was disheartening to me that a few women in leadership resented the time and attention I bestowed upon her. They scorned her. These particular women of affluence within the church just couldn't figure out "what was so special" about a 300-pound welfare recipient who was rough around the edges. The Bible says, "Man looks at the outward appearance, but God looks within the heart" I Samuel 16:7. Unfortunately, it's the busybody and meddling women who often cause devastating church splits.

But today, after losing weight, Tina developed an outreach to street gang teenagers, young children and their mothers in her low-income, inter-racial neighborhood. In her former home, Tina taught a Bible study to teens and single moms. Last year, about eighty-five young people crammed into her home to hear "Mamma T" share the love of Jesus Christ through heartfelt exhortation from the scriptures. She is currently on the pastoral staff of an inner city, multi-cultural church. Her citywide ministry is called *Redemption Doors.*

In addition, Tina is a volunteer advocate within the courts, working side-by-side with teens, parents, social workers, drug counselors, and probation officers to help troubled kids go straight. She admonishes the kids to stay out of trouble and off the streets. She has also been assisting *Habitat for Humanity* to find volunteers among the older teens, so that they can learn some useful job skills.

"I don't allow no drinking or drugs in my home, and I make um put a quarter in the cuss jar every time I hear them swear."

Tina has a love and passion for music, dance, drama, and the arts. She has inspired several teen rappers to turn to Jesus Christ. Their message now glorifies Jesus Christ instead of the usual misogyny and violence of many rap lyrics.

Tina calls her ministry *Redemption Doors Outreach* because she wants everyone to feel welcome, regardless of his or her plight in life. Inner city people are usually too filled with guilt and shame to grace the doors of a traditional church. Perhaps they don't have clean clothing or nice shoes to "fit in" so they stay home on Sunday. Taking the Gospel of Jesus Christ to the streets is a simple way to overcome those barriers.

Through several church engagements within her Mansfield hometown, Tina also ministers in dance to anointed Christian music. Tina is teaching her many spiritual daughters prayer and worship expression through spontaneous dance movements. It blesses me to see her dance very gracefully. When she was overweight her desire was to dance before the Lord, but she felt too awkward. However, within her heart Tina always worshipped the Lord in spirit and truth. In spite of severe abandonment and rejection, Tina has developed an openhearted ministry that reveals Christ's redemption to the lost and lonely. It's been a joy to see her fulfill the call upon her life. I am so grateful that God allowed me to see the power of His love transform a life that many would have given up on.

Do not store up for yourselves treasures on earth, where moth and rust destroy, and where thieves break in and steal. But store up for yourselves treasures in heaven, where moth and rust do not destroy, and where thieves do not break in and steal. For where your treasure is, there your heart will be also. Matthew 6:19-21 (NIV)

Discussion Questions

1. Has anyone recognized a buried dream in your heart?

2. Have you denied a goal in life because you lack the financial means to attain it?

3. Do you have a message you'd like to share with young people?

Chapter Eleven

Women Empowering Women

My friend, Sarah Moseley, is someone I enjoy being around. She has an infectious smile and an inner Holy Spirit glow that warms your heart any time you're with her. Some people can make you feel good, but it borders on insincere flattery. Sarah is the real thing and there isn't anything phony about her. Her genuine humility was produced from a lifetime spent in prayer and fasting while experiencing tremendous trials and tribulations in her marriage and personal physical problems. Today, both marriage and body are very healthy by the grace of God!

As a devoted wife to Tony and the proud mother of three teenage sons, Sarah is also an award-winning freelance writer and the director of donor relations at a worldwide Christian publishing conglomerate. She's had many accomplishments in her lifetime, including the past production of her own television program called "Friend-to-Friend" on a local Christian network. She's also written scripts for a myriad of other media related programs, too. I consider her a true evangelist and one of the most gifted women I've ever met.

About ten years ago, she started a foundation called Grace Connection, a non-profit organization that ministers the Gospel of Jesus Christ through women's retreats and couples seminars. In addition, she developed "Freedom Through Grace," which is a weekly Bible study she teaches at a correctional facility in Columbus. The Lord has produced priceless wisdom to share with other women because Sarah has weathered many storms and gone through many wilderness places. However, by the grace of God, she learned to turn every personal trial into a pearl of great price. God desires that we become women of influence to empower other women by deed and example.

Since we live in the same area, Sarah and I occasionally walk for exercise when we can coordinate our busy schedules. While out walking one day last summer, we both concluded that women need women to grow spiritually and emotionally. Therefore, it's always a blessing to spend a few hours with my friend whenever I can.

One of the most impressive aspects about David C. Cook, the publishing company Sarah represents, is that they equip grassroots church leaders in developing nations with God's Word and helpful Christian resources for a minimal financial donation that goes 100 percent to this cause. Last year, donations through Cook's Global Mission provided spiritual growth resources to more than 5 million people.

Recently, while visiting family in Colorado, thanks to Sarah, Daryl and I were taken on the grand tour of David C. Cook's headquarters in Colorado Springs. Eric Thurman, the president of global missions came out of his board meeting to personally greet us.

Later, Sarah filled me in on this impressive man, explaining that Eric co-authored a book called *A Billion Bootstraps*, which introduces the microcredit movement in third world countries.

"Really? Tell me more about this concept." I was eager to hear all about it.

Sarah's face lit up as she explained how it works. "Well, we extend business loans of about $200 to help women grow their small businesses. It might be a seamstress in Pakistan, or a basket weaver in Kenya, or someone selling baked goods in India. When these women make a profit they're always faithful in repaying the loan. We get small checks of $10 or $20 and it's such a blessing to know these women are becoming successful and overcoming financial hardship."

A few weeks later, Oprah devoted an entire television program on the microcredit movement, which empowers women to combat poverty. As I researched this concept I noted several national organizations that assist women in third world countries.

Oprah interviewed Secretary of State, Hillary Clinton during this micro-financing segment. I appreciated what Mrs. Clinton had to say about lending money to impoverished women. She said, "Well, we've discovered that if we loan money to a man, he's apt to spend it all to brag to his friends in the village. But when a woman receives this same amount of money, she's apt to buy a goat and sell the milk for a profit."

By God's perfect design, women are life-givers by nature. We were born with a womb that produces life and our breasts nurture our babies with life-saving sustenance. We are also gifted with unique talents that inspire others to achieve their greatest potential. We need each other for empowerment. And when we reproduce ourselves in others, we become the express image of God the Father in Heaven.

I'm greatly encouraged by humble women like Sarah and Oprah…both, in their own unique way, have overcome tremendous difficulties in life to use their media savvy talents to inspire others for good with a microphone and a willingness to be *real*.

Although Oprah may have differing views on the deity of Jesus Christ and the way to get to

Heaven, I respect her stance on helping women overcome poverty and shame. I'd like to see Oprah package all her past humanitarian programs into a gift package to use in schools and prisons. It would be a tremendous resource to teach young women the strength of education and philanthropy.

It's too bad I can't just package Sarah. She's the best thing going for a cloudy day or anyone in a bad mood. Her next bright idea is to produce a Christian program similar to *The View*. Wouldn't that be something? Go Sarah!

God, who at various times and in various ways spoke in time past to the fathers by the prophets, has in these last days spoken to us by His Son, whom He has appointed heir of all things, through whom also He made the worlds; who being the brightness of His glory and the express image of His person, and upholding all things by the word of His power, when He had by Himself purged our sins, sat down at the right hand of the Majesty on high. Hebrews 1:1-3 (NKJV)

Discussion Questions

1. Have you ever thought of launching a fundraising program within your sphere of influence?

2. Do you have the leadership skills to organize a food pantry in your church? Your Community?

3. Have you ever thought of organizing a 5-K run to raise money for the poor in your community?

Notes

Chapter Twelve

Faith Overcomes Fear

Our son was nine-years-old when I began desiring another child. But he was a difficult birth. My obstetrician said that my Native American Indian blood must have taken me into gestational diabetes during pregnancy. This was before ultra sound was invented, so we weren't prepared for such a large baby. During labor, it was two days of pain and no sleep before I finally gave birth.

On February 3, 1975, our son was born after much agony. He weighed 10 pounds, 7½ ounces and needed to be delivered by high forceps. His head came out, but his shoulders became stuck in the birth canal. I had a spinal tap, so my husband and I were able to watch the whole nightmarish ordeal in a mirror on the opposite wall. At one point, the nurse was up, off the floor, on the delivery table next to me, pushing on my huge stomach. After the delivery and the excitement of seeing our beautiful baby, it took exactly forty-five minutes for my doctor to suture me back up because I watched the clock as he chatted with me. I was hospitalized for five days, but didn't see my doctor again until the last day. He was home in bed for four days on prescription codeine because he threw his back out pulling my son out! He said, "That was the most difficult birth I've had in twenty-four years." I believe it. When I went to his office for my first check-up, one nurse teasingly said, "What did you do to our poor doctor?"

Needless to say, I was apprehensive about having more children. I vacillated between the joys of motherhood and terror of another difficult birth.

Sometime in 1984 I couldn't stand the heaviness of it anymore. The weight of that decision was too much for me. I asked my husband to make the decision for me. It was very difficult to trust God to speak through my husband because I knew that Daryl was leaning toward no more children. He had been at my side during my trial giving birth; so, naturally, he wanted to protect me from possible future pain.

It took several months to surrender to the sovereign will of God through my husband. By submitting to my husband's choice regarding more children, I was receiving his verdict as God's answer for us. I quietly prayed for the answer. A few days after placing the decision in his hands, Daryl announced that he would have a vasectomy. My heart sank.

After returning from a consultation with a surgeon, Daryl reported that the physician talked him out of it. The doctor explained that a certain percentage of men with vasectomies become impotent. I felt relieved the Lord had intercepted a "wrong decision," and I became very confident that God was going to give us more children.

Growing up in my neighborhood there were three sets of twins within a five-house radius. Two doors to our left, the Borden family had two sets of twins. Two doors down, on our right side, lived the Norton twins, Debbie and Danny, adorable kids that I would often babysit.

Since growing up "to get married" was never an ambition of mine, I never verbally acknowledged a desire "to have twins someday." The infatuation was there, but it was never exposed until I was in a ladies' Bible study sometime in 1985. It was a year after we helped pioneer a church, so I was no longer worrying about having or not having more children. After the Lord intervened, I felt peace about the decision. I joyfully went on about "my Father's business" being consumed with church work.

One afternoon, a large group of church ladies were gathered for a Bible study held in Judy's home. Our associate pastor's wife, Patty, expressed a desire for personal prayer because she was unable to get pregnant with a third child. Patty and her husband, Dean, had two teenagers. They felt a desire to have more children.

Judy chided, "Well, what about you, Barbara? Are you planning on having more children, too?"

My response surprised me.

"Well, if I could have identical twin daughters, I'd get pregnant tomorrow...."

Then I turned to Janice, the gal sitting to the left of me. Janice had identical twin daughters attending high school.

Smiling at Janice, I said, "It must have been such a blessing to rear Stephanie and Suzanne."

The next day as I was doing dishes in my kitchen, my words about having identical twin daughters came to my mind. In fact, I could not get it out of my head for several days. It was to the point that I was being harangued about it, but I didn't know why. Another week passed by, and as I relaxed in a bubble bath on a Saturday afternoon, those same words came to mind. My husband was reading at the other end of our newly remodeled bedroom. In the process, I got my much-desired Jacuzzi, a small soaking tub just big enough for me in the limited space below a window.

As I relaxed in my little pink tub, the thought of twins came to mind once again.

Okay, Lord what's up? Why do I keep thinking about twin daughters? I mused.

Within my heart, I immediately heard, "Because I put that desire there to fulfill the desires of your heart." It seemed like the Lord said, "Glad you finally asked!"

I sat straight up, startled by such a profound revelation from the Lord.

I called out to my husband. "Hey, honey, the Lord just spoke to me. We're going to have twin girls!"

Daryl put the newspaper down to talk back over his shoulder.

"What are you talking about? You mean adopt?"

I thought it was a very odd response.

Did my husband forget that he had *not* had a vasectomy, I wondered?

A few months later, I had a prophetic dream. In my dream I addressed someone whose face was not revealed. I spoke to this person very emphatically.

"Well, why would God tell me He was going to give me identical twin daughters, unless He's intending to?" *End of dream*

Early the next morning, as we dressed for church service, I shared the dream with my husband. All the while I continued dressing the dream was on my mind. Before long, I began plotting on how to pull the whole thing off. Now I know how Abraham's wife Sarah felt after being told she'd have a child in her old age. Doubting God, she got her handmaiden, Hagar, to have a child with her husband. The conniving spirit of Sarah completely took over my thought process. Driving to church I thought of in vitro fertilization to see if science could pull off twins in a dish. My lack of faith was apparent.

Our church rented out space at an adult education career center. My husband, along with some volunteer men, always arrived early to set up church. They brought out the piano and organ from the storage room. Yellow chairs were set up theatre-style. We met there for about two years before building a beautiful church sanctuary.

About twenty minutes before Sunday morning service began, a gal named Beth came rushing over to me, extremely excited. She pulled up a chair alongside me and another lady who had been chatting with me.

"Barbara, Barbara! Listen to this! I have an urgent prayer request. Remember Jane? She's my friend I brought to church last year. Well, there's a woman in Jane's church with twin girls. They are looking for a good home for them because the mother is unable to care for them. It is a very bad situation."

Every hair follicle on my body was standing on end. I had goose bumps running up and down my head, arms, and legs. I could hardly believe my ears.

Beth was married to a Viet Nam veteran who was struggling emotionally. Her husband was unemployed, and they had come in for marriage counseling.

However, I knew that Beth had a hysterectomy and was unable to bear children. She had been involved in a failed adoption about four years earlier.

"Were you thinking of adopting these girls, Beth?" I was sensitive to her desire to have children.

"Oh, no, I haven't even told my husband, but I would be willing to keep them for a while just to get them out of a risky situation. You wouldn't believe how horrible it is."

I looked intently at her before speaking again.

"How old are they?"

"They are three years old," she said.

"And they are identical?"

"Yes, you can't tell them apart. It's so funny."

After hearing that information from Beth, I shared my dream with her because I knew these twin girls to be ours.

Beth became elated, and she couldn't wait to call Jane after church.

My dear, analytical husband thought it was too "far-fetched" to be possible. But, during the previous months, he couldn't refute that God had spoken to me twice about identical twin girls.

Our twin daughters were in our home the following Saturday, six days after my dream. With the help of some dedicated Christians who were in relationship with the birth mother, the girls were rescued out of a deplorable and life-threatening situation.

The little girls were adorable. They had fair complexions with sandy blond hair and hazel brown eyes. Unfortunately, they were not without health problems. Both had severe ear infections when they arrived. At three years of age, they were unable to utter a single syllable of speech because of gross neglect. After hearing tests and speech evaluations, they were deemed eligible for a federally funded pre-school program that my pediatrician highly recommended.

Bo was ten years old and affectionately welcomed his two little sisters. When we first approached Bo with the idea of adopting twins, his initial response was, "Well, I won't be alone at Christmas anymore."

We all looked forward to their arrival, but we were unprepared by their inability to do simple things. Not only did they not know how to talk, but these oppressed little girls also did not know how to play with toys. If I placed a doll or stuffed animal in their lap they just stared down at it, not knowing how to relate to it. The birth mother, Ann and her partner, Kim, were both heavy smokers, so the girls were always congested with runny noses and coughs. Jane informed me that the two women and the twins had been sleeping on a urine-stained floor mattress. You hear about impoverished families living in cars with little children who can't talk, but it is still hard to fathom, especially in this day and age with welfare so available to the poor and disadvantaged.

An attorney in Jane's church represented Ann, pro bono, covering the legal aspect of the adoption. Ann was made fully aware of her legal rights, and she wholeheartedly offered her children to a Christian family so they would have a better life. I spoke to Ann by telephone, knowing that she could easily change her mind and take the children back before our actual court date, several months away. During our pleasant phone conversation, we talked about Ann's life and her mother's death from cancer when Ann was only five years old. I brought up the Bible account of Hannah and how this courageous mother gave up her son Samuel to the Lord when he was about five years old. Ann also knew the story and shared her thoughts. This mother of twin daughters did the right thing before the Lord, too. I know that Jesus gave Ann supernatural grace to surrender her children to Him. The adoption process took six months to complete in court. When it came our time to sign the legal documents, I wept.

Every day with the twins, renamed Elisa Lynne and Leanne Alexandra, was an adventure because there was so much catching up for them. A mini-sized yellow school bus pulled in to our driveway every morning. Elisa and Leanne were thrilled to climb aboard and drive off, waving bye-bye to me from their window seats. They loved school. Each had a different teacher who was equally qualified to help children delayed in motor skills and speech development. They partook in pre-school activities with Down syndrome children and other preschoolers with temporary delayed development. Mrs. Risky, Leanne's teacher, was a jolly elderly woman. She said, "Leanne's favorite thing to do in school is to 'cut and paste.' I always know if she doesn't feel good when she doesn't cut and paste during class." Elisa's much younger teacher said to me, "I love her very much. I have never been this attached to any child before her."

Within weeks we saw vast improvement in the little girls. Soon syllables were formed as they ventured into exciting language development. They started out saying, "Ba" for banana, or "da" for drink. Just as a five-month-old baby learns to make sounds, these little girls were starting to form words in the same way. They were extremely happy to express themselves in a safe and clean environment.

Our generous church ladies gave me a huge baby shower, so Elisa and Leanne were now dressed in the latest fashions – so different from their former tattered clothing.

When Jane and her church friend, Anne, arrived to deliver the twins, I guided the two women into the twin's new bedroom. Their room featured an antique double bed with a white, lace-eyelet coverlet covered with stuffed animals and dolls. The little girls had a closet full of matching Polly Flinders smocked dresses purchased at an outlet store. When Anne saw all the pretty dresses hanging in the closet, she started to weep. With tears streaming down her cheeks she said, "Barbara, you will never, never know how bad it was for them . . . I am so grateful God rescued these little babies."

One afternoon, after returning from school, our adorable little girls rushed into our living room gleefully singing a nursery song they had just learned in school. They were giggling, bobbing their heads to the rhythm, both singing the same tune, over and over. It was the first time they "found their voices" to sing. They were joyfully looking up at their daddy and me, hoping we'd twirl with them and join their celebration. We were delighted to unite in the joyous movement of discovery, but we didn't recognize the song! With limited, single word syllables, the girls sang out the same thing in perfect harmony. Months later, I finally recognized the words of "Ten Little monkeys jumping on a bed, one jumped up and bumped his head. Mom called the doctor and the doctor said, no more monkeys jumping on a bed." They both knew what the other was singing even though they sang out nonsensical single syllables! I love to remember that the twins were *singing songs* before they could actually form a sentence.

My mother, Shirley Ann, arrived from Michigan shortly after their arrival, late March 1985. It was instant love among the three of them. When Mom got out of the car to greet them the first time, the tiny tots ran toward her with their arms held up. In early June, after Bo got out of school for the summer, we drove to Florida in my minivan to spend two weeks on Siesta Key beach. The first day on the beach, we took a large umbrella to shade their unexposed skin from the sun. Jane had informed me that the twins had never been to a park or touched grass with their bare feet. They must have felt like they were in paradise.

At the beach, the twins each wore a red and white polka dot bikini with matching sun visors and little white terry cloth cover-ups trimmed in red. Every single beach stroller stopped to speak to them. Ten-year-old Bo splashed in the shallow shoreline with them as waves gently lapped at their toes. They laughed at everything Bo did and never took their eyes off of him. He built them sand castles, to their sheer delight of having an amazing big brother. Later, the twins ate their lunch and also napped side-by-side under the umbrella. It was a typical, magnificent "day on the beach."

About 4:00 o'clock, Mom and I shook out the towels and quietly loaded up the red wagon to return to our beachfront condo to prepare dinner. As our group leisurely headed back across the pure white sand, strolling away from the cerulean blue water, Elisa panicked. She didn't understand that we'd return again the next day. Without language skills or an ability to shout, "No!" this little girl communicated the only way she knew how. Elisa ran in front of us to prostrate her entire body in protest. Both her arms and legs were extended out with her entire frame face down in the warm sand! I will never forget her clutching the ground with every fiber of her body. Her body language screamed "I love this glorious place so much that you're going to have to drag me away!"

In the year 2001, we celebrated the twin's graduation from high school at a large family picnic in Michigan. All their aunts and uncles gathered, along with about sixty family members, including most of our first and second cousins.

For their graduation party, I selected my favorite picture of them to be centered on the large sheet cake. They were sweet three-year-old's, contently sitting side-by-side on the shaded lanai during that first trip to the beach. The gloom is completely vanished from their bright smiles. Their beaming faces are rosy tan, and Leanne is clutching a baby doll. The beautiful blue Gulf of Mexico is behind them, shining as radiant as the future before them.

Elisa became a paralegal. She worked at the largest banking network in Columbus before working in sales on a large transatlantic cruise ship for the past eight-years. Leanne also has a very good job working in sales at a successful family-owned company. God has surely been faithful. Our girls are virtuous young ladies who still love to sing. In high school they sang in a most prestigious choir and traveled to Washington, D.C to represent Ohio in the Centennial celebration. Following high school, they attended *Christ For the Nations* in Dallas and sang in the international choir as well.

I wonder where those little girls would be if I hadn't trusted enough to believe the voice of God? My husband has been my rock and totally supportive of my outreach to others. What if we had been too self-consumed with our lives to sacrifice them to take on toddlers with tremendous emotional needs? We answered "Yes" to God, in faith. Rearing the twins was not without difficult challenges. However, the Lord has had His hand upon their lives for a very special plan that is still evolving. Our daughters have been a tremendous blessing to our entire family. We are grateful that God plucked them out of the miry clay and placed them in our laps to love.

On Sunday morning, January 4, 2009 Pastor Parsley called "the twins" up to the platform during an anointed time of prayer. Pastor placed his hands upon their heads to pray for them and he uttered the spirit of prophecy: *"The spirit of worship is upon you says the Lord, pouring forth by My Spirit, callings from deep to deep says God. Power in your praise, in the secret place of your private worship, says God, I will break bands of wickedness. I will loose the heavy burdens and the oppressed will go free. And when you are in this place, you will celebrate the shallowness of the depths that were broken loose up out of the river of your belly – rivers, rivers, rivers, rivers, rivers, rivers, rivers of living water."*

Discussion Questions

1. Do you believe that God will go to any length to rescue abused and neglected children?

2. Do you pray for families in crisis in your church or community?

3. Are you aware there is a national crisis for abandoned children due to poverty, drug addiction and domestic violence?

4. Have you thought of solutions to this problem?

Chapter Thirteen
The Mountain Man and the Mountain Mover

About forty-years ago, two bright young men taught together at a public high school that seemingly had no significance on the worldwide scale. These two men prayed together and formed a weekly Bible study to learn more about the mind of God. Both Christians were also dedicated coaches for intramural sports programs at Taylor Center High School located in a small suburb of Detroit. One coach would go on to coach football at a prestigious college level and ultimately start a Majar movement across America that moved mountains for the Lord. The other coach would stay put at a high school level, but would produce some Olympic champs for the world to esteem.

During their time together as fellow high school teachers, Coach Bill McCartney, founder of Promise Keepers, affectionately called his buddy, Mickey Turcheck, the "Mountain Man," because my Uncle Mickey was a wonder to behold in terms of physical strength and endurance. At 78 years of age, he still roller blades like a teenager and works out to maintain a physically fit body of a thirty-year-old!

Mickey recently retired after thirty-eight years as the head coach for high school boys and girls track and field. As a former record holder in college pole vaulting, Mickey was also able to hurdle his way through the impoverished community by organizing record breaking blood drives for the American Red Cross and numerous community fund raisers for the poor and disadvantaged.

My Aunt Claire was just as involved in the community service that brought recognition to her husband, such as teacher of the year, a Mickey Turcheck Day in their city of Taylor, and the most distinguished alumni award. Mickey was inducted into the Michigan High School Coaches Hall of Fame in 2003. But it was not public recognition that motivated Mickey – no, not at all. It was a struggling athlete needing a morale boost or special attention because his or her home life was in shambles. That's probably why sport programs have become a way out of poverty for many of the world's athletes. However, it takes a very dedicated coach to dig them out of the miry clay.

In addition, it takes more than raw talent to win an Olympic medal or make it to the NBA or NFL. It takes a committed motivator able to see beyond a student's flaws to bring out the best in them. My husband was one such inner city kid who made it to the NFL. He credits the Cleveland YMCA and his high school basketball and football coaches who helped pave the way for a college scholarship at The Ohio State University. Football Coach Woody Hayes also brought the best out of Daryl to become a number one draft choice for the Detroit Lions.

Sometime in 1980 during track and field try outs, sixteen-year-old Earl Jones came to Mickey asking for help to avoid being sent to a boys group home. His caseworker went to bat for him hoping a change of schools might keep him out of further trouble since he was on probation. Earl was getting straight Ds on his report card and was falling through the cracks in the system. Both parents were illiterate so he wasn't getting any help with school assignments at home. His previous high school was located in the center of a prostitution and high crime area. The kid didn't stand a chance unless someone ran interference for him. When Mickey followed up with his caseworker, she appealed to Coach Turcheck to "take responsibility for Earl and keep him accountable."

Since Claire and Mickey were always up for the challenge, they accepted Earl on the condition he bring up his grades and make it on time to all the track and field practices and meets. A few weeks went by without incident. Then they were put to the test. One night the police called Mickey in the middle of the night. "We have one of your athletes in custody." At about 2:00 AM Mickey went down to get him out of jail. Hungry, Earl had stolen a large salami to eat because there was no food at home. Mickey escorted him home. He attempted to knock on the door to arouse his parents, but he found a sheet covering the doorway and several children sleeping on bare mattresses on the floor. His heart went out to this family and quickly rallied community support to help them. Claire gathered donated furniture, beds, bedding, lamps, kitchenware, and other necessities to make the home more livable. Food was also provided whenever the cupboards were bare. The Jones family was very grateful and a close relationship developed over the years.

Mickey accompanied Earl to court for his arraignment and appealed to be allowed to take responsibility for his athlete and keep him out of trouble. The Judge said, "I've never done this before, but okay."

Now it was time to make Earl buckle down since it was a court mandate to keep him in line. To be deemed eligible for track and field, Mickey required that his athletes maintain a 2.3 GPA. Coach Turcheck also prayed with his team before and after every meet. Much to everyone's amazement, Earl brought up his grades to a 3.75 GPA. The first cross county track meet was another eye opener, too. Earl was competing in a three-mile run and lagging behind all the other runners by about a quarter of a mile. With only a half mile left to run Earl suddenly "put on a kick," and sprinted up to the runner in the lead and came in second by a hair. Mickey said, "In all my years of coaching, I've never seen any runner able to do that, so I knew Earl had the potential to be a world class record holder." And he did become a record holder. By the time Earl entered college on a scholarship he was the most sought-after runner in the United States.

A few years later, nineteen-year-old Earl Jones won a bronze medal at the Olympic games in Los Angles in 1984. Just before the gun went off, Earl made eye contact with Mickey who was smiling at him from a place in the stands. Claire's sister, Bonnie, and I were watching the race on television, jumping up and down screaming as Earl ran the 800-meter course, setting a new personal best of 1:43.83 minutes. It was before cell phones, so I immediately sent Mickey a telegram to congratulate him on Earl's success. We were all so proud!

Tragically, a short time later Earl injured his knee in a car accident on the way to the Los Angeles airport for a European competition. His fiancé was driving because they were to be married and honeymoon in Europe. This injury abruptly ended his successful career. He returned to Eastern University and graduated. For a while Earl was helping Mickey coach track and field before moving on to Texas.

Uncle Mickey also coached sixteen nationally ranked athletes. Four were Olympic qualifiers: Deby Lansky, Sherice DuChamp, Paul Babbits, and Earl Jones.

My dear aunt and uncle made significant investments in all of their special students. Each athlete was treated with equal respect. They lived on Mickey's meager teacher's salary with three children of their own, so their kids shared the joys by being just as involved. Their door was always open to any student to drop by and hang out.

Over the years Mickey developed a training course called *World Class Fast Lane Speed Assisted Training,* which *guarantees* an increase of speed for every athlete who takes this training. He is in great demand in high schools and colleges to conduct seminars on his unique teaching methods, which obviously work, since they produced world record holders!

Mickey introduced Daryl to Bill McCartney through their Bible study all those years ago in Taylor, Michigan. In 1990, among the massive mountain ranges in Colorado, Bill formed *Promise Keepers.* Bill asked my husband to be on the founding board, but we were planting a church in Columbus, so Daryl had to decline this honorable invitation. Whenever Bill and Daryl talk he says, "I still pray for you and Barbara every day." I have felt those prayers over the years and I'm truly grateful. As a result of his prayers, I'm hopeful that this book will motivate my readers to get involved with those who need Jesus. That's my sincere heart's desire.

Coach McCartney has reached millions of men through Promise Keepers. He said, "Way back before Promise Keepers had a name, we looked up the word integrity in *Webster's Dictionary*. It gave six definitions: utter sincerity, honesty, candor, not artificial, not shallow, no empty promises."

The name "Promise Keepers" also derives from the covenant that God fulfilled through Jesus Christ. In Christ, God kept all the promises that he made to mankind and we rely upon God as the original Promise Keeper to keep our promises. As a man of prayer, Coach McCartney imagined a revival among Christian men who were willing to take a stand for God in their marriages, families, churches, and communities. Revival and discipleship are the two elements that became the foundation and focus of Promise Keepers. He has been a true mountain mover because countless marriages have been saved and lives transformed for Christ. Countless millions have attended the Promise Keeper conferences held throughout America in Majar cities.

The core beliefs of the Promise Keepers, outlined in the *Seven Promises*, consist of the following:

A Promise Keeper is committed to honoring Jesus Christ through worship, prayer, and obedience to God's Word in the power of the Holy Spirit.

A Promise Keeper is committed to pursuing vital relationships with a few other men, understanding that he needs brothers to help him keep his promises.

A Promise Keeper is committed to practicing spiritual, moral, ethical, and sexual purity.

A Promise Keeper is committed to building strong marriages and families through love, protection, and Biblical values.

A Promise Keeper is committed to supporting the mission of his church by honoring and praying for his pastor and by actively giving his time and resources.

A Promise Keeper is committed to reaching beyond any racial and denominational barriers to demonstrate the power of Biblical unity.

A Promise Keeper is committed to influencing his world, being obedient to the Great Commandment

(Mark 12:30-31) & obedient to the Great Commission

(Matthew 28:19-20).

These two remarkable coaches of integrity may not have made it to the big screen, but the Mountain Man and the Mountain Mover each hold a significant place in Heaven for advancing the

Kingdom of God in their own humble and unique way. We can certainly learn from them because it takes the sincere heart of a coach to reach those with the greatest needs.

Preserve me, O God, for in You I put my trust. O my soul, you have said to the LORD, "You are my Lord, my goodness is nothing apart from You." As for the saints who are on the earth, "They are the excellent ones, in whom is all my delight." (Psalm 16:1-3 (NKJV)

Discussion Questions

1. Did you have a coach in high school that help you achieve better grades or more confidence?

2. Did you have special teachers that seemed to bring the best out of their students?

3. Can you think of ways your words might encourage others to strive for excellence?

Notes

Chapter Fourteen
Our Reason for Hope

Jesus is our everlasting hope for eternal life. Nothing ever prepares us for the sudden death of a loved one, especially the loss of a child. But as Christians, we are prepared to meet death with a holy anticipation of the pearly gates. Through His death on the Cross our Lord removed the sting of death, granting us grace to make it through tremendous grief and despair. If you're reached my age, then you've lived long enough to suffer the loss of a loved one along life's way. We've mourned the death of precious family members, close friends, and certainly our beloved pets. None of us are exempt from the sorrow associated with loss of life or perhaps the death of a marriage. Our tears are stored in vials like costly perfume the Bible tells us, so we can be certain God values our pain and longs to comfort our breaking hearts.

One evening, Steven Curtis Chapman was a solemn guest on the James Robinson television network seen all over the world. From Chapman's latest CD collection of songs entitled, *Beauty Will Rise,* he sang a tribute to his daughter, who was tragically killed a few years ago at the age of five. Maria Sue was their adopted baby from China, a cherished child loved by the entire family, which included teenagers. A few weeks before the accident, Maria asked her mommy several probing questions about Heaven, expressing a sincere desire to see Jesus.

Strumming his guitar, Steven sang, "Heaven is the Face," a heart-wrenching tribute to Maria, who was "a little girl with dark brown eyes that disappear when she smiles." A joyful photograph was shown of Maria laughing and sure enough, her eyes had become slits on her sweet cherub face. As he continued to sing, another photo showed his daughter as an infant sleeping on her daddy's chest. What makes this tragic death far more devastating is that his teenage son had accidentally run his little sister over while driving out of the family driveway, certainly compounding the tragedy beyond human comprehension.

As tears rolled down my cheeks my heart was stirred, recalling another adopted child from China through the expansive ministry of James Robinson. Since this book was ready for press, this morning I called my publisher requesting permission to add a final tribute to some ordinary people doing extraordinary things for the Lord. This particular testimony took place about fourteen years ago.

My mother was a blushing teen bride and had a huge white wedding with several bridesmaids. Her little sister Margaret was the flower girl. I've already mentioned that my mother had six younger sisters, so my three youngest aunties, Bonnie, Claire, and Margaret have been more like my own sisters. My Aunt Margaret eventually married as a teen, as well. At one time Margaret had four children under the age of five! As a teenager I used to baby sit for her on occasion, so I witnessed the tremendous demands on her home life. When I finally married at the age of twenty-five, Margaret and I had more things in common, so we developed a closer relationship through the years.

After her divorce, my Aunt Margaret decided to attend college with four elementary school age children to care for at home as a single mom. It was a brave move, but she managed. However, it was not without extreme sacrifice because she worked her way through college with no financial assistance from the government, or much encouragement from family members. It was a very difficult journey because certain people questioned her motives and felt she was neglecting her children by doing such a lofty thing as attending college. She graduated with academic honors in the field of special education. Within a few years she obtained her master's degree in blind education. For the past thirty-nine years, as a loving and dedicated teacher, she's taught countless blind children to read and write in Braille. Over the years she's organized field trips for her students to experience cities like Chicago and Washington, DC, along with visits to famous art museums, amusement parks, and other outings like horseback riding. Her four kids, now grown and married, are proud of their mother and very thankful that she was a courageous role model to them. My aunt recently retired from a very rewarding teaching career and is affording world-wide travel when she's not enjoying her seven adorable grandchildren, all living in Michigan.

From Ohio, one early Friday evening in the spring of 1996, I picked Margaret up in her Michigan home to travel "Up North" for a weekend away with other women in our family. We call it our Yahoo weekend because twice a year about twenty-five of us cousins and aunties gather to enjoy each other for a great time eating, reminiscing, laughing, and doing various crafts at someone's cozy cottage or home on a lake.

"This has been such an emotional day for me," Margaret commented as we drove away from her house that day. "At school today, all of the teachers watched a video of an overseas adoption of a student of mine from China. It is such an amazing testimony of how this little blind girl arrived in our country through an organization called 'Life Today,' with James Robison."

"Oh, my goodness!" I gushed. "My friend Marcus Vegh is the television producer for that ministry. He's been working on assignment in Beijing for several months, so he must have been involved in her adoption!"

During this time era James Robison had visited various orphanages in China. Marcus had filmed and produced many of the visits that were featured as part of their daily broadcasts in an attempt to raise awareness and financial support. One day this little girl sat on James Robison's lap as he appealed to his television viewers for help. He said, "This little girl will probably never get adopted because she is handicapped." She sat contently on his lap touching his face and fiddling with his wedding ring as he talked to the camera. He passionately challenged his worldwide audience to consider the tremendous need to place older children because most Americans favor newborn infants or babies under the age of two. A Michigan couple had been thinking about foreign adoption when they saw that particular broadcast. Jesus touched this Christian lady's heart. "That is your child," the Lord said within her spirit. After this brave family brought this little girl home a doctor estimated her to be between seven and nine years of age according to her bone structure. Her new parents named her Hope.

Margaret commented, "Hope is the most gifted child I've ever taught. I tutored her one-on-one for about six months because she couldn't speak English. Children like her make my job so rewarding."

Months later, Margaret came to visit me on her birthday weekend and I prepared a special day in her honor. As a big surprise for both of them, I planned to get Marcus on the phone to discuss their mutual admiration for Hope.

I first met teenager Mark Vegh at his dad's church in Findlay, Ohio more than thirty years ago. Ironically, the church Pastor Moses Vegh pioneered was called "Hope Temple." Pastor and his devoted wife Betty remain dear friends of ours. Out of their six children, Mark seemed the most likely to follow his dad's footsteps into national ministry. Mark was also so much like his dad in personality and temperament, along with the same handsome Hungarian dark complexion. Mark also had the same zeal for Jesus and constantly spoke of future vision for a worldwide ministry. It took me and his family awhile to get used to calling him "Marcus," but we eventually accepted the name change. There was not a doubt among anyone who knew Mark that this ambitious and vivacious kid was going to be a shaker and a mover for Jesus. He had world vision, and it was quite obvious that the Lord had His hand on his life. There were matchmakers, including me, throughout many churches that were trying to find a bright faithful Christian wife for him, someone deserving of such a special guy, because he was quite a catch. He married at age thirty-two to a young Swedish girl from California. All of us who adored Marcus had such high hopes for this Christian marriage.

About fifteen-years ago, Daryl and I stayed a few days in Budapest with Pastor Vegh and Betty on our return from Russia. They were living there for an extended ministry engagement that lasted a few years. We had a rich time of fellowship while staying in their rented home wedged on a mountainside. They drove a van and we all held our breath as Pastor Vegh zoomed around sharp curves to reach the restaurant we dined at each night. Moses greeted every waiter with a hug, speaking Hungarian. He never failed to sail back to the kitchen to personally thank the chef for our delicious food, speaking the language with an old-fashioned dialect he learned from his Hungarian grandmother. Moses is quite a character. I remember Marcus calling his dad every night for a brief transatlantic conversation, which could be overheard throughout their house. I visualized Marcus on the other end, grinning from ear to ear while sharing exciting news related to evangelism. I concluded that Marcus and his dad were two peas in a pod when it came to enthusiasm. You couldn't be around them for more than two minutes without getting caught up in an arousing Jesus moment!

During that 1996 Ohio birthday visit with Margaret, I telephoned Marcus in Dallas, knowing he'd be genuinely thrilled to hear a great report about Hope from her school teacher. He explained that her foreign adoption process had turned political because Hope was completely blind. The Chinese bureaucrats considered children like her "undesirable." Therefore, due to Chinese pride, they country wouldn't release a child less than perfect. In addition, the officials involved in the adoption process couldn't comprehend why an American family would desire a handicapped child over adopting an orphan with normal vision. It looked hopeless for this child to get out of the country. Undaunted, Marcus continued to pressure them to release her. For many weeks it was no-go until Marcus threatened them with national exposure. He warned, "Listen, every Majar U.S. news station has run this unusual adoption story and all of America knows about this blind child you are trying to hide, so keeping her will make it look bad for your country."

Before I put Margaret on the phone Marcus asked me for the latest news. "Well, the biggest news is that I turned 50 this year." I knew he'd react as he did.

"What! Are you kidding me? You're FIFTY? I can't believe you're FIFTY!" He shouted. He was genuinely shocked while we laughed together for several moments. But I took his exuberant response as a compliment since I didn't really feel or act that old. We laughed about my BIG milestone, but sadly, how could we ever know, at that moment in time, that Marcus would not live long enough to reach his own fiftieth birthday? How could we have ever known that this bright young man, with so many God-inspired hopes and dreams, would never live long enough to experience the fruition of many of them? How could we know that Marcus would not live long enough to walk his daughter Annelisa down the aisle on her wedding day or live long enough to see his two darling young boys, Mathew and Hunter, graduate from high school? Or that my dear friend would not live long enough to read this book that he'd be so proud of for me. Or that he wouldn't live long enough to realize how much he was admired by so many of us that had such high hopes for his life because he was so wonderfully gifted and Marcus loved God with all of his heart? That moment on the phone, how could we possibly know that he would not live long enough to learn that Hope, the little girl he helped get out of an impoverished orphanage in China is about to graduate from college? Or that Hope had some of her eyesight restored through corrective surgery, something that wouldn't have been done for her in China.

On October 20, 2007, my dear friend died after a long and courageous battle with throat cancer. Marcus was only forty-seven years old. Pastor Rick Warren conducted his funeral and many other Christian leaders also gave tribute to an outstanding young man who loved Jesus with all of his heart.

Recently his dad spent the weekend with us while fulfilling some preaching engagements in Columbus. Daryl and I cherished our meaningful time with Pastor Moses, relishing fellowship as old friends do. We talked about Marcus with such fond memories. I cried at the mention of Marcus' name because I had not come to terms with the horrible circumstances surrounding his death. It almost felt like an unsolved crime in the annals of Heaven.

Marcus looked so full of radiant life at the July 2007 Hope Temple family reunion with the Vegh family and former church members. It was wonderful to see him and so many old friends. He was brimming with testimony about the faithfulness of God he had personally experienced through his extensive cancer battle. Countless Christians across the nation were praying for him. The answers to those prayers were electrifying. Daryl and I left Findlay later that day, marveling at his regained strength and stamina. We were so confident that Marcus was going to continue to accomplish great and glorious things in the kingdom of God as prophesied to him as a teenager. His media company, called Progressive Vision, had produced hundreds of hours of media resources in more than thirty languages, which are used around the world today. His legacy will be continued under the leadership of Hector Tamez in Puebla, Mexico, reaching people groups in Latin American and other countries around the world who had not been reached before.

My heart celebrated hope for Marcus. I was confident that he had beaten the disease. When we talked privately that day, I kept exclaiming, "Oh Marcus, you are SO healed!" He grinned with that beautiful smile of his knowing it was so true. In fact, his doctor had written a letter documenting his cancer remission, which was evidenced by his thick black hair and the fact that he had gained all of his weight back after chemotherapy. Without a doubt, this vibrant young man was on his way back to victory and would soon be once again moving mountains for Jesus in full-time ministry.

However, my dear friend still battled a private conflict on the home front. He remained under tremendous stress because the past pressures of his original death sentence and painful chemotherapy brought considerable stress to his home life. His dear mother Betty nursed him throughout the most critical periods of his cancer ordeal. When a deadly disease strikes a marriage, the sacred wedding vows are certainly tested. Throughout this critical family adversity, Marcus informed me that certain well meaning, but meddling church counselors, as well as his wife's family members, influenced her to give up on him. Sadly, the painful divorce proceedings began in August, just weeks following our glorious July church reunion with Marcus and the Vegh family. Obviously, such stressful court sessions drained Marcus of strength, thus weakening his immune system. He became emotionally exhausted from the heartbreaking mêlée and certainly must have longed for complete peace in his life. He was a faithful husband and devoted father and did not want his marriage to end. It saddens me to realize that Marcus suffered a broken heart in the midst of it all.

Just three months after the glorious Hope Temple family reunion, Marcus died. I was stunned speechless when his dad called us with the tragic news. We learned that throughout Marcus' intimate deathbed vigil, his parents, friends, sisters, and brothers, along with their spouses bid good-bye to their favorite brother when the end was near. His mother told me that her brave son never lost his bright smile or the spunk to make people laugh right up until the very moment he took his final breath. As close family members and friends surrounded him, Marcus never lost his smile because he was ready to meet the Lord.

As a brave young soldier, he surrendered to the serenity of death. He fought the good fight of faith until the end. The Lord certainly must have welcomed him with: "Well done my faithful servant." My friend left this Earth filled with genuine hope in his broken heart. He never lost hope even in the midst of his greatest trial. Perhaps he chose Heaven rather than succumb to the emotional fatality in the marriage arena. The end of his marriage must have felt like a dagger in his heart. Life without being a hands-on full-time dad to his three adorable children, now torn apart by the unresolved conflicts swirling around their tender little hearts, surely must have been the final blow to his compromised immune system.

Writing this tribute to him has helped ease my personal grief for the loss of this outstanding young man, who touched so many lives. He had such a bright future. My hope is that we'll spend eternity together. Marcus accomplished more for the Lord in his short time on earth than most Christians do in an entire lifetime. At our joyous Heavenly family reunion, we'll celebrate Jesus together as a true homecoming. We'll glorify Jesus for everything the Lord accomplished in the committed lives of those who worship Jesus, our truest reason for hope.

Love bears all things, believes all things, hopes all things, endures all things. Love never fails.... I Corinthians 13:7-8 (New American Standard)

Discussion Questions

1. Death of a loved one is especially heartbreaking. Does your church have a support group to offer anyone who has lost a parent, a spouse or child?

2. Whenever someone in your congregation has suffered loss, do you send a card or letter expressing sympathy?

3. Does your church offer the building for memorial services with food following in the fellowship hall?

4. Have you ever thought of supporting international organizations that save children?

Notes

Chapter Fifteen
A Burglary Gone Right

When Christ is at the helm, there is no telling where life will lead us. Our lives living in Connecticut suddenly took a turn when the owner of the Bridgeport Cadillac agency decided he wasn't going to retire after all. Since he was elderly with failing health, he had good intentions to sell his agency to my husband. However, it felt as if we had been robbed when he reneged after two years of this buy-out arrangement.

The Detroit corporate brass felt responsible since they unsuccessfully tried to replace this ailing dealer with a few previous potential buyouts. Therefore, Daryl became top contender for a new Cadillac agency in Columbus, Ohio. Daryl graduated with a business degree from Ohio State University and had played football in the Big Ten under Coach Woody Hayes.

During our time in Connecticut, we had reconnected with fellow OSU football teammate, Bob Vogel and his dear wife, Andrea. Since Bob had played for the Baltimore Colts, they lived with their three young children on several acres in Havre De Grace, Maryland. As a city-girl, I loved visiting their mini-farm complete with livestock. A corn field served as their front lawn on both sides of a long drive up to their sprawling, brick ranch home they personally designed and had built while Bob played for the NFL.

Andrea baked homemade bread each morning. I stood in awe at her brimming pantry shelves stocked with jars of food from her garden. Her bread & butter pickles are the best I've ever eaten. Andrea Vogel quickly became my ideal role-model. Bob and Andrea were dedicated Christians who led a very structured and disciplined lifestyle.

After Daryl was awarded the Columbus Cadillac agency, it was a scramble to get financing to build this multi-million-dollar project. Motors Holding was financing most of it, but we had nothing but our good looks and Daryl's football status to make it work. Thankfully, my widowed mother refinanced her house and made us a sizable contribution loan. Bob offered a small fortune in exchange for a percentage of the company and a role in management. It was a perfect fit. I cried with heart-felt emotion at the thought of Andrea moving to Columbus to mentor me in the ways of mothering and homemaking.

In the prior months of planning, Daryl and Bob spoke regularly on the phone, usually late at night. Bob was up early to feed the hogs, so these business discussions were burning the midnight oil. On one such after-hours conversation, Bob was intent on going back to sleep when he heard an attempted break-in.

Their screened porch stretched across the back of their home from the kitchen, along the dining room, and ended at their master bedroom. The bedroom French doors were open, so Bob clearly heard someone attempting to pry open a closed window with a crowbar. He flicked on the outside light and witnessed a burglar caught in the act.

He awakened Andrea to call the police before taking off after the man, now running down the long, front driveway. After being tackled to the ground, landing on his back, the intruder began beating Bob on the forehead with the crowbar with all his might.

Within minutes, a string of police cars lined the driveway with flashing lights, loud sirens and real-life drama.

After being handcuffed and led away, the burglar looked back at Bob's bloody face. He said, "I am sorry."

After calling the police, Andrea had remained inside praying. She said, "With all the sirens, flashing lights and loud radio dispatches, our kids slept through the entire thing. Their bedrooms were in the front of the house and if they had awakened to peek out their windows, they would have been completely traumatized."

The next day, Bob called Daryl. His bludgeoned head required several sutures performed in the emergency room. He chuckled about being "the hero of Havre de Grace" since the notorious cat burglar had robbed several homes in the area. The police wanted Bob to press additional charges of "attempted murder" since his gashed forehead was key evidence.

However, as fate would have it, the man sitting in jail, apprehended by a Super Bowl offensive tackle was about to abruptly change his ways of robbing from the rich to support the poor.

The next day, Bob visited the jail to talk with the burglar, face-to-face. Majar Bowling, was a short, sturdy African-American in his fifties. Bob learned Majar had lost both parents at a young age and was raised by his grandmother. This man had no comprehension of right-from-wrong. In fact, he had never heard of the Ten Commandments or what it meant to live as a Christian. He seemed sincere in his desire to change and intently listened as Bob shared his faith in Christ Jesus.

Most likely, it was the first time Majar had ever heard the Good News.

Andrea and Bob often visited Majar in jail and went to his arraignment. Through their kindness and desire to see a lost sinner saved, Majar eventually gave his life to Christ and repented of all his past sins.

During his jail time awaiting trial, Bob and Andrea pledged support for his welfare by becoming his advocate through the court system. While in prison, Andrea kept up with Majar through letter writing to encourage his growing faith in God. After serving a fairly light prison sentence, Majar spent Christmas with the Vogel family as a week-long guest in their Ohio country homestead.

Daryl and I met Majar at church during his family visit to Columbus. While talking with him before and after the Sunday service, Majar impressed us as a polite, soft-spoken, little guy with a giant of a God now residing inside him. He had surely been arrested in his tracks by our loving Lord Jesus Christ.

So often, our local news report victims getting shot and killed by *a burglary gone wrong*. But in this incredible case, it was truly *a burglary gone right!*

The Sheep and the Goats

"When the Son of Man comes in his glory, and all the angels with him, he will sit on his glorious throne. All the nations will be gathered before him, and he will separate the people one from another as a shepherd separates the sheep from the goats. He will put the sheep on his right and the goats on his left.

"Then the King will say to those on his right, 'Come, you who are blessed by my Father; take your inheritance, the kingdom prepared for you since the creation of the world.-For I was hungry and you gave me something to eat, I was thirsty and you gave me something to drink, I was a stranger and you invited me in, I needed clothes and you clothed me,-I was sick and you looked after me. **I was in prison** *and you came to visit me.*

"Then the righteous will answer him, 'Lord, when did we see you hungry and feed you, or thirsty and give you something to drink? When did we see you a stranger and invite you in, or needing clothes and clothe you? When did we see you sick or in prison and go to visit you?'

"The King will reply, 'Truly I tell you, whatever you did for one of the least of these brothers and sisters of mine, you did for me,

"Then he will say to those on his left, 'Depart from me,-you who are cursed, into the eternal fire prepared for the devil and his angels. For I was hungry and you gave me nothing to eat, I was thirsty and you gave me nothing to drink, I was a stranger and you did not invite me in, I needed clothes and you did not clothe me, I was sick and in prison and you did not look after me.'

"They also will answer, 'Lord, when did we see you hungry or thirsty or a stranger or needing clothes or sick or in prison, and did not help you?

"He will reply, 'Truly I tell you, whatever you did not do for one of the least of these, you did not do for me.

"Then they will go away to eternal punishment, but the righteous to eternal life." (Matthew 25 NIV)

Discussion Questions

1. Have you ever extended mercy to someone who hurt you or deeply wounded you with words of rejection?

2. How important is it to understand the background of people who commit crimes?

Chapter Sixteen

Miracle Fundraiser Connections

One afternoon sixteen years ago, I drove out to a farm to interview my longtime friend who cared for discarded babies born with crack cocaine addictions or other critical problems. That day, Andrea Vogel, a former nurse, was tending to the needs of another gravely ill infant born on July 15, 1993.

Along with photographs of her and a special needs baby, I planned to write an article for a fundraising project for One Foundation in an attempt to raise community awareness of special needs children.

Andrea pointed out the new breathing apparatus that had been set up to take in medically fragile infants.

This tiny blond, blue-eyed newborn's distorted head was the size of a cantaloupe. He was a hydro anencephalic baby. Such babies have no cerebrum or cerebellum but they do have a brain stem. The brain stem allows them to breathe and allows their hearts to beat. But the babies cannot see, hear, or feel anything. They will never be able to think or achieve what is considered a "personhood."

I sat in a comfortable chair across from Andrea on their cozy sun porch, as she loved on this tiny infant. She never put him down the entire time we spent together and we talked for hours. I enjoyed watching love in action and sharing our mutual Christian fellowship. Before I left, we placed our hands on his little body, asking the Lord Jesus Christ to heal him and watch over him. At that point in time we did not know that this infant was also born without a brain, which is a completely hopeless condition.

I said, "Where will he go? To an institution?"

She said, "The Eckfelds are taking him. Do you know about them? They are from World Harvest Church…they have a ministry for special needs children."

About five years later, I was watching a five o'clock local NBC news report with Cabot Rae and Colleen Marshall, who are both Christians. They preempted their upcoming report on a "modern day miracle."

Their story was about five-year-old, Cody Eckfeld, shown writing at his desk while attending Kindergarten at Harvest Preparatory School. They reported that Cody had been born without a brain and the Lord healed him. The news anchor team showed the viewers the before and after CAT scan film of Cody's missing brain. Then the camera broke away to another clip of Pastor Rod Parsley praying over infant Cody when the Eckfelds dedicated the baby boy to the Lord during a morning service at World Harvest Church. I watched in complete amazement as the medically documented miracle unfolded before my eyes. I had no idea this was the same baby boy Andrea had delicately cared for years earlier.

Heading up a fundraiser, my friend Stephanie Lindsay called one day requesting that I write a story on the amazing Eckfeld family and their ministry entitled *Progeny*. I was glad to oblige and set out across town with my camera and tape recorder to write their story. *Progeny* is a family training center that provides multidisciplinary support services to keep families with medically fragile children intact by hands on education and ongoing support and encouragement. If I had not accepted Stephanie's fundraiser assignment I would have missed out on a tremendous blessing that continues to unfold!

More than twenty years ago, Tom and Linda Eckfeld started adopting special needs children that were left with no parent or home to go to. With three now-grown children of their own, they have adopted 27 special needs children altogether. Nine children have gone to be with the Lord, so they currently have 18 special needs children living in their large home staffed with 24-hour nurses and other dedicated volunteers.

When I entered the Eckfeld's sprawling ranch style home, the peaceful atmosphere instantly touched my spirit. Linda greeted me with genuine warmth and gave me a quick tour. Christian praise music was softly playing throughout the immaculately clean home. Linda led me to a large room that closely resembled a neonatal intensive care center for critically ill babies. Respiratory machines beeped as babies and toddlers sustained breath under tracheotomy placement and medical care. *Progeny* has volunteer RNs scheduled around the clock to monitor each child's medical needs. Sometimes, children come for a short stay and Linda and her team counsel and educate the parents for permanent care in the child's own home.

Later, Linda and I sat down in the kitchen to continue discussing *Progeny*. Soon children began arriving home from school. Brittany and Bethany, who were delightful twelve-year-old's, greeted me with happy faces.

Linda said to Bethany, "Tell Mrs. Sanders what God did for you." I have to admit I was not prepared for what I heard.

Bethany looked at me with a bright smile. "I was born blind and deaf."

Brittany, born very premature, had a trach scar on her throat. She never left my side. Bethany continued chatting up a storm without any sign of sight or hearing impairment. Actually, Bethany was born without optic nerves. Talk about an astonishing P.R. rep for *Progeny*!

That afternoon Cody came by to greet me, too. As I peered into the face of that angelic 7-year old, I vividly remembered his blue eyes. It was then that I realized he was the same little boy I had witnessed that day in Andrea's loving arms!

Today, those amazing kids are now adults. Cody is about to graduate from World Harvest Prep. Nearly every Sunday I see Cody wearing a white carnation buttoned on his dark sports jacket as an usher at our church. I still marvel whenever I see his bright face at all the sports events at our football stadium. The Eckfelds also have three grown children of their own and eight grandchildren. It's been a joy to witness this dedicated family display the wonderful working power of love combined with unconditional love.

At a planning meeting in preparation to launch a second Columbus location for World Harvest Church, I met Connie Will, a close friend of Andrea's daughter, Lori. While talking to Connie, we also discovered other mutual friends — the Eckfeld family!

Out in the parking lot that night, still chatting, Connie's fundraiser testimony inspired me to include this chapter about the Eckfelds in this book.

Last summer 2008, with fundraising ever on his mind, Pastor Parsley proclaimed, "Someone needs to give the Eckfelds an Extreme Home Makeover!" The World Harvest Church congregation clapped in wholehearted agreement, especially Connie, whose six-year-old daughter, Avery, was born with a rare chromosome disorder. She and Avery spent years in *Bethany's Place*, our church nursery set up for special needs children. Therefore, Connie and Linda became friends over the years.

Later that Sunday afternoon, Connie was praying about the much needed Eckfeld home addition. The Lord spoke to her heart.

He said, "Why don't you do it?"

"I can't build a house!" she exclaimed.

He said, "You can do something!"

As a personal trainer by profession, Connie seriously considered the challenge. She thought of putting on a 5K race to raise some money and community awareness. But as the idea began to germinate she said to the Lord, "But this will barely bring in enough money."

He said, "Do what you can do."

As Connie planned the fundraiser race, stepping out in faith "one step at a time," the Lord began orchestrating the bigger picture. Connie hired a race consultant who caught the vision with excitement. He said, "Oh my goodness! You have a big vision to fulfill. I have goose bumps. I want to be a part of it!"

The next step was to find a builder/general contractor to remodel the Eckfeld home, but finding one in the midst of tough economic times would be difficult. Connie personally knew three builders and purposed to contact each one of them. The first builder turned her down.

Connie was a friend of another builder's wife, but she hadn't seen Amy in two years. Jon and Amy had a special needs child, too. God quickly connected their paths allowing Connie to share the vision of *Progeny* with them. They didn't hesitate to get on board with wholehearted enthusiasm.

In the midst of fundraising for the Eckfelds, six-year-old Avery fell into a sudden and unexpected grand mal seizure that stopped her breathing. Gary and Connie rushed their precious daughter to the E.R by emergency squad. They also have a two-year-old son.

When Connie called Linda Eckfeld for prayer, she learned that Linda was also in the hospital with their little adopted boy, Jalen, who was having uncontrollable seizures. Despite the enemy's attack, Gary and Connie remained confident that they were in the middle of God's perfect will. Therefore, they expected a miracle for these two hospitalized children, and the building project vision fulfilled by the mighty Hand of God! The Lord proved faithful!

Undaunted, Connie continued fundraising by mailing out letters requesting building supply donations. Jon, the builder, also stepped up to the task and used his contacts for additional materials. The Lord moved on the hearts of countless suppliers and the donations came pouring in while the community became more aware of the powerful work done within the ministry of *Progeny*.

The community rallied for the fundraiser 5K race and the much needed Eckfeld "Extreme Home Maker" is still well under way! Although additional funds are still needed to complete the project, God has proven Himself faithful because as the circle gets bigger, the truth goes deeper. As Pastor Parsley often shouts, "Deeper with distance! Be a sign and a wonder beyond the closed walls of your church!"

Praise be to the God and Father of our Lord Jesus Christ, who has blessed us in the heavenly realms with every spiritual blessing in Christ. For he chose us in him before the creation of the world to be holy and blameless in his sight. In love he predestined us to be adopted as his sons through Jesus Christ, in accordance with his pleasure and will—to the praise of his glorious grace, which he has freely given us in the One he loves. Ephesians 1:3-6 (NIV)

Discussion Questions

1. Using nursing skills in creative ways in your home is a valuable ministry. Have you thought of ways you can help critically ill children through home care or foster care?

2. Have you every volunteered in the nursery at church?

3. What would stop you from being part of the Sunday school program for young children?

4. Have you ever considered volunteering one day a week rocking babies in a hospital?

Notes

Chapter Seventeen

Laborers Beware!

It is amazing how quickly a beautiful sunny day turns into a thunderstorm by circumstances beyond our control. Too often our best intentions get twisted and misconstrued by the very person we're attempting to help. That's probably one of the underlying reasons why some Christians are reluctant to extend a hand of mercy. Hands get bitten.

About twenty years ago, while meandering down a quiet river road, lined with trees, I pulled up to a peaceful four-way stop in a lovely residential area. It was a bright autumn day and the leaves were at their glorious crest of red, orange, and golden yellow. The crystal clear cerulean blue sky brightened my spirit as praise music played on the radio. I felt thankful to be alive in Christ. That morning I was driving back home after dropping my three children off at a private Christian school. It was a perfect day.

As I pulled to the stop, a red pick-up truck also pulled up to my left. Just as I was about to drive through the intersection, a small dog appeared out of nowhere. The dog sat down smack dab in the middle of the road. Even after I tapped my horn, the shivering dog didn't budge. The other driver looked over at me and I glanced back at him. I shrugged my shoulders and got out of my minivan to lead the dog to safety. The frightened Shih Tzu breed was obviously a pampered pet with I.D tags on its gilded neck collar.

There was a large, grassy knoll off to the right with fancy houses dangling off a high cliff overlooking the two, or three-acre grassy park. The dog scampered over to the park area. As I got back in my van to drive away, my conscience got the best of me. I knew the dog owner living in one of those luxury homes was frantically searching for his or her dearly loved pet. Therefore, deciding to be a Good Samaritan, I drove my car onto the grassy knoll to rescue the dog. Keep in mind that this was before the day of mass cell phones, so I needed to capture the terrified dog, read the phone number off the tag and drive to the nearest phone booth to call the owner.

Since this was my first canine rescue I wasn't banking on having to chase the dog down. Out of breath, I finally caught up to the pooch because it had also run out of steam and rolled over in surrender. The little guy was quivering on its' side attempting to shield itself from me. I bent over, speaking softly to coax the fellow to simmer down. As I reached for the tag, the dog growled and snapped at my fingers with razor-sharp teeth. I jerked my hand back in the nick of time. I sincerely desired to help, but I wasn't about to shed blood in the process.

Undaunted, I remembered my cotton jacket on the front seat. I could use it as a blanket to scoop up the dog and keep from getting bitten. I rushed back to my van, parked about twenty yards away. With jacket in hand, I hurried back to scoop up the dog, now running away from me again.

Suddenly, a late model, shiny black Mercedes screeched to a halt. A lady jumped from her car obviously overjoyed to see her precious little guy. I felt like a true hero. I now know how the firefighters must feel when they carry a terrified child out of a burning building. Just imagine the elation the fireman must experience when a tearful parent realizes his child is alive and not dead.

I stood beaming with blissful tears in my eyes as I observed the tender reunion. Having once lost a beloved pet, I knew the agony this owner must have been experiencing while frantically searching for her dog.

Expecting a gushing sentiment from this lady with heartfelt gratitude, I was not prepared for what happened next. This lady thought I was attempting to steal her dog! Clutching the dog in her arms she glared at me as if I was a terrorist attempting to blow up a schoolyard. If looks could kill I would've been dead instantly.

I went from a smiling super hero to a condemned dog thief in two seconds flat. And before I had a chance to absolve myself, she sped away after giving me another menacing glance.

It was obvious by her hostile reaction that this lady considered me nothing more than a lowly criminal. I stood there feeling helpless. For a few moments I felt degraded, shamed, and humiliated by a stranger who thought I meant evil and not good. It took a while, but I eventually found my center in Christ Jesus and all condemnation fled my soul. But the experience left me reeling for hours.

In my helps ministry, I can't begin to tell you how often recipients with suspicious minds and callused hearts have falsely accused me of insincere motives. Like frightened animals, unredeemed rebels often bite the hand that feeds them because of trust issues and severe emotional childhood trauma that has gone unresolved.

When attempting to extend a helping hand to someone less fortunate, be prepared to get your hand bitten more than once. A lifelong captive held in Satan's bondage is apt to misjudge your motives or slander your character and create strife within your circle of friends at church because that's all he or she has ever known throughout life.

With the love of Jesus motivating me to help young women escape their emotional prisons and extreme bondage to sin, I've often been shunned for my sincere intentions. However, that has never stopped me from doing what is right or confronting their irresponsibility with the love of Christ. The Lord never said it was going to be a piece of cake. We are imperfect, born with a fallen nature. None of us can claim to be perfect. We all make mistakes, but we're forgiven by the Blood of the Lamb.

Therefore, throughout my forty-years of helping troubled youth, I've come to the conclusion that *ingratitude* is the underlying cause of *all* conflicts in life.

At a stoplight intersection, whenever I encounter a vagrant holding a cardboard sign that reads "Will Work for Food," my immediate prayer has been "Lord deliver that man from the root of bitterness and lead him back home with a repentant heart." If a beggar catches me by the light turning red, I usually hand him some change or a few dollars because I have a soft spot in my heart for anyone who is hungry enough to beg. We aren't to judge anyone. Besides, somewhere on earth, that man most likely has a mother or grandmother praying for his safe return home.

The Bible cautions us about returning to beggarly elements after we've been set free by the Blood of Christ. Our Lord says it's like a dog returning to its own vomit.

The Prodigal Son ultimately ended up in a pigpen eating garbage before coming to his senses. Hunger will bring a new perspective to everything. With a repentant heart, the wayward son returned to the loving arms of his father who had been anxiously waiting for him to return. He received unconditional love from his father, just as our Heavenly Father extends to us.

My sincere hope is to inspire you to become a laborer. Yet at the same time, I must also warn of the possible risks in volunteerism and mentoring. People bite. Words sting. You'll get falsely accused, rejected, and hurt, I promise you that much. But God has need of you. Your reward is in Heaven.

The Lord cautions us about casting precious pearls to swine. My pearls of wisdom have cost me dearly, even though the recipients may not always value my Christ-centered life, or appreciate what the Lord Jesus Christ has done to help me become an over comer.

In God's harvest, my best advice, to every laborer, is to remain prayerful because the Lord will lead you and grace you to endure till the end. After all, it's God's love that leads us to repentance. Someone reached out to *you* with His unconditional love.

How then shall they call on Him in whom they have not believed? And how shall they believe in Him of whom they have not heard? And how shall they hear without a preacher? And how shall they preach unless they are sent? As it is written: 'How beautiful are the feet of those who preach the gospel of peace, who bring glad tidings of good things. Romans 10: 13-15 NKJV

But in your hearts set apart Christ as Lord. Always be prepared to give an answer to everyone who asks you to give the reason for the hope that you have. But do this with gentleness and respect, keeping a clear conscience, so that those who speak maliciously against your good behavior in Christ may be ashamed of their slander. It is better, if it is God's will, to suffer for doing good than for doing evil. I Peter 3:15-17 (NI

Discussion Questions

1. When you have given someone, (less fortunate) a gift, do you expect a thank you note?

2. Have you ever been falsely accused for having ulterior motives?

3. Have you ever given up on helping someone because you thought they were ungrateful?

4. Have you ever needed charity or help paying a bill?

5. Has someone every borrowed money from you and not payed it back? Did that end your relationship with that person?

Chapter Eighteen
Out of the Miry Clay

I didn't think I had the emotional energy to write Candy's story, so I purposely left her out. But since she is such an important part of my life, I need to include my special daughter in this journey. Candy was already mentioned in Tanesha's story. In fact, Candy was a little miffed that I almost didn't include her.

You might know young women like Candy; those all too common, heart-wrenching testimonies of abuse, neglect, and abandonment by family members. It makes you wonder how children manage to survive such horrific circumstances, but they do. Kids growing up in abusive homes usually turn out to be drug addicts or alcoholics, but they do manage to survive. But, often they survive only as broken and bruised misfits in society unless God heals them and breaks the chains of bondage off of them. God is willing and able to set the captives free!

Sadly, life as an abuse victim becomes a cycle of pain with self-medication used as a method to ease the bad memories of childhood. Childhood molestation is what usually drives both men and women into prostitution or into self-destructive relationships that perpetuate the agony. Abuse victims also manage to sabotage positive experiences coming their way. Sufferers of childhood atrocities are also drawn to other self-destructive people as adults.

Candy was no different than any other victim of these circumstances, but thankfully God rescued her from the miry clay. Candy came into my life over twenty-years ago. She was someone left for dead in all aspects of her personal life. In fact, her mother and older sister figured she was long gone because they had not heard from Candy in more than five years. Candy was on the run all those lost years until she ran into me. I'm a seasoned crusader for the injustices done in society. God put Candy in my path to help rescue her from the depth of despair. Even though she was slippery and very difficult to hang on to, I never let go of her. My grasp was as tight as my determination for her to experience the miraculous healing and restoration power of Jesus Christ.

This book serves as my weapon to expose the evil tactics of the enemy. The devil is the destroyer because all mental torment begins with a lie. Through Biblical truths every false belief system is exposed to the healing balm of God the Father. It is the love of God that leads us to repentance and a change of heart.

Perhaps the Lord has placed a self-destructive person in your path. Maybe it's your own son or daughter. Don't be dismayed. This story will encourage your heart and inspire you to go the distance, no matter how difficult it gets to help someone who's gone astray and lost his or her way.

Naturally, I was stunned to learn that Candy had been alienated from her mother and sister for all those years. As a mother, I couldn't imagine losing one of my children to the world. Therefore, I instinctively put on my detective hat to investigate her mother's whereabouts. With small bits of information obtained from Candy during casual conversations, I managed to track down Candy's mother. She was a business owner in another state, several hundred miles away. When Candy spoke to her mother by telephone it was a tearful reunion. Of course, her mother was overjoyed to discover that her daughter was actually alive. Years earlier, fearing the death of Candy, her sister had gone to the city morgue to identify a woman's badly charred body. She was never certain that body wasn't her sister. Truly, the family had given her up for dead. Therefore, when Candy "rose from the dead" and called her sister at work, Laurel began to hyperventilate.

Laurel cried, "No, this is some cruel joke you're playing on me. You aren't my sister!"

When Candy finally convinced her by sharing certain details from their childhood, she heard Laurel collapse to the floor. Thankfully, a co-worker came to her sister's aid.

However, the damage was done. Too many Christmases had passed without a telephone call or a post card from Candy. Their hurt was deep and resentments ran high because Candy caused tremendous worry and anxiety in the family. Certainly, there are two sides to every story. It's been said that during a conflict, each opposing force usually accepts only ten percent of the blame. The end result is that 80 percent of the problem goes unresolved.

Perhaps Candy had valid reasons for leaving home at such a young age. However, I've worked with enough troubled teenagers to know that rebellion often leads to flawed character and life-threatening choices.

After years of refuge in foster care, she and Laurel were reunited with their mother, a virtual stranger. Their mother was a very strict immigrant woman set in her foreign-culture ways, so it was a difficult reunion for these frightened little girls.

Eventually, Candy dropped out of school after the eighth grade and fled from what she felt was another unbearable situation. On her own, she lived a life of hell, exposed to the wicked dangers of darkness.

When trust is broken on both sides, it takes years of right living before a broken family structure gets mended. Without Christ in every heart, true reconciliation most likely will never occur in a fragmented family unit. Our fervent prayers have been expressed for true healing and complete restoration for these broken relationships. With God, all things are possible. May the light of Candy's newfound life in Christ be a testimony to all those who remain skeptical of her true transformation. Candy longs to be close to her family and has made sincere efforts to be forgiving, loving, and kind.

Her mother has also made great strides in recovering the lost years. She's been very generous to Candy. She purchased a brand-new car for her daughter, as well as nice furniture for an apartment near my home. The first year her mother paid the rent, which helped Candy eventually become solvent through public assistance to single mothers attending college.

Candy's come a long way. I'm very proud of her. About twenty-ears ago, she was living with an African-American family that took her in as a run-away teenager. For years, the mother and her daughters used her for babysitting, cooking, and cleaning. Candy was also romantically involved with the woman's son. The mother was dying of black lung disease. With the love of Christ in my heart, Candy and I were able to lead this frail woman to the Lord before she died. There were times when I brought meals and cleaned her kitchen when I came to pick Candy up for school. Getting to know this family was a blessing the short time I knew them. The Lord put it upon my heart to purchase art supplies and pay for her son to enroll in art classes. When I contacted his high school art teacher in West Virginia she informed me that he was a gifted artist but he couldn't read. Therefore, I immediately found help for his illiteracy with a private tutoring program for reading.

Since Candy had a warrant for her arrest, the fear of prison was another way the devil kept her in bondage. Candy did not have a driver's license or a G.E.D to get a decent job. The unresolved warrant for her arrest became a monkey on her back with no hope for a future.

However, we have contacted the district attorney in that state. Arrangements have been made to eventually deal with this serious offense involving a firearm. Fortunately, no one was hurt. Candy will appear before the judge to be accountable to these charges. They are aware that she lives in Ohio.

After passing her G.E.D course in only one class session, I taught her to parallel-park using the empty garbage cans as guides along my long driveway. Candy finally obtained her Ohio driver's license. It was time to attend college since the Lord had spoken to my heart about her "genius I.Q." Her basic language skills were underdeveloped and sometimes it seemed as if she had just gotten out of a cave and entered life. She had limited skills for the work force.

Candy is endearing. Everyone who meets her loves her, but she didn't always love herself. Self-hatred drove her down a destructive path. A fear of rejection has held her in bondage.

When she attended church with us it was always emotional. She has a tender heart for the Lord. She made numerous trips to the altar to surrender her life to the Lord. However, despite her open heart and desire for God, it was hard for her to continue her walk in Christ.

A few years ago, in spite of church attendance, she continued to keep company with the fast crowd and ended up in prison for possession of marijuana. The entire six months she was incarcerated I wrote her inspirational letters filled with scriptures to express my love and concern for her life. When she got out, it was back to the fast track. Sometimes I actually think I've been to hell and back many times with her. I marvel at God's grace to enable me to stick it out.

One day I was at my computer attempting to find suitable jobs for Candy. Daryl was seated nearby. I turned to him in frustration because she had so few skills and no education.

"Agree with me in prayer that one of these employers will hire Candy."

Within days she was hired as part of a college group that sold promotional merchandise to business owners in various parts of town. With her outgoing personality she excelled in sales and gained more self-confidence. During one of her sales pitches, she met an older man that I'll call Grim because he has such a dismal outlook on life. She dated him until he exposed his true colors. After showing signs of domestic violence and extreme control, she broke it off with him. It was another self-destructive path she chose to take, much to my dismay.

Self-destructive patterns were not yet broken in Candy. Therefore, she was easy prey to abusive men like Grim.

A few weeks after leaving this abusive relationship Candy discovered she was pregnant. She didn't think it was possible because a doctor once told her she couldn't conceive. It was bittersweet news. I wondered about her ability to care for a child with no education or life skills. In her third trimester I encouraged her to re-enroll in community college and give it another try.

Except for the 2007 summer term, when her baby was born, Candy has been a fulltime student at a reputable two-year community college. She plans to further her education at a four-year university. For the six consecutive terms she's attended she's maintained a 4.0 grade point average. In fact, she's now a member of *Phi Theta Kappa International Honor Society.* She's been getting out-of-state college scholarship offers right and left in the mail. She was recently awarded the most prestigious scholarship offered at her school. More than 3,000 students had also applied for it, but Candy received the award!

A few months ago, in our kitchen, Candy was reading aloud a homework assignment to Daryl and me. It was a short story from her Latin class. He exclaimed, "Are you translating that from *Latin!*" It *was* astounding. Without faltering on a single word, she had translated the entire one-page story into English. Considering her past and all of the handicaps she's overcome, it was a remarkable ability.

When her baby was about twelve months old, I accompanied Candy to the doctor's office for his check-up exam. Her very nice female physician had treated Candy throughout her entire pregnancy. Now she was also the family doctor. Dr. Olson smiled brightly. She studied Candy's face with admiration in her eyes. She said, "You've done a complete 180 degree turn for the better. When I first met you during your early pregnancy, I didn't think you'd ever make it as a mother. Now look at you!"

Chuckling in agreement, I said, "Will you put that in writing?" I've been hard at work keeping record of all Candy's accomplishments. It's been a labor of love to keep her motivated and active in church, but as the Lord leads, I follow.

Look on me and answer, O LORD my God. Give light to my eyes, or I will sleep in death; my enemy will say, 'I have overcome him,' and my foes will rejoice when I fall. But I trust in Your unfailing love; my heart rejoices in Your salvation. Psalm 13:3-5 (NIV)

Discussion Question

1. Have you ever rescued someone from a very destructive lifestyle?

2. Do you understand that people need rescuing from sex slavery or adult entertainment?

3. Have you ever met someone who has overcome an addictive lifestyle of drugs?

4. Does your church lovingly welcome men and women who have experienced the dark side of life?

Notes

Chapter Nineteen

Inner City Gangs

You'd have to be a former gang member or a wayward youth to have a heart for this kind of outreach. Many ex-drug addicts do. Tina's outreach to troubled teens is admirable. She had fulfilled her dream of becoming a nurse and was feeling a burden to use her new station in life to reach troubled youth.

During a visit to Tina's weekly Bible study last year, I met a beautiful Christian lady named Tammy, a dedicated drug and alcohol counselor with the Urban Minority Alcoholism & Drug Abuse Outreach Program (U.M.A.D.A.O.P). I brought my tape recorder with me to interview this reformed crack addict. Tammy said, "We need more people like Tina to invest in our youth. Because these kids are our future, they are our precious jewels, and if we don't put anything in them, then we can't expect to get anything out of them. It does take a community to raise a child, and that's what we all need to do."

Tammy went on to say, "You can't solve the problem of the drug and alcohol abuse unless you touch all aspects of their lives – meaning family, support system, structure, discipline, basically meeting the kid where they're at, which is my approach. This city would be wonderful if we could just get some men to be positive role models; to be fathers to these fatherless kids. Unfortunately, because of what society brings today, talk is cheap, and seeing-is-believing, so our kids need something tangible. We have to show our youth that 'you can make it, that you are someone and you can reach your potential and you can achieve your dreams, but we have to give them a hand in doing so. We have to give them something to believe in. So many of them have been misled by broken promises, then we as a community and a society come in and break more promises, so we lose them. We can really make a difference if we have some positive roles models to mentor and get involved."

In my walk with Christ, I've observed that many sincere Christians like to preach, counsel, or dish out advice to the down trodden, but talk is cheap. Genuine Christian ministry will touch you where it hurts, in the wallet.

It's true that I've made sacrifices in order to give to those less fortunate. I have no regrets for the time or money spent because no worldly possessions compare with the blessings that come from witnessing a life transformed in Christ. My one true regret is that I don't have greater resources to help more people.

It doesn't take much. Don't excuse yourself if your household budget is tight. While she was living, my friend Shar used to clip coupons for diapers, toilet paper, feminine products, and cleaning supplies because these necessities aren't covered by food stamps. Shar would stock up on these items to give away because most single mothers struggle to have enough money at the end of the month to cover these additional expenses. All of us have a few dollars left over from our food budget. If not, skimp to find a way for added cash. Your family will never notice and besides, leftovers are always better the next day.

Occasionally filling someone's vehicle up with gas is helpful for a single mother getting to work or attending college. Slipping ten bucks in a pocket to purchase incidentals is another way.

However, my most valuable commodity is *time* spent driving a single mother to a doctor's appointment, to a court appearance, or to the Ohio Department of Jobs and Family Services to help a qualified person sign up for public assistance or to show up for necessary follow-up appointments with assigned caseworkers. I've spent countless hours waiting with a friend to be called by the bailiff or a caseworker. This is a long tedious process. However, this one-on-one time is an excellent occasion to bond with a lost soul and share the principles of Christ through natural conversation. Most people don't like to be preached at or told how to live. Use caution when quoting scriptures. The world is not receptive to reform or to getting told what to do by Christians. It's always best to share how God has changed your own life because there can be no argument about the power of a testimony. Make sure you're not being condescending or lording it over someone who isn't as enlightened as you are. "The fruit of the spirit is love, joy, peace, longsuffering, kindness, goodness, faithfulness, gentleness, and self-control." (Galatians 5:22-23)

The most successful opportunities for serving and giving are discovered in soul searching prayer. Earnestly seek the Lord to reveal practical ways to meet the needs of those less fortunate. Our Heavenly Father will direct your path and orchestrate "divine connections" if you have a sincere heart to bless others. Just doing dishes or folding clean laundry for a busy mom or a frazzled college student is a blessing beyond words.

You'll be tested. Sometimes appreciation isn't always expressed. You might start to feel that your good deeds have gone unnoticed or your important time has been taken for granted. Growing up, my mother always used to tease, "You'll get your reward in Heaven" whenever my two brothers and I expected payment for some accomplished household chore. The Lord will challenge your heart by the ingratitude of others. If your motives are pure you will not be offended if someone doesn't express instant appreciation or send a thank-you note by mail. Our reward is not in this lifetime.

When Tina came into my life, she was an emotional mess for good reason. There were many times when she felt like throwing in the towel and giving up. Many of us can certainly relate to despair and tremendous discouragement.

The Bible teaches us that the *Key of David* unlocks prison doors. I found this principle to be true, but it would take an entire book to share my personal revelation about the power of praise and worship.

Tina granted me permission to share this following testimony.

Twenty years ago, Tina telephoned me one evening after being emotionally beaten down by her abusive husband. Domestic violence is about the control of one human being by another. This control begins with verbal abuse and is similar to mind control. Verbal abuse attacks one's spirit and sense of self. Verbal abuse attempts to create self-doubt so the victim becomes fearful. She was in the midst of a divorce trying to cope with the oppression of past physical and mental abuse. The financial pressures of poverty also created feelings of complete hopelessness. Even though Tina was separated from this man and was no longer being physically abused, the telephone became a weapon when her abuser verbally assaulted her sense of worth. His threats continued and she didn't feel safe either. Her world had caved in around her. She was a young woman with a two-year old son and an infant baby boy.

Through halting sobs of anguish, she managed to choke out these words, "I can't take it any longer. I'm dropping my kids off at an emergency room then I'm going to kill myself."

"No, you're not," I said with firm authority. "You're going to get off this phone and go straight to your bedroom to get on your face before the Lord. Then you're going to praise Him until He gives you a song of deliverance."

That directive might sound insensitive to someone actually threatening suicide, but I knew that Tina had a tender and sincere heart to worship the Lord. She needed a breakthrough. God needed to set her free. Jesus was waiting for her to seek Him.

Tina called back within twenty minutes with a new song to sing. She was gushing with joy because God had set her free. Years later, sometimes I still hear that song playing in my spirit because it is a beautiful melody. At the time, we also sang it in church, too. Perhaps the words to

Tina's Heavenly song will minister to your emotional pain . . .

> *Holy and Righteous are You, Lord*
> *Holy and Pure is Your Name*
> *The Lamb of God,*
> *The Healer of our transgressions*
> *Holy and Righteous are You.*

You can praise your way out of anything, which is why the Bible calls it a *sacrifice* of praise.

I'm a worshipper because I love Jesus with all my heart. My life has been dedicated to serving and doing whatever I can to help someone succeed or discover their God-given talents. If I had my life to live all over again, I wouldn't change a thing. When I enter Heaven, by the Blood of the Lamb, I long to hear the Lord greet me with *"Well done, thy good and faithful servant."*

Whoever is generous to the poor lends to the Lord and he will repay him for his deed. Proverbs 19:17 (NIV)

Whoever sows sparingly will also reap sparingly, and whoever sows generously will also reap generously. II Corinthians 9:6 (NIV)

Tina recently posted this "Food for Thought" on her Face Book page recently…

"Some Don't Know About"

Food for thought: Everybody knows about food stamps & Ramen Noodles, but some don't know about walking to the laundromat with big bags of clothes, or boiling water on the stove for baths, lighting candles in the house because the power went off and not because it was storming. Some don't know about hand-me downs, second hand clothes, sleeping on the couch or on the floor. Some don't know about getting groceries at a food pantry or waiting in a lunch line for a meal, or turning the oven on to heat the house. Some don't know about hand-washing clothes in the bathtub or sink and drying it on a clothes line. Some don't know about showering at someone else's house.

If you haven't struggled, I don't expect you to understand. I never ate from a silver-spoon; therefore, I will never make fun of another person who struggles…where much is given, much is required. It made me who I am today. We adapt, we overcome & we survive! Stay humble!
Copy and paste if you understand!

Discussion Questions

1. Are you aware that teenagers from broken homes are most susceptible to gang involvement?

2. Does your church offer youth programs for teens?

3. Are you alert to lonely teens who are vulnerable to sex-trafficking?

4. Are you alert to social media and other Internet traps that entice young people into dangerous situations?

Notes

Chapter Twenty

Forsaking All to Follow Jesus

After asking a stranger to lift a lone purple vase off the top shelf to place in my basket, I continued to mosey around house wares. "Thank you, sir." He smiled, but his wife gave me the evil eye.

As I turned the corner, our mini carts nearly collided in a kitchen aisle near an end cap containing stainless steel gadgets. The tall, stunning redhead looked like a movie star and slightly out of character in the discount department store. Rodeo Drive in Beverly Hills might have been more appropriate for my dazzling friend, who was golden brown from the sun, looking fabulous in an all-white cotton jacket. Susan's polished nails were long and perfect. Nearly every finger was enhanced with her signature diamond rings – the only woman I know who might wear that many glistening baubles for breakfast each morning.

"Well, hello! What are you doing at my end of town?" I asked, grinning from ear to ear. Susan and Don were our dearest friends, but it had been many months since we'd seen each other. She was hunting for a child's quilt for her granddaughter's bed.

"Oh, look at these *huge* garlic presses! Have you seen any like these?" I gushed.

"Yes. And they really work *great*," Susan said, taking the press from my hands. "Look, see how this extra piece slides back and forth? The outer skin doesn't get stuck like it does with the other presses. I'm buying two – one for our condo in Florida and another for a shower gift."

"Then I'll get one, too." I said. You can always count on Susan to be up on the latest of *everything*. She's a gourmet cook and a fabulous hostess.

Decades earlier one could never imagine this glamour queen serving on the mission field in India using a rock to hand wash clothes. Susan's husband Don, a beloved Christian physician, heard the voice of the Lord. Like Abraham, in faithful obedience, he sold his large family practice, his opulent home in Muirfield Village, and both of his swanky cars. Within months Doc and Susan, along with their two children, Bethany, 5, and Joshua, 4, moved to South India to serve in an impoverished orphanage and help build a new medical facility within the compound.

There are more than 11 million abandoned children in India, where a growing number of newborn babies are being dumped anonymously in cots placed outside orphanages in an initiative to deter infanticide. About 90 percent of those abandoned are girls whose poor young mothers cannot afford to keep them. These children face a bleak future as beggars, prostitutes, or menial laborers if families cannot be found for them.

Through their church affiliation, this dedicated couple had been sending monthly financial support to an orphanage in South India for several years. When the director, "Brother Samuel," passed through Ohio he called Susan and Don to personally thank them. Susan cooked a beautiful dinner for him in her home. Brother Samuel graciously invited the Furci family to India for a few weeks to help raise awareness for his three orphanages. They accepted the invitation, but decided to make it a permanent relocation. Obviously, this was not an easy decision. It was a bumpy road that caused great anguish before they departed on this faith journey.

Years earlier, as a new physician starting out in the medical field, Don's faith was tested with tremendous financial hurdles. As a Christian doctor he often felt tempted to join up with various medical mission teams as a means to escape, but all doors were mysteriously shut. The Lord spoke to his heart one day. "Running is the easy way out. I will see you through every financial obstacle." Over the few years that followed, the Lord was faithful to His word.

Soon Don's family medical practice was flourishing. Financially, it was everything he hoped for as a doctor. He was like the rich young ruler, so God began to test the motives of his heart. After prayer one afternoon the Lord directed his attention to the diplomas and awards on the wall. He said, "The Lord spoke to my heart by saying, 'all these are nice and fine achievements, but in the end, they will be burnt up and mean nothing.' In that instant, I knew the choice was mine. I could continue serving man for money or follow the true riches from God, my Heavenly Father. In that moment I immediately felt the presence of a doorway. My response was, 'Lord, I want to follow You.' Not long afterwards, the door opened to go to India."

Susan told me that accepting a three-week invitation to visit India was not a problem. However, when her husband of ten years began acting sullen, she knew something was amiss. Finally, on a Thursday evening, Don confessed that God had spoken to his heart to "go and don't make plans to come back." Needless to say, Susan was stunned beyond words. As a highly organized planner, she made detailed lists for the grocery, vacations, the mall, and various daily errands. Susan loved the Lord, but she was not willing to give up her children to an English-speaking boarding school like other missionary couples had done. She dug in her heels. She wasn't budging until God spoke to her about a permanent relocation to a third world country that considered cows more sacred than human life.

After Don told her about "not making plans to come back," her life was turned upside down. During the next three days Susan felt like Jonah in the belly of the whale. She agonized every possible scenario in her mind. She wrestled with God. Then came Sunday.

"As I walked around the lovely lake near our home, I stopped at a stone bench to wait upon the Lord," Susan reflected. "I remember lying down on my back to gaze up at the blue sky above me. It was so quiet and beautiful, but I felt absolutely no peace within my troubled soul. I closed my eyes to blot out my tormenting thoughts of living in India forever. I purposed to hear the word of the Lord because I sensed He wanted to comfort me. My spirit tuned into His voice, which was gentle and reassuring. He said, 'don't go because you're afraid of losing your husband. Don't go to keep your Christian reputation. GO because it is MY will for your life and I will keep you. And if you don't go, I will still love you.'"

Unless you are extremely wealthy, life in India is horrible, especially for committed missionaries who live among the lower class of people.

Rats roamed freely at the orphanage where Doc and Susan served. One day a little boy had been hurt. Doc sent Susan to fetch his medical bag out of their room. When Susan dashed into the apartment, she came eye-to-eye with a large rat on top of their small refrigerator. This same varmint had been eating bananas off the kitchen table each night for more than a week. The morning of discovery a few bananas were half-eaten. The next morning, all the bananas were on the floor. After Don and Susan prayed about this serious rat problem, a cat mysteriously appeared on the compound. The Lord solved the fearful rat dilemma in both situations.

With the grace of God, Don and Susan adjusted to the extreme culture barriers. Susan's letters were filled with delightful stories of the orphanage. She gave the children much needed affection and her own two children became fluent in the native language.

Sweet deprivation seemed the hardest to bear for Susan. I always included Hershey chocolate bars or Bit-O-Honey candy in my letters. These flat candy bars fit perfectly inside an envelope. When I heard about the hardship of Susan washing clothes on a rock, I mailed her a zinc scrub board, "a modern convenience" from America. I wasn't about to let my "Sister Susan" suffer such hardship!

Each morning the gate to the orphanage opened up to natives who had walked for miles for medical treatment. Along with two other Indian doctors, Doc helped treat hundreds of men, women, and children every day. Two hundred and sixty-eight were allowed through the gates each morning. Peasants not making it through would spend the night outside, camping out till the next morning. Tuberculosis was very common there. Field hands often showed up with serious machete cuts on legs, arms, or hands. The medical needs were vast.

All those making it through the gate would patiently sit around in the large courtyard, waiting their turn for medical attention. The native women, dressed in traditional saris, sat on the ground with their children. To pass the time they'd nit-pick lice eggs from the hair of infected heads of children. This was a common sight at bus stops and other public places. Susan quickly learned to use a small comb to clean the lice from heads of orphans under her care.

Doc frequently traveled throughout the countryside with Brother Samuel, bringing additional medical aid and much needed awareness for financial support. It was a rewarding and productive time for this young, handsome physician.

Don experienced blood poisoning from a rat bite on his arm while sleeping one night. Fortunately, he was able to medically treat himself. He said to Susan, "If I pass out, promise me you won't take me to a hospital." The medical conditions in India were below our American standards and he wasn't taking any chances.

Due to difficulties with their visas, Don and Susan needed to leave India after only four months. They had planned to stay indefinitely. However, God had alternate plans.

Returning to Ohio was no longer an option because starting up another family practice would be unethical. Doc had sold his practice and all of his former patients would desire to return to him. Thus, he honored his non-compete clause. Fortunately, he was also licensed in Florida, so he opened a family practice in Sarasota. At their Christian family medical center, Don and Susan touched countless lives with the love of Jesus. Doc prayed with many of his patients whenever they expressed a desire for spiritual guidance. Don and Susan Furci were blessed to see their staff personnel and numerous patients enlightened for Christ. I'm very honored to call them my friends.

Years later the Lord brought them full circle back to Ohio. Doc is now a medical director in a large family clinic that trains medical students and residents. His gift for teaching is another way the Lord has used him as a physician.

Once a year Doc faithfully leads a team of doctors and nurses to Belize in Central America. These countless short-term mission trips have raised awareness of the critical needs of another impoverished nation. These teams of medical professionals have provided support to under-developed villages by empowering local people to collaborate, learn new skills, and improve their own communities.

On one such infamous Belize mission trip, Susan decided to accompany the team as the "official cook." From home she brought food for her carefully planned delicious meals. The first morning, Jim Hill, a seasoned member of the American team, came down early to start coffee. He had been on numerous trips in the past, so he was able to show Susan the way around the kitchen. He also had another reason for being up so early.

Jim nonchalantly banged a frying pan on the pipeline running from the sink to the open hole in the ceiling. "That's to keep the rats away." Undaunted, Susan also banged the pipes before preparing breakfast or other meals. Thankfully, she had been initiated in rat patrol in India.

Perhaps God is calling you to short-term mission outreach. He may not require you to sell all your earthy possessions, deal with snakes, or sewer rats. However, the Lord may be calling you to a local clinic in your own city. Piece of cake!

For I know the plans I have for you, declares the LORD, plans to prosper you and not to harm you, plans to give you hope and a future. Jeremiah 29:11 (NIV)

Discussion Questions

1. Have you ever considered going on a short-term mission trip to a foreign country?

2. Do you encourage your teens to do community work during the summer months?

3. Do you offer encourage your children to extend charity to those less fortunate?

Notes

Chapter Twenty-One

Foster Care for Families in Crisis

My dear friends, Debbie and Eva, were housemates for several years. They met in California. Eva was a short, Mexican gal with a cherub face and a temperament to match. The first time I was introduced to sweet Eva, I shook my head. I chuckled, "You're going to have Crowns in Heaven for living with Debbie." It took someone as angelic as Eva to live in harmony with ironclad Debbie, who never learned the meaning of "no." Just ask her mother. I should also add that this was a pure friendship in the Lord.

Unfortunately, Eva was severely handicapped from a broken hip that happened at birth, when a drunken doctor delivered her. Failed surgeries in her lifetime caused her to walk humped over with a tremendous limp. Eva was very pretty with a loving, and cheerful personality, but tragically she was maimed for life.

Debbie was a big gal with blond hair and beautiful, expressive blue eyes. She had a flair for glamour and was always trying to jazz me up with heavier make-up, which just wasn't my style. Deb was also a hairdresser with her own beauty salon. Eva did acrylic nails for the steady customers who were mostly Deb's numerous friends. However, once you got in Deb's salon chair, it would be hours before you got free from her artistic clutches. She'd come up with any excuse to keep you there all day long because she wanted to improve your looks and enjoy your company. It was a new hairstyle, a different color to try out, a total hair weave or just ordering food to enjoy fellowship with good friends. Then she'd say, "Hey, do you want to go to the movies?" If Debbie was in a bad mood you were likely to get a lousy haircut. No one ever complained because Debbie had such a magnetic personality. She never let go of anyone she liked. If you were her friend, it was for life.

One day I was in her salon and overheard a new customer expressing heavy sighs. This poor lady with wet hair was obviously exasperated. She was tired of waiting on Debbie as she flitted back and forth between two or three other haircuts or shampoos. Undaunted, Debbie looked at me and whispered. "I haven't broken her in yet."

Debbie and I could laugh our heads off over the silliest things. We shared the same sense of humor, so she was always fun to be around. Years ago, Debbie would show up at my house to give my kids haircuts and stay for two or three weeks. There was a time when she lived out of her trunk and went from one friend's house to another for months.

When Debbie announced that she and Eva signed up for emergency foster care my eyes widened in disbelief. I couldn't imagine Debbie jumping in to rescue helpless children. But I was terribly wrong. For the next few years these dedicated women lovingly took in 35 children in desperate need of safety.

Foster care could last for many months or just a few days. Regardless of the need, these two dedicated women would be available, day or night. It was not unusual to get an emergency call in the middle of the night to pick up two or three little children taken by authorities from domestic violence or other potentially harmful situations involving guns and drugs. Their three-bedroom apartment was set up with bunk beds, cribs, and toys. The social workers at Children's Protective Services in Columbus loved them because they were two Christian women with more flexibility than most of their foster care providers.

Debbie got emotionally attached to a two-year old named Samantha. This troubled child had two older sisters that were placed in a different foster home. It was a terrible situation with the birth parents, so Debbie was hoping to adopt Samantha. She spent tireless months working with this little girl to help her overcome fear and other negative behaviors. But Samantha was taken from Debbie and placed in another foster home. Debbie appealed with a ten-page letter to no avail. Yet, a year or so later, Samantha returned to Debbie.

A few years after that, Debbie was awarded permanent custody of Samantha. She changed her name to Nicole. We had an adoption party with grandparents, aunts, uncles, and all of Deb's friends. Of course, everyone was thrilled that this little girl was now in a safe and loving Christian family.

About this same time, a social worker called Eva to announce that a little Mexican boy needed a loving mother. Nathan was four years old and looked like he could have been Eva's natural born son. Eva had Nathan for a few years before the adoption became final. Eva was thrilled because this child was very loving and bonded with her immediately.

One autumn, Debbie and Eva were attending a women's retreat put on by our church. A woman name Anne was also among a crowd of women gathered in the main lodge for fellowship one evening. Anne's husband was an orthopedic surgeon who specialized in hips and knees, so I knew her heart would melt seeing Eva's severe disfigurement. I turned to Anne and whispered, "See that pretty girl sitting over there? Watch how she walks from a deformed hip." Anne and Dave were loving and generous Christians. A few weeks later, Dave performed corrective surgery on Eva's hip and didn't charge her for this expensive operation. Eva's insurance paid for her hospital stay. Eva now walks with a straight back and no longer limps! Her father couldn't believe it was true. He actually flew in from California to see his beautiful daughter finally free from the deformity that had plagued her for more than 35 years. Naturally, all of Eva's friends also rejoiced because no one was more deserving of this miracle blessing than our sweet Eva.

Debbie planned a surprise adoption party for Eva and Nathan, but she was too fatigued to carry out her elaborate plans. Debbie sat in a kitchen chair while I prepared all the finger food for the party, which was the next day following church.

We laughed and yakked it up till midnight as I prepared tuna salad, egg salad, an array of chip-dips and other delicious food items for the next day. I also decked out their dining room table with all my nice serving pieces from home. It was something I did with little effort and was more than happy to do because Debbie just wasn't up to it. She kept saying, "I could have never pulled this off, Barbara. Thank goodness you came to my rescue."

Debbie had taken in a new dog from the shelter. Tawny was a sheltie and beagle mix and a nuisance. She was under your feet at all times. If you were seated, she managed to squeeze in behind your knees when you were seated on the couch. I recall both Debbie and Eva yelling at the dog for nearly getting stepped on. Tawny kept following me into the garage each time I needed to store prepared food in the spare refrigerator. At one point I lost my shadow. I said, "Where's Tawny?" She was accidentally trapped in the dark garage.

After that, I said, "I'll take Tawny home with me so she won't be underfoot with all your guests tomorrow." Debbie thought that was an excellent idea. The odd thing about that suggestion was that I had often reprimanded Debbie for bringing that stray dog home. She had a pampered purebred named Brittney, the reigning princess of the household. When Tawny came along as second fiddle, Brittney often attacked her. One time, during a quiet prayer meeting, the two dogs went at it again like two pit bulls. As I often exclaimed on previous visits, I yelled "Debbie! *Get rid* of that dog!" We talked to each other like genuine sisters because we had known each other since 1976.

A few weeks later, we found out why Debbie was so exhausted. She had ovarian cancer. The night before her surgery she made another good friend, Bonnie White, and I stayed with her until she fell asleep. Debbie needed to drink some awful tasting concoction and needed our moral support to finish it off. Of course, she managed to find an excuse to keep us there by taking small sips every half hour to pass the time away. That was so Debbie.

We prayed with her before she drifted off to sleep. About midnight Bonnie and I stood on each side of her bed to pray over her before we left. I noticed Debbie was breathing "funny," so I called for the nurse. When the nurse came in to check on Debbie she immediately hit the "code blue" panic button. Within seconds, two doctors and three nurses were frantically tending to Debbie. They rushed her out of there because she was in trouble. Bonnie and I ended up spending the entire night waiting to see if she was okay. I had to call her mother, Darlene, at 3:00 a.m. As it turned out, Debbie was fine. Leave it to her to have Bonnie and me, along with the entire medical ward, in a complete state of panic. That was so Debbie.

Her surgery revealed that the cancer had progressed throughout her body. Her last few days were spent in Hospice Care near the large hospital that had done her surgery six months earlier. Bonnie called me that morning to tell me that Debbie was now in Hospice care, but I thought she still had a few remaining days. Several hours later, I stopped by to see Debbie. I leisurely got out of my car that cold January afternoon. But I hurried along when I heard the Holy Spirit say, "Death is knocking on the door." When I entered Debbie's private room her mother, brother, aunt, uncle, Bonnie, and Eva were surrounding her in a holy-hushed, deathbed vigil. A pillow had propped the door ajar. When I entered, her mother said cheerfully, "Debbie, Barbara is here!"

I reverently slipped in next to Eva who was clasping Debbie's right hand. Her mother stood on the opposite side tearfully gripping her other hand. They had been like that for several hours waiting for Debbie to take her final breath.

Eva stepped back so I could take Debbie's hand. As soon as I took Debbie's hand, she gave up her spirit. In fact, I felt the Lord take her and my knees buckled from the spiritual witness of that divine moment. The nurse jumped up from her chair with a stethoscope to listen to her heart. Debbie was gone in that instant from this earth. Debbie had been holding on until I got there to bid her farewell. That was so Debbie.

Before the funeral, Eva gave me a huge box of pictures to put together a photo collage of Debbie's life. I sat at my dining room table for a few days sorting through pictures. I had many tearful moments seeing Debbie's life unfold before my eyes. A few times I felt Debbie standing over my shoulder to make sure I selected the best pictures to display. That was so Debbie.

Bonnie and I both spoke at her funeral. Debbie has been dearly missed. I've never found another friend like her and I never will.

Sadly, a few months later, Eva left for California with Nathan. Darlene and husband Bob, along with Bonnie and I, helped Eva load up the van. In fact, we all had been packing for days. Bob was going to miss Nathan very much. He often took him fishing and they had formed a special bond. Bob told me about his dream about Nathan. He saw Nathan as an adult preaching to a crowd of people in a large auditorium. I believe that will come true. Nathan was a very special little boy, just as sweet as his mother. Truly God's hand was upon him when he was placed in Eva's care.

Another gal was helping Eva drive back home. It was so sad to see them drive off. They arrived safely back in Los Angeles and quickly reconnected with Eva's large Mexican family. I called a few weeks later. Eva laughed when she told me that Nathan fit right in with all his cousins. She said, "He looks just like them!"

Before her death, Debbie made legal arrangements for Nicole to live with the young Christian family who had adopted Nicole's two older sisters. Eva kept in touch with Nicole and they were eventually reunited because it didn't work out with this family. Nicole joyfully came to live with her other mommy, Eva, and her little brother Nathan in California.

Debbie's pampered dog Brittney went into a "nursing home" ministry, getting affection from the elderly all day long. And Tawny, the misfit dog, the one I often complained about, became the most beloved dog in our long history of family pets. My son lovingly nicknamed her Tay-dee. She lived out her life for several more years sitting on our laps and getting all the loving attention she needed. We were all heartbroken when she suffered with liver failure and had to be put to sleep. After several days in the hospital, the vet called me with the sad news. I brought Tay-dee home for our family to say our goodbyes. She arrived with instructions for her I.V. drip because she had stopped eating and drinking. I bathed her and tearfully called the twins. We took her pillow and our other dog, Taffy, back to the veterinarian's office the next morning. I sat on the tiled floor beside Tay-dee, as she rested on her warm pillow. She was so sick. The attendant wanted to take her away for the procedure, but I insisted on petting her as she took her last breath. Elisa and Leanne tearfully watched in moral support. After she was gone, our tears of grief were inconsolable. It was one of the saddest days of my life.

Foster care extends to many areas of family life. It's very painful at times. You have to say goodbye to precious children you've grown to love. However, the triumphs far outweigh the tragedies. It's very rewarding for all who take the risk.

Eva came to Ohio in faith. I, for one, was most apprehensive about her future away from her close-knit family in California. However, the Lord had plans for this friendship. Eva gave our dear friend Debbie the courage to enter into the risky business of foster care. She was also there for Debbie's cancer ordeal. Eva had a beautiful, loving spirit, but she was physically handicapped. For her obedience, the Lord blessed her. Five years later, Eva left Ohio with a healthy new body, free from pain. She walked with a straight back and no hideous limp. Best of all, she adopted a precious little boy who looks just like her. Both Nicole and Nathan adore their mother.

That is so God. And I know Debbie is in Heaven smiling down on us. The Lord used her in a very special way, during her brief time on earth. She touched many children who were in harm's way. Debbie was a prayer warrior and a genuine woman of faith. God used her feisty ways and steely determination to boldly crusade for a part of society that most people selfishly shun or simply ignore. God placed those needy children in her care for a reason. God has certainly honored Debbie and Eva's faithful prayers to cover these children with His divine protection throughout their difficult journey.

Perhaps the Lord has called you to reach out to children in need. May Eva and Debbie become an inspiration to you to consider foster care or legal adoption. Go ahead, take a chance and get involved. There is a child in need waiting for your loving arms and dedicated prayers.

Command those who are rich in this present age not to be haughty, nor to trust in uncertain riches but in the living God, who gives us richly all things to enjoy. Let them do good, that they be rich in good works, ready to give, willing to share, storing up for themselves a good foundation for the time to come, that they may lay hold on eternal life. 1 Timothy 6:17-19 (New King James Version)

Discussion Questions

1. Have you ever considered Foster Care for infants, children or teens?\

2. What would stop you from taking in a child in need or nurturing?

3. Do you pray or give financial support to local charities that offer shelter to abandoned children?

4. As a doctor, dentist, or lawyer have you offered your services to someone in need?

Chapter Twenty-Two
Faith is an Adventurous Journey

Have you ever wondered how some Christians seem to be able to walk on water? I don't mean the Christians who teach or preach on television. They have sacrificed and the Lord has taken them through hell-on-earth to be proven fit for a national platform, so don't ever envy them. I'm referring to ordinary, everyday Christians you meet in church. I've wondered about such things. I've longed for that kind of genuine faith. How does one obtain faith that is so strong? During hard times these warriors in the faith never waver, never grow cold, never stammer, stutter, or falter. They are unshakable, unmovable, unflappable and never blame God for unfortunate circumstances. What a place to be! Unfeigned faith is genuine faith. It means "without hypocrisy, without a mask." Abraham was the Father of Faith–he certainly had it. The New Testament says that Timothy's grandmother Lois had genuine faith. Her daughter, Eunice, mother of Timothy, also had it. The Apostle Paul exhorted his spiritual son, Timothy, to get a hold of his inherited faith and not to be afraid. Through prayer, Paul stirred up Timothy to stand strong, to walk in his inheritance of faith.

Faith moves mountains, faith conquers death, faith removes prison walls, faith removes darkness, faith stills the storms and breathes in light. Faith is not in a pill form. We can't buy it. Faith can't be faked or conjured up when we're faced with insurmountable problems. Faith is more like a redeeming force that takes over when we're in the middle of a panic attack or ready to jump off of a bridge.

Faith is tangible and transferable. Faith is unseen, but it can be felt. Faith is like a blood transfusion. Faith surges. Faith arises. Faith takes over. Faith ignites and sets us on fire. Faith renews and helps us to recover. Faith calms the storm. Faith refreshes. Faith brings life out of death. Faith is stubborn and won't be moved or smothered. Faith is what we need.

Faith originates in the heart of God. Our Heavenly Father expects us to get faith from Him. It pleases Him to supply our needs. He is a loving Father. Whatever He gives us is for our own good and overall wellness. If we ignore God and act on our own, we fall into trouble. Faith is dependent upon God. Faith never fails. Faith shows up on time and is never late. Faith is like the bail bondsman. We may end up in jail before we realize we need faith to get out. Faith will bail us out of jail, but not if we don't want it. Faith lets us know that God is in charge. Faith is the doorkeeper. Faith is a key to get close to God.

My journey in faith began with a fairy tale wedding when I married Daryl Sanders, my handsome prince. He was a successful businessman who was vice president of a Fortune 500 company in Dayton, Ohio. Before we met, he was playing in the National Football League. Before being selected as an NFL number one draft pick, an offensive tackle for the Detroit Lions, he played for Coach Woody Hayes at Ohio State University. He played in a championship game and has a dedicated chapter in the book, entitled *Woody's Boys* and later in the documentary *"Beyond the Grid Iron: The Life and Times of Coach Woody Hayes.*

We were in love and life was good. In the first two years of marriage, we enjoyed executive travel to exotic places like the Canary Islands, Acapulco, Morocco, Paris, Madrid, and Paradise Island in the Bahamas. I had a full-time maid and lived in a beautiful historic home with five bathrooms and six fireplaces. We gave elaborate dinner parties and had many good-looking and successful friends.

My stepchildren, Tammy and Scott, ages 12 and 11 were the only snag in this romantic picture. At age 17, Daryl had married a pretty, but troubled girl right out of high school. She was his first love and being responsible, he married his pregnant 16-year-old girl friend. By the time Daryl finished college, he had two babies to support. He also worked a third job to pay for his wife's private psychiatric sessions. After ten years of a tumultuous marriage, his kids were an emotional mess. Divorce was imminent.

Crowns in Heaven are awaiting suffering stepchildren and their stepparent. It's no wonder divorce is a grievance to God and considered sin. Oh, the mess we make of our lives by willful decisions and wrong thinking. God is never in the scenario when the selfish choices land us in bondage through financial failure or broken relationships. Living outside of the will of God is a path too many take, which is why divorce is rampant and the lives of children suffer. Our society is paying a high price for the damage done when married couples split.

Marriage was never a goal for me. I grew up as a tomboy. Climbing trees and playing softball from noon to dusk was my favorite warm weather pastime. When the farmland behind my grandfather's house turned into a subdivision, I used to collect wood scraps for my prize tree fort in a perfect tree across the street. During the summer, I also sold lemonade to the thirsty construction workers.

In the empty lots behind Grandpa's house, whenever new basement foundations were dug, I'd ride my bike along the edge, within an inch, as fast as I could, along the bumps of the gravel and fresh dirt. A true daredevil. But one day I tumbled down, with my bike and all. Fortunately, my dad was looking out of the second story window of our home. I have a feeling he had been watching me drive through that construction zone. Dad must have been quite alarmed to see his nine-year old daughter take a critical nose-dive into the deep, freshly dug foundation. It's a wonder I didn't break my neck. Within a few minutes Dad was there to rescue me. He didn't find me crying or afraid. Rather, I was angry that I couldn't get out by myself! My dad must have been surprised to find me standing on top of my bike seat, straining with all of my might to reach the top. All he had to do is reach down and pull me out by my up stretched hands.

God is like that, too. He waits until our foolishness lands us in a deep pit. His compassion and mercy never waver, so when His hand reaches down to pull us out, He never says, "I told you so." My dad was so relieved to find me alive, he didn't fuss at me. My scrape with death already taught me the lesson I needed to learn. There was no need to yell at me or warn me of the dangers of getting too close to the edge. Many of us go through life like that: taking chances and taking risks for the sheer thrill of it.

God promises to never leave us or forsake us. He is always watching and waiting for us to need His help. His Hand is always there to pull us out of the pit we're in by our own foolish actions or making decisions without consulting Him in prayer. It might be the pit of despair, the pit of financial ruin, the pit of sickness, or the pit of divorce.

In junior high school, I was a member of Catalina, a synchronized swim club. Our coach, Miss Natalie Herbster, drilled our team with a good workout in the pool for several hours after school every day. For fun I used to dive off the edge of the pool, jackknife-style to see "how close to the edge" I could get. One day, I felt the ceramic tiles slide down my chest as I dove down the side of the pool. When I came out of the water, Miss Herbster was lying on her back with her arms shielding her eyes, pretending to be passed out. I got the message.

Being athletically able, I was bold and seemingly fearless. In my entire childhood, I don't ever remember crying or becoming afraid of anything. In junior high, my best friend Judy Koester and I were voted "cutest girls, best dancers and most popular" by our ninth-grade fellow classmates. We entered high school feeling confident with many adoring fans.

Therefore, confidence in myself was strong. It was centered on an ability to get things done and make things happen. Therefore, at the age of twenty-five, taking on two troubled children was a task that didn't scare me. I expected Tammy and Scott to adore me, too. Boy, was I wrong! It seemed like the harder I tried to be the perfect stepmother the more I failed. Not being accepted by these children was difficult to comprehend in my own state of survival. I sincerely tried to win them over. However, their unresolved emotional conflicts caused them to distrust me. The children's rejection of my attempts to be a good mother was a jolt to my ego because I considered myself a genuine person, liked by everyone.

Consequently, I was confronted with a situation I couldn't change. In retrospect, I realize that I needed to deal with some root problems in my own shaky emotional makeup. Without the comforting guidance of the Holy Spirit, that necessary healing and an inward journey into the deep recesses of the heart for wholeness is not impossible. Jesus heals and restores a bruised and broken heart. There was an internal work to be done in our lives, especially in my own un-redeemed soul. God desired to use my life, but not until my own character deficiencies were acknowledged and surrendered at the Cross. That would happen in time, but in the process of discovering my need of God, the road was turbulent. I was truly lost and so was my family.

Before encountering these impossible obstacles that led to acknowledging my sinful nature and my need of a Savior, I considered myself quite wonderful. I was blind to the pride which was motivating me to be the "best stepmother" around. Whenever these two lonely and frightened children scorned my gallant attempts at motherhood, I felt rejected. Rejection produces anger. Since I was not anchored in Christ, I was thrown off-balance and thrust into frequent bursts of anger. My character defects were magnified by many problems that I encountered with my children. In turn, it brought pressure into our marriage because I took out my frustrations on my husband. Thankfully, our love and commitment to each other created a strong bond that nothing negative would penetrate.

The character traits I needed to develop in order to be their new mother were unconditional love, wisdom, patience, and self-control. These "fruits of the spirit" are developed by faith and trust in God. At that point in my life, I considered myself a Christian, but Jesus Christ was not in the foremost of my mind. Rather, He was in the fringe of unconscious thought, therefore Jesus Christ did not rule and reign in my life. I was calling all the shots, living independent of daily prayer, Bible reading, or asking God for the positive traits my character lacked.

After about six months of my marriage, I suffered from physical symptoms related to stress. I was not happy. In fact, I felt trapped. The future seemed as bleak as my empty and futile thoughts. Growing up I felt fearless, but suddenly I was riddled with fearfulness. I felt hopeless. I had no faith in the future at all. But God stepped in because He had a wonder plan for my life with Daryl and for our family.

At that point in time I felt hopeless without a future and my friend Sherry introduced me to a clairvoyant, who could see into the future. I went on a lark to see if Mrs. Goodman could tell me something *hopeful*. I went several times and compared notes with Sherry who was also visiting her. Then Sherry became a Christian.

After the Bible study where I accepted Jesus Christ as my personal savior in 1974 Sherry and I left the house to head for her car, I heard a voice inside my head. *So, are you going to get on your soapbox like Sherry? Are you going to preach like her and have all your friends laugh at you?* I was mortified at the thought of me proclaiming Christ to anyone. My cheeks flushed.

Sherry had already turned to a Bible passage before I closed my car door. Little did Sherry know that there was a future call of God on my life that would take me to the nations to share the love of Jesus. Her urgency to get me straightened out was valid.

"Here, read this out loud," she said, pointing to a key scripture in her open Bible.

"When you enter the land the LORD your God is giving you, do not learn to imitate the detestable ways of the Nations there. Let no one be found among you who sacrifices his son or daughter in the fire, who practices divination or sorcery, interprets omens, engages in witchcraft, or casts spells, or who is a medium or spiritualist or who consults the dead. Anyone who does these things is detestable to the LORD, and because of these detestable practices the LORD your God will drive out those nations before you. You must be blameless before the LORD your God." Deuteronomy 18:10-13 NIV

After reading the scripture passage aloud, I asked, "So? What's that got to do with me?"

"Well, that means you can't continue going to see Mrs. Goodman because she's satanic, that's why!" She exclaimed. "What does Sa-tan-ic mean?" I asked, genuinely puzzled.

"It means that she is of Satan!" Sherry admonished. Her bright blue eyes narrowing with a severity that I couldn't comprehend.

We argued because Mrs. Goodman was such a sweet old lady. I refused to believe Sherry. There was no way that Mrs. Goodman could be from the devil! After all, my checks were made out to the *Church of God*. But still…I had read something from the Bible, and it mattered, even though I was leery of Sherry's stern warning.

Later that evening, Sherry dialed me up on the telephone, asking me what Daryl had to say. She was still grinning.

"Say about what?" But, of course I knew what she meant.

"Well, you know! That you became a Christian today!"

"Oh, that. Well, we didn't get on the 'subject of religion' at the dinner table, so he doesn't know."

Sherry's bubble burst. I could hear it deflate through the phone. She was no longer smiling from ear-to-ear. My response was a huge disappointment to her. In her opinion, I didn't experience genuine salvation experience if I wasn't willing to tell the entire world that Jesus was my Savior.

The Bible states "that if you confess with your mouth the Lord Jesus and believe in your heart that God has raised Him from the dead, you will be saved. For with the heart one believes unto righteousness, and with the mouth confession is made unto salvation. For the Scripture says, "Whoever believes on Him will not be put to shame" (Romans 10:9-13 NKJV).

Little did I know that within 48-hours, I would tell the world on national television something I could not confess to my own husband.

Forty years ago, the Phil Donahue show was as hot as Oprah is today. Millions of viewers tuned in each day. In its pioneer days, it was taped live at 9:00 am from Dayton, Ohio. Since my husband knew Phil Donahue, anytime I wanted to be a guest in the studio audience, I was ushered to the front row like a privileged character. They had played basketball together when Phil was a fellow employee in the E.F. MacDonald Company. I never needed advance tickets to get on the show. After the show, my friends would get to meet Phil in his office for pictures. During the taping, I would ask a question so that all of us got on camera. At 2:00 pm, at home in our living room, we'd watch the taped version and giggle to see our faces on national TV. Out of the group of friends or relatives who accompanied me to the show, I'd always be the brave one to raise my hand and ask a question relevant to the topic being discussed by guests on the show.

The day after I accepted the Lord at the Wednesday Bible study, my brother, David, and sister-in-law, Lorraine, came to visit us from Detroit. They arrived Thursday evening so we attended the Phil Donahue Show on Friday morning.

It was another God set-up. That day, Phil Donahue's two guests were the late Godfrey Cambridge, a popular black actor/comedian and an attractive female companion who was his personal "spiritual advisor."

As I listened to this psychic brag about her past predictions, such as a plane crash that had come true, it occurred to me that she was exploiting fear. The veil was lifted from my eyes.

I raised my hand to ask her a question. Phil darted up the aisle with the camera crewman close behind him.

My question would solicit a certain response from her, so I asked it purposely.

"Where do you get your power from?" I smiled innocently. The spiritualist was four feet away from me, so I could see her eyes narrow to glare at me.

"From God," She answered defiantly.

"Well, if this *gift is from God*, do you read the Bible?"

"Sometimes," she said with a distinct hiss.

"Well, if you read the Bible, then you should already know what it says in Deuteronomy 18:10. God says that it is wrong to predict the future by using divination or charms through witchcraft. The reason I know this is because I've accepted Jesus Christ as my personal savior."

Phil Donahue was the precursor to Jerry Springer and he became energized by the possibility of a heated debate on camera. He quickly stuck the microphone back in my face. "So, are you saying she is of the *DEVIL?*"

But I didn't fall for the bait. I responded with poise and dignity. "I didn't say that, I just quoted what God says about what she does." Then I calmly sat down. But I began to tremble by what I had just said on live television.

Sherry was home watching the show. Needless to say, she was grinning again.

Confessing Jesus Christ as my personal savior on national television was the beginning of my faith journey contained in this book. When you say "yes" to God you never know where He's going to lead you, so hang on for the ride! You'll never be sorry.

"For I know the plans I have for you, declares the Lord, plans to prosper you and not harm you, plans to give you hope and a future" Jeremiah 29:11 (NIV).

"Before I formed you in the womb I knew you, before you were born I set you apart; I appointed you as a prophet to the nations" Jeremiah 1:5 (NIV).

"But when Jesus saw the multitudes, He was moved with compassion for them because they were weary and scattered like sheep having no shepherd. Then He said to His disciples, "The Harvest truly is plentiful, but the laborers are few. Therefore, pray the Lord of the harvest to send out laborers from His harvest." Matthew 9:36-39 (NKJV).

Discussion Questions

1. How important is it to make your faith in Christ Jesus known to your co-worker?

2. Is sharing your faith with others difficult for you?

3. Have you ever been prompted to offer prayer for a friend or neighbor expressing a problem to you?

Notes

Chapter Twenty-Three
Heavenly Songs of Deliverance

When I was four-years-old I used sing to God with my whole heart. In the summer time, I would often climb up on the back of the toilet seat to sing through an open screen window with a wide windowsill. That special place became my own little sanctuary. Towering oak trees shadowed the back of the near silent alley behind our little house on Hanna Street. The sun sparkled through creased tree branches as the lush trees, chirping birds, and gentle breezes created a sound stage straight to Heaven. I sang to God with all my heart in my enchanted asylum. Sometimes I reached such sacred notes, tears rolled down my cheeks. The angels accompanied me because I could hear them in my heart. I didn't care who heard me.

One day, tragedy struck. That little girl lost her song. I still remember how I stopped singing as if it happened yesterday, and it still brings a lump to my throat. Seated as a guest at a dining table, I quietly ate lunch with my mother and great grandmother, Lydia Brant. She was a full-blooded Mohawk Indian, a direct descendant of Chief Joseph Brant from the American Revolution. He was an interpreter for missionaries and translated the Book of Mark into the Mohawk language.

Out of the blue, Lydia looked across the table at my mother. "Shirley Ann, who sings the best of all your children?" Grandma Brant and my mother both played the piano, so she probably hoped her grandchildren had musical talent, too. It was a perfectly innocent question.

I straightened up, expecting my mother to praise my beautiful singing. After all, I was the only one who actually sang. Since my brother, David, was a late bloomer, at age three, he rarely talked, much less sang. My baby brother, Dennis, was still in a crib.

"Oh, *David* sings the best," Mother replied with pride. Even though my mother didn't say I *couldn't* sing, that is what I comprehended. I stopped singing. Twenty years later, I found Jesus, the lover of my soul and I found my inspiration to sing again.

As an adult, I understand why David was so special to Mother. During the nine months my 18-year old mother carried me, she desired a boy. After the doctor delivered me, he announced, "Oh, it's a beautiful girl!" In stunned denial and disappointment, my teenaged mother spouted out, *"HE is NOT!"* Unfortunately, rejection from her womb and from her spirit affected me. Tragically, I never bonded with my mother. However, I am confident that God called me from the womb because He knew me and loved me in spite of any rejection I experienced as a child.

My father fought a few bloody battles in the South Pacific during World War II as a young marine. However, Dad never spoke to us about the war. He had a photo album that we often looked through as curious kids, but without details. But a few years ago, my cousin Tommy heard some war stories after he and my dad drank a few beers while painting the walls in our living room. Years later, Tommy repeated these stories to me. I learned that my late father survived a foxhole, air raid from Japanese forces. After the spray of bullets stopped, my dad discovered that all three of his buddies were dead. Years later, I sought the Lord about this story while grieving the loss of my dad. The Holy Spirit spoke to my heart. The Lord said, "I saved him because you were in his loins..." God has revealed that to me because I needed to know that He has plans for my life.

God began giving me little songs about twenty-five years ago. Pastor Dean Demos, former choir director for Pastor Moses Vegh, admonished me about keeping track of my simple, child-like choruses. He cautioned, "Barbara, you won't lose your salvation on Judgment Day, but you'll lose some of your crowns if you bury your talents."

In 1987, I was in the midst of planning a Columbus worship conference. Following about five hours of prayerful intercession, the Holy Spirit birthed a song in the night through my willing vessel. It is entitled "O Glory to the Lamb." The next morning, I sang it to Dean Demos and he transcribed it to sheet music. It is a beautiful choral arrangement that many choirs have sung throughout the country.

In 1988, Daryl and I attended a national conference at a church in Pasadena, California. While we there, we also heard about an upcoming international worship conference, which was honoring Steve Fry, an outstanding music composer, whose anointed cantatas have spanned the globe. More than 3,000 Christians registered for that weekend worship conference. As the music director of the Pasadena church, Dr. David Fischer was also involved with the worship conference coming up the following weekend. When Dr. Fischer met Daryl and me at his church conference, he remembered us from Columbus. He said, "Barbara. I am conducting 'O Glory to the Lamb' as the *grand finale* on Saturday night with a full orchestra." Daryl and I weren't able to stay over, but I obtained a video. Dance troupe, Ballet Magnificat, processed with beautiful banners as the choir sang, "O Glory to the Lamb." To think that Steve Fry was given a tribute with *my* music is mind-boggling.

Traveling evangelist, Rev. Daniel Cason, a music minister, informed me that as a guest artist, he conducted a 400 voice-choir that sang "O Glory to the Lamb" in Philadelphia. My husband was a keynote speaker at a church conference in Indiana a few years ago. The Pastor informed Daryl that his church choir performed "O Glory to the Lamb" when dedicating their new church!

Prophetic songs are birthed from Heaven to bring glory to the Lamb. I am humbled by this testimony because the Lord allowed me to experience a new song from the chambers of paradise where angels never cease singing praises to our Lord.

Prophetic worship comes from a heart yearning for God. We cannot have a relationship with God without a heart of worship and adoration. Music has been a profound key to my deliverance and walk with the Lord. But before I could worship God I had to make Him Lord of my life. I also needed to swallow my pride and confess Him as my savior.

O Glory to the Lamb
Words and Music by Barbara Taylor Sanders
Arranged by Dean Demos

O Glory, O Glory to the Lamb
O Glory, O Glory to the Lamb
His Power and His majesty, our crown
Our Savior has risen from the ground
Praise Him, all ye people
Praise His Holy Name
Jesus, the Messiah has been found
Jesus, the Messiah has been crowned
His blood has been sprinkled on the mercy seat
The sacrifice is complete
Satan is now under His feet
Angels shout for joy
Sin is atoned for all mankind
O Glory to the Lamb
O Glory to the Lamb

© Copyright 1987

Discussion Questions

1. How important is singing Christian music to you?
2. Have you considered joining the choir at your church to develop lasting friendships
3. Do you play a musical instrument that could be used at church?

Chapter Twenty-Four

The Fires of Revival Are Still Burning

"You a preacher?" asked the elderly woman seated in a wheelchair. Mom Beall intently gazed at my husband as we were about to walk past her. We were in Detroit attending an "Understanding God" seminar conducted by her daughter, Rev. Patricia Beall Gruits, the author of the nine-month Bible course. It was early spring 1979.

Rev. M.D. "Mom" Beall, a delicately frail woman was parked at the rear of a very crowded church conference room filled with pastors and lay leaders from all over the country. My handsome husband, a former NFL player for the Detroit Lions, was dressed in a dark, three-piece navy suit and looked very distinguished walking up the aisle at my arm.

"No," he chuckled, "I'm a car dealer!"

"Well, you will be," she chuckled back with a twinkle in her eye. But we kept moving toward the dining hall with the hungry lunch crowd, not comprehending her prophetic peek into our future.

Rev. Myrtle Dorthea Beall, the founder of Bethesda Missionary Temple must have sensed we didn't value the significance of her prophetic word to us about Daryl becoming a preacher. So, from that point on she kept a watchful eye over us throughout the entire three-day conference. That evening she personally invited us to sit beside her at dinner. She told me her amazing testimony during our meal time together.

The year before, in August 1978, we had encountered evangelists Fred and Florence Parker during their brief visit to Columbus. They were lay leaders at Bethesda and enthusiastic volunteer counselors for the "Understanding God" "catechism" course taught to hundreds of adult students every year. They urged us to get involved, so we attended the instructional seminar to learn more about teaching the course.

Through our developing friendship with the Parkers, we were enlightened on the benefits of establishing the six foundation stones of faith based on Hebrews 6:1-3.

Without hesitation we opened a large conference room at Daryl Sanders Cadillac Dealership to offer an evening "Understanding God" Bible course. About thirty people signed up for the maiden course. Daryl had already been offering a weekly luncheon Bible study to the community for several years.

With the blessings of their pastor, Rev. James Beall, Canadians Fred and Florence drove to Columbus from Windsor, Ontario each week to conduct the initial course. They made a tremendous sacrifice to be with us each week. Through the subsequent years, my husband became the teacher and hundreds of Christians gained a significant foundation in the Lord Jesus Christ. In 1985 we pioneered a local church through the faithful guidance of the Beall family.

In 1980 we sold the Cadillac dealership, but continued teaching the "Understanding God" course in various locations in the community for several years. Each nine-month course was well-attended with an average of seventy-five people in each class. We also remained faithful members of our local church. Through the blessings of our pastor we began a new local church, with its first meetings occurring on Sunday evenings. In January 1985, during a formal ordination ceremony, six governing pastors ordained my husband to continue preaching and teaching the Gospel of Jesus Christ. In good faith, Rev. Harry Beall, Rev. James Beall, Rev. Willard Jarvis, Rev. Samuel Farina, Rev. Paul Stern, and Rev. Moses Vegh placed their hands on my husband in order for him to continue the work of the kingdom.

Mom Beall passed from earth to Heaven in September 1979. We were blessed to hear her speak since she usually gave closing remarks following her son's sermon. A second pulpit stood on the platform, low enough for her to speak from her wheelchair. One Sunday morning we were in the packed 3,000-seat auditorium after another weekend conference. After Rev. James Beall delivered an eloquent message, we sang a closing song before Brother Jim delivered the benediction. We were all standing waiting to be dismissed. I felt uplifted by the rich deposit of God's word heard through various guest speakers and grateful to be in the company of so many gifted ministers from all over America. It had been a tremendous event, as always.

Suddenly Mom Beall wheeled to her podium to say something. "When we sang that last chorus, the Lord brought the story of the lost coin to my mind," she began reflectively. The microphone amplified her soft, tender voice. "Scripture tells us that the woman searched and searched her house until she finally found the missing coin. She was so overjoyed that she called her neighbors to rejoice with her. Jesus said that the angels rejoice when a lost sinner is found…"

Before she said another word, I began to tremble. I had read that familiar parable many times. The Holy Spirit quickened my understanding of His wondrous love in a deeper measure. Something like warm energy shot through my body, stirring my emotions. I began to weep. Then

I realized I wasn't the only person reacting this way. Within seconds the entire congregation was also weeping, as a few thousand people reverently and quietly slipped out of their seats, onto their knees, using the back of their chairs as a makeshift altar. I could not stop crying even if I tried. In fact, I continued crying throughout our four-hour drive back to Columbus. My eyes were nearly swollen shut by the time we arrived home. But I felt renewed, refreshed, and thankful for the cleansing experience. God had certainly done a deep work in my heart.

Thirty years later, I remain in total awe of the anointing of God expressed through this compelling woman. Her anointed words caused the Holy Spirit to sweep through that auditorium as a sovereign visitation from Heaven above. It was the most profound experience I've had with God in a corporate setting. If this dear lady uttered a few syllables and had an entire auditorium humbly sink to their knees in tears of repentance, I could only imagine what the revival must have been like during the 3 ½ years it lasted in the 1950's. After that experience I'm convinced the revival fire has not died.

Through the years our friendship with the entire Beall family grew because we frequently traveled to Bethesda for Sunday morning service or conferences. Realizing her end was near, Mom Beall assigned resident prophet Manley Higgins to personally exhort us with his unique prophetic mantle whenever we were at Bethesda. He'd see us in the crowd of visiting ministers and make a beeline toward us. In a good way, he'd always made me tear up by his exhortations about ministry.

Therefore, I spent a lot of time in the bathroom cleaning my smeared mascara because this elderly gentleman always spoke life into our spirits. One time he said to me, "You're like Mother Sarah, many are going to nurse from your breast as you feed them what God produces in you." At that time in my life I had no idea that he was speaking prophetically.

Following one such prophetic moment with Brother Higgins, I washed my tear stained face in the ladies room. In my haste to get back into service I left my purse in the restroom. Right before the offertory, Mr. Comedian, Harry Beall held it up in jest. He announced, "Sister Sanders left this very nice Gucci bag in the lady's room, so we took the liberty to take all the cash out of it for this morning's offering." Everyone laughed, so they knew he was just kidding.

In 1989 we dedicated our beautiful new church building. To my husband and the planning committee I said, "I don't care who comes from the Beall family, just as long as Brother Higgins is here." Along with a delightful delegation from the Beall family, Brother Higgins was also present with a special place of honor, representing the heart of Mom Beall who would have been very proud of us.

A few years following Mom Beall's death I had an opportunity to chit-chat with Rev. Garland

L. Pemberton, a minister who was very close to her. At the personal invitation of Pastor Jim Beall, Daryl and I attended a Louisiana conference with him, hosted by our friends, Rev. Charles and Barbara Green, the founders of Word of Faith Temple, New Orleans. Evangelist Garland Pemberton, a big jolly man, sat on the platform at every meeting, clicking his ballpoint pen whenever he agreed with the guest preacher's high points.

Rev. Garland L. Pemberton was born in Cameron, Texas in 1917, but he planted numerous churches throughout Louisiana and Mississippi during his lifetime. He died in July 2008. Sometime in the early 1950s, Garland attended an outdoor revival tent meeting in the southwest. He was curious to hear "the preacher woman" from Michigan. As Mom Beall approached the pulpit she suddenly glanced over at Garland. The young man was seated, not knowing what to expect from her. She spoke to him in passing. "You're going to be close to me until my end," she said, matter-of-factly, and kept walking. Naturally he was startled. But, true enough, after thirty years of close friendship with her, like another favored son, Garland Pemberton delivered an emotional eulogy at her funeral.

One afternoon at the 1981 Word of Faith conference, I slipped into a vacated chair next to Garland following lunch. "Tell me some more stories about Mom Beall."

His face lit up. "Well, let me tell you about her trip to New Orleans in November 1975. A blizzard had hit Detroit, so we worried that it wasn't safe for Mom to travel, but she insisted on coming." His deep southern drawl was engaging as he continued the story.

"The next morning, I picked her up at the High-Rise Holiday Inn. Mom, you don't look like you slept very well last night. How are you feeling?"

"'I'm okay, Brother Garland, but I've been praying half the night. God put a word in my mouth that He said 'All of America will hear.'"

Garland went on to explain that author Peter Jenkins and fiancée, Barbara Pennell, a postgraduate college student from New Orleans, was in attendance of the Word of Faith service that Sunday morning. A few years before all of America had read his *New York Times* bestseller, *A Walk Across America*. Peter and Barbara had come to a standstill about their future plans for marriage. Deeply in love but filled with doubt, Barbara had been praying "for a sign from God" that she should marry Peter. Marriage meant traveling with him for his final trek across America, which included thousands of miles of territory to finish in the Pacific Northwest.

Peter writes about his seemingly hopeless situation with Barbara. After hearing that she was praying for a sign from God at Word of Faith church that morning, Peter was *not* hopeful. This is an excerpt from *A Walk Across America*. The following passage is how the book ended.

Peter writes: "There was nothing more to be said between us and all I could do was wait. I knew this situation was impossible and nothing could happen, God never did anything like that."

The six or seven ministers entered together from their room at the side of the stage. I was shocked to see the pastor, Reverend Charles Green, push in an old lady in a wheelchair. The pastor always delivered the sermon on Sunday mornings, but today he told us Mom Beall had come all the way from Detroit to speak a special message. A microphone was bent down for her since she had to speak from her wheelchair. She had founded a church in Detroit called Bethesda Missionary Temple over forty years ago and it had grown beyond five thousand members.

Mom Beall was at least eighty years old, and her hair fluffed, light red. I looked at her with prejudiced eyes and she looked sickly and pale. I had just reached the part where I believed in God and now an old woman in a wheelchair was going to preach. It seemed even more impossible for anything to happen to save Barbara and me now. I wanted to step out of the side door and not waste any more time.

When Pastor Green finished his introduction of Mom Beall, the whole church erupted with deafening applause. Whoever she was, everybody seemed to know her and was anxious to hear what she had to say. Mom Beall began to speak. Her voice was as quiet as a leaf dropping to the ground, but it was so truth-tuned that every word was loud and clear. She captured everyone's attention instantly—even mine.

This wheel-chaired grandmother began telling us about all the snow in Detroit but said that the Lord God in Heaven had told her to come to New Orleans regardless of the weather or anything else. She didn't know why she was to come, but she had learned to obey.

She spoke, "Everyone, please turn to your Bibles to the book of Genesis, Chapter 24." The pages in hundreds and hundreds of Bibles turned with a sound like walking through a pile of raked leaves. Whoosh, whoosh, whoosh.

The old and wise lady began to tell us a story from the Old Testament. It was like sitting at your grandmother's feet and listening to her kind and gentle voice as she began to tell a story.

The story was about Abraham and his Son, Isaac. Abraham was old and about to die, but he wanted to find a wife for Isaac. He sent his best servant to Mesopotamia with many camels and gifts. Mesopotamia was Abraham's homeland and he wanted Isaac to have a wife from there. The servant stopped in a city called Nahor to water his camels and get a drink. It was hot and dry when the servant reached the well. He prayed, "O Lord God, let the maiden who says she will water my camels be the one whom thou has appointed for thy servant, Isaac."

Mom Beall continued the story sweetly. I sat fascinated and had forgotten about the aching situation with Barbara and me. I had to know how the story would end.

"A beautiful maiden named Rebekah came to the well with a water jar balanced on her slender shoulders. When she saw Abraham's servant at the well, she drew water for him to drink. Then she began to draw water for his thirsty camels. The servant knew this was the girl for Isaac. When she left, he followed her home with the jewelry of silver and gold. Soon, he would ask her if she would come back with him and marry Isaac."

The next day, Mom told us, "Rebekah's family called her to them because the servant was ready to ask her and give her the gifts."

At this point Mom paused, ready to emphasize a point as dramatic as any I had ever heard. Her pause was long and over a thousand people were totally silent.

Although Mom was over eighty she now looked full of the most powerful energy in life. A radiant glow circled her entire body, she pounded the arm of her wheelchair with her right fist and half-yelled and half-quivered, "Will you go with this man?" The simple phrase, one of thousands in the Bible, burst through me with a surging power; it echoed and shot through my body like holy electricity-this was Barbara's sign! I knew it as I glanced over at her for the first time since Mom's story had begun.

Again, with fantastic power, Mom shouted those words from Genesis: "Will you go with this man?" The impact of the message pushed Barbara back into her cushioned chair. She was sort of slumped down, her eyes staring nowhere. She had prayed all night, yet this direct message from God seemed to shock her.

"Will you go with this man?" Mom's lily-white hand banged the wheelchair, emphasizing each and every word. Barbara gasped as though each word hit her heart with the force of a sledgehammer pounding on iron.

She sat up straighter, blood flushed her pretty face and her hair seemed to stand out fuller than before.

"One last time," Mom cried, *"Will you go with this man?"* I couldn't believe this was happening. I looked over at Barbara again. She knew that I knew. Her eyes were wide and clear except for the crystal tears that gathered in the corners. She leaned close to me and whispered, "Peter, I'll go with you."

Very slowly we stood as the service ended. I wished I could slap myself in the face just to be sure all this had really happened. Even though I now believed in God, this kind of thing was impossible. Yet, in that church on that Nov. 16 in 1975, among a thousand people, God had pointed his finger at the two of us.

The lights of the tall sanctuary dimmed and everyone began to leave. Coming toward us against the flow of people was a smiling man with dark hair. When he got to us he stopped abruptly. He handed me a plastic container, which I recognized as a cassette tape and said, "We record all our services here at Word of Faith. Perhaps you'd like to have this." God had not only given us the sign Barbara had prayed for, now He was offering us proof!

"Thanks," I said, stunned. Barbara was staring ahead, deep into what had happened to us. She had not noticed the tape. As we stepped through the doors into the blaring Louisiana afternoon, Barbara leaned toward me and said with wonder in her voice, "Peter...Peter did that really happen?"

I felt the cassette in my pocket. Someday we would listen to it, and hear those words again that joined us together.

"It sure did," I said. "It sure did."

I reached down to take her hand. From now on that's the way we'd be, hand in hand.[4]

Peter and Barbara were married in February 1976. On July 5, 1976, they started their two-year honeymoon hiking and camping across the remaining U.S. territory that included Louisiana, Texas, New Mexico, and into Colorado.

In 1975, Mom Beall's eldest daughter, Patricia Beall Gruits, "Sister Pat," as we affectionately call her, opened a medical clinic and maternity ward in Haiti with her husband, the late Peter Gruits. Following her husband's sudden death, Dr. Gruits continued their ministry, Rhema International, along with their four sons and wives. Today she continues to write books, teach seminars, and preach the gospel throughout the world. Mom Beall left quite a legacy. Her granddaughter, Analee Dunn, now pastors Bethesda Christian Church.

It's been rewarding to know the Beall family history. I marvel at God's power at work through the simple obedience of a young mother who studied scripture and taught the neighborhood children and their parents prior to WWII. This dear, faithful woman, with the approval and blessings of her husband, started a mighty revival that is still going strong today. During dinner, the first time we met Mom Beall, she told me how she left the Catholic faith to the Pentecostal movement. She was engaged to Mr. Harry Beall, even though he was a not-so-strict Methodist. Since she was such a devout Catholic, she naturally assumed he would convert to her religion. But he didn't budge even though they were very much in love. Like Peter and Barbara, they came to a standstill in their relationship.

---

[4] A Walk Across America, Peter Jenkins, Harper Perennial 1979, p. 287 Spring Hill, TN.

Young Myrtle and Harry were invited to dinner at a relative's home. It was to be their last date as an engaged couple before Myrtle planned to break off the engagement over their religion conflict. While waiting for dinner to be served, Myrtle picked up a small devotional off the coffee table and began reading the story of Ruth. When her eyes met the challenge, "Where you go, I will follow, your God will be my God," she told me that the words jumped off the page and into her heart. "I couldn't stop thinking about what I had read. I ate those words all through dinner with each bite of food." She surrendered to Mr. Beall's God and they were soon married. She followed him and his God in simple but sacrificial obedience. Like Ruth, her obedience eventually had significant worldwide impact.

There are countless thousands of people who have been touched by Mom Beall and the ministry of Bethesda Missionary Temple, currently known as Bethesda Christian Church. In 1934, this young mother of three children started preaching in a small storefront location. Today, Bethesda is a 200,000 square foot church and education facility occupying hundreds of acres. In addition, the ministry has launched countless missionaries currently serving Haiti, East, Central and South Africa, Uganda, Indonesia, Far East Asia, Ecuador, South America, and other parts of the world that are still planting churches and preaching the Gospel to the lost. The revival fires are still burning.

Ask of me, and I will make the nations your inheritance, the ends of the earth your possession.
Psalm 2:8

Discussion Questions

1. Do you believe that the Holy Spirit speaks through Christians by a Word of Wisdom or Word of Knowledge?

2. Have you ever had a departure from one direction to another direction by the counsel of a parent? By the counsel of a pastor or church leader?

3. If yes, how did that new direction impact your life? Was it positive or negative?

Chapter Twenty-Five

The Power of Prayer

After learning that the unborn baby was a boy, it was time to find a suitable name. My friend, Katrina Brown, wanted a "non-traditional" Bible name. I suggested consulting my husband since he is very knowledgeable of the Bible. The three of us were out to breakfast the morning she asked my husband for a name.

Sitting across the table from her my husband said, "What about Shem, Noah's righteous son?"

Katrina said, "Oh, I love that name! I've never heard it before." So, it stuck.

Months later while reading in the Old Testament, I came across Josiah, a righteous King who started his reign at age eight. Katrina loved both Hebrew names. Shem means "fame and renown" and Josiah means "the Lord saves."

She was in mild labor pain while taking her final exams that June. Our Shem Josiah was born June 24, 2007. I coached Katrina through labor with many trips to the maternity ward before they finally let her stay. After that third trip I think I would have checked in myself.

I had the joy of being at this precious child's delivery. Baby Shem let out a loud, healthy cry upon arrival into the world. Katrina touched him and I captured it all with my digital camera clicking away. He was whisked to the warming unit for clean up by two attending nurses. Katrina was talking to the female OB/GYN who was tending to her post-delivery needs. The atmosphere was electrifying because a new life had entered the world. With all the prayer that went up for this baby, I am certain the angels were rejoicing, too!

When Shem suddenly stopped crying I observed urgent commotion across the room. One nurse placed an oxygen mask on the baby while the other attendant dashed to the wall telephone close by. A tall, male physician arrived within seconds. I heard him say, "Why isn't he breathing?" Katrina was unaware her son was in danger because she was chatting it up with the female physician who was delivering the afterbirth.

I quietly, but quickly went into action, too. I slipped over to the lounge sofa I had been sleeping on through the night hours of Katrina's labor. While sitting with my knees pulled up to my face I began calling down Heaven in fervent prayer. My heart pounded. After a few minutes of prayer, I felt the need to "do something," so I darted over to the baby as the two nurses and doctors stared at him, waiting for something to happen. I kept saying, "Jesus, Jesus, Jesus" in reverence as I ran my hand lightly over his motionless little body. Then Shem reached out and grasped my index finger with his left hand. His little hand wrapped around my entire finger and it felt strong. It seemed like a desperate grasp. In fact, he communicated, "Don't ever quit praying for me, Nana. I need your prayers in my life." He started to cry again to our relief. It was the happiest sound I've ever heard in my life. From that moment on I felt a spiritual connection with this child.

Then the baby was whisked away to the Neonatal Intensive Care Unit for a procedure to clear his lungs. He was diagnosed with pneumothorax, which is a condition that causes air leaks into the space between the chest wall and the outer tissues of the lungs. If undetected, it can be fatal. However, we did not know these facts until much later.

When Katrina was informed that her baby was in trouble the nurse did not give us any details. She said, "I'm sorry, but you won't be able to see your baby until tomorrow. He is in the NICU for observation."

"Will my baby be okay?" she asked.

"I don't know," the nurse replied.

Katrina began to cry out, "Jesus, Jesus, save my baby." And the Lord did. An hour later, a very nice nurse "sneaked" us to see the baby. Although baby Shem was hooked up to scary looking wires, seeing the tenderness in Katrina's face as she gazed upon her baby was precious. He seemed healthy and content as he slept. She had such a look of awe and wonderment to view the life she had created. It brings tears to my eyes remembering those treasured few moments with her.

As a new parent and a single Mom, she was conscientious and alert as are all young mothers bringing such a tiny baby home for the first time. For the health of her baby, Katrina breastfed for several months.

Shem turned two years old on June 24, 2009. He loves church and attempts to sing Christian music whenever he hears it on the radio. He's been the joy of my life, and I adore this precious little boy with all my heart. He loves his Nanna just as much. He is very attached to me and frequently spends the night with our family.

This past November during church, our pastor announced that it was "baby dedication Sunday." Katrina was in the service that morning, sitting near the back with the baby. I nudged Daryl and whispered, "Oh, I wish we'd known. We could have had Shem dedicated this morning." It had been something on my heart to do for months.

About forty couples began lining up on both side of the platform with their infants. There were two lines. Pastor Parsley began praying for the babies on one side while his wife, Joni, began praying for the opposite side.

Suddenly, Katrina appeared at the end of a line holding Shem. I was delighted that she had gumption enough to dedicate her son without previous church instruction. Katrina walked up on the platform but, somehow, she and Shem got blocked from Pastor Parsley's view. All the parents holding babies were now off the platform, so Pastor Parsley and Ms. Joni turned to face the congregation. One of the ushers nudged the pastor to acknowledge Katrina. Pastor quickly turned around to face her. He said, "Well, you get the double blessing." He said that because *both* he and Ms. Joni placed their hands upon Shem for the prayer of dedication.

I was delighted that happened because the "double blessing" is truly an honor to bestow on a child, and Shem *is* a special child deserving of that tribute.

After church Daryl and I explained the Biblical meaning of a double blessing to Katrina. She was also very pleased to know that Shem had been singled out for such a prayer.

My husband planned to drive out of town on business following church. Therefore, Katrina drove me home that Sunday afternoon. She desired to return to church that evening.

When we got to my house I fixed a light meal for us and spent quality time with the baby. It's always a joy to visit with him since Katrina no longer lives nearby. She's now living on her own in low-income housing and no longer financially dependent on her mother's monthly support.

When Katrina left my house to drive back to church, it was getting dark and raining hard. The baby was buckled in his car seat in the back. The peculiar thing about that day was that as I watched them drive away, I started to weep. I'm always sad to wave goodbye and somewhat choked up. However, when I closed the front door I felt an overwhelming sense of grief, as if I was never going to see Shem again. It was the first time in my life that I felt a sense of impending doom of a loved one. Naturally, I began to pray for protection with extreme emotional intensity. After being doubled over in agony for several minutes, the grief sensation lifted, and I experienced peace in my soul.

I inquired of the Lord because I thought maybe He was trying to teach me a Bible lesson on prayer. I pondered in my heart, "Lord, should I be praying with that kind of same intensity each time they leave my house?"

Within minutes, Katrina called my cell phone. She was hysterically screaming, but unable to speak or tell me what was wrong! I could hear a lady trying to talk to her. The woman asked, "Where's the baby?" It was a car accident. Then the phone went dead. I thought that our sweet little boy had been killed. Everything in my body went numb. In fact, I could hardly move my legs.

I managed to call Daryl to inform him that Shem had probably been killed in a nearby car accident. He had already arrived in Michigan. He said, "Calm down. Don't drive by yourself, go get Bo."

When my son and I arrived at the accident scene there were two fire trucks, three squad cars, and two medical cars with their lights blinking. It was on the interstate highway. It looked like the scene of a ten-car pileup, and we still did not know the condition of the baby! I continued to cry and pray fervently with all my heart and soul.

Suddenly, through the rain I saw Katrina with Shem in her arms climbing into a fire truck to fill out an accident report. I still could not move, so Bo jumped out of the car to assist Katrina.

Later, we learned that as Katrina was getting off a main highway to approach the interstate, out of nowhere, a drunken truck driver crossed her path and spun out of control in front of her. She couldn't avoid crashing into him. When Katrina's small, 2007 silver KIA crashed, the baby started screaming. The fast moving, oncoming cars almost hit her car several times. A lady in a van stopped to help. She also stood on the highway attempting to get the speeding traffic to slow down because Katrina's car and the red truck were blocking a lane of traffic.

What made it extremely dangerous was that Katrina was trapped in the car because the electrical power shut down. She couldn't open her doors or windows. In a panic she crawled across the seat to see if the baby was hurt. There was just enough juice left to get a rear window halfway down. She was able to crawl out of the window and pull the baby through to safety as cars sped close by at high speeds.

The right front side of Katrina's car was severely damaged. The male truck driver was bleeding and taken to the hospital. He was also placed under arrest because he was so drunk. Later we've prayed for his salvation and ultimate sobriety.

When Pastor Parsley heard about the near fatal accident, he rejoiced with us because the Lord truly intervened in something that could have been tragic. In fact, this testimony on the miraculous power of prayer first appeared April 17, 2009 on the Breakthrough network for the world to see.

Together, when Katrina and I watched the documentary of her accident on television we both cried. She looked at me with tears in her eyes. "God has really saved my life. I'm so thankful for all that's He's done in my life."

That's the best happy ending for any chapter!

Do not be anxious about anything, but in everything, by prayer and petition, with thanksgiving, present your requests to God. And the peace of God, which transcends all understanding, will guard your hearts and your minds in Christ Jesus. Philippians 4:6-7 NIV

Discussion Questions

1. Do you ever sense an intense burden to pray for someone or a situation?

2. Do you keep a prayer journal? Do you write out your prayers?

3. Have you ever seen a dramatic answer to prayer?

Notes

Chapter Twenty-Six

Tolerance and True Hospitality

"I just don't understand how this man can be so closed-minded. Of all people, he should realize how important it is to reach out to wayward teenagers. His own son was messed up on drugs for years before getting saved," sighed Pastor Ross. "But Clem just won't budge. He insists the new community center should be restricted to just our own church members. Now others are agreeing with him."

Our friend was facing another hurdle concerning the new church addition. The vision of this pastor was to reach out to the poor and disadvantaged in his community. Sometimes new, clean buildings are like new furniture, and we try to keep the kids away until the newness wears off.

Debates over their church expansion program were wearing down our friend. He was experiencing a challenge with Clem, a respected leader and board member,

My husband, Daryl, is a retired senior pastor. We sympathetically listened as Ross and his wife, Sherry, expressed concerns with us during lunch. These out of town friends of ours have been in fulltime ministry for decades. Understandably, discouragement was at an all-time high for our dear friends, who were weary from controversy and waging the battle over the use of their nearly completed building project.

Ross and Sherry have an admirable goal of reaching neighboring families with the Gospel of Jesus Christ. The new education and multi-purpose gymnasium is aptly called The Community Life Center. However, a different perspective being voiced by certain irate board members had dashed their hopes. It wasn't long before more and more church members began to chime in protesting non-members "messing up" the sparkling clean community center.

"After all," vented Clem, in a previous congregation meeting, "Our families have made tremendous sacrifices to build this new gymnasium, so why should any of our kids have to wait in line for strangers to get off the basketball court? And besides, non- members won't have any respect for it and will probably damage our new facility." He had a valid point.

Costly wisdom is usually learned the hard way. Having been in full time ministry for many years, Daryl and I experienced our own share of people problems. We gained wisdom through mistakes made while pioneering a church, which grew to about six hundred members. God is faithful to teach constructive lessons in life, as long as we remain in tune to the direction of the Holy Spirit through prayer.

Through the years, Pastor Ross has invited Daryl to fill in whenever he's away from the pulpit. Therefore, we feel a kinship to this church family even though it's not our regular place of worship because it is out of town.

Our hearts are linked with Ross and Sherry through our mutual love of Christ and each other. Over the past few years we've heard first hand, the agony and the ecstasy of this building program. Over the past decade, we've received or given objective biblical counsel to each other whenever needed. Discouragement often creeps in like a black cloud to hinder God's perfect vision for the church.

This mainline denominational church has flourished since Ross took over the post as Senior Pastor twenty years ago. Ross and Sherry have served in full time ministry for more than thirty years, with humble beginnings in churches throughout the region. They certainly have proven faithful to the call upon their lives as God continues to use them to impact their local community.

With mixed emotions and heavy hearts, this committed couple prepared a special dedication service to the Lord as the church officially opened their new beautiful education and sports center to "the community."

Pastor Ross and Sherry sincerely desire to reach the lost in their working-class neighborhoods by offering the community Christ-centered outreach programs. Certainly, many lost kids would walk through their doors. However, this noble purpose had been challenged with growing opposition within the congregation.

Building expansion projects are a blessing on one hand, but too often, a pastor's worst nightmare. Church growth is an admirable thing. Studies have proven that if the increase of people and outreach projects causes cramping in the existing facility, chances for healthy growth *cease*. Under crowded conditions, a church becomes stagnant.

Members often oppose spending money for larger church buildings, challenging the motives of leadership. The pastor gets accused of "being on an ego trip" if he suggests building a larger sanctuary, especially if the existing one seems to be fulfilling its purpose "perfectly fine."

A wise pastor senses the right time to appeal to his congregation and propose plans for enlargement. At the drawing-board stage committees are appointed, followed by the long arduous months of fund raising. However, change can bring out the worst in a congregation, and most often, it's the pastor who takes a beating.

Throughout the building and fund-raising campaign, a pastor needs to be on his toes at all times. Dancing between the pew and the pulpit, he makes sure everyone remains in tune and in step as the Lord leads.

Sometime along the way, the pastor usually experiences the painful "death of the vision" when criticism is voiced, especially if financial commitments are not readily fulfilled. Thankfully, an all-knowing, powerful God raises people and projects from the grave.

Sherry and Ross have always been concerned for the poor and disadvantaged in their congregation, as well as the surrounding community. Giving food and clothing to shelters, they serve as an example to be involved with the less fortunate. With a true shepherd's heart, Ross is usually the first one to arrive at the hospital, ready to pour out his heart to anyone in need from within his flock. Their genuine care and sacrifice is a shining example of Jesus Christ.

Last Sunday while Ross was away at a national church convention, my husband felt privileged to preach in his place. Early that morning, as Daryl knotted his neck-tie, I asked about the sermon he had prayerfully prepared for a congregation filled with dissention over the use of their new facility.

"The Lord has given me a message on love and unity, so I am asking Him to guard my tongue." He didn't need to explain. It's inappropriate to bring correction as a visiting minister, even though we're a respected part of this large congregation.

Katrina and I made plans to make the hour-long, out-of-town trip. Since my husband was preaching at both services, we decided to drive separately. The Lord planned to use what happened in our home the night before to bring revelation about being a church with an "open door to those less fortunate."

It was tempting to stay home from church that morning because I was worn out from the dinner party we gave to honor our missionary friends the day before. In fact, I had worked hard the entire month – wallpapering and painting a remodeling project. Our two dogs are no longer allowed back on the new carpeting. Now we go to great lengths putting up and taking down a wooden board that prevents Taffy and Tawny from sneaking back into the remodeled lower level family room.

Our Christian fellowship had been open to many children as well. Included on my guest list was Carletta, a single mom, I've helped over the past ten years. Carletta brought her single friend, Shauntelle, a pregnant young woman with an autistic 7-year-old son, Tyler. Shauntelle's father accompanied her. As single mothers, Carletta and Shauntelle were economically less well off than the rest of the white, middle class couples gathered in my home. These sweet ladies were given a loving welcome even though they had never met my other guests. In the course of the evening, God used their visit to teach me a powerful lesson in tolerance through their participation in our Christian fellowship.

Following dinner, our twenty guests gathered downstairs to watch a promotional video produced by Edward and Linda McPherson, our guest missionaries from the Ukraine. As the room filled up, I scrambled to knock down a folding table to make room for additional seating. My entire focus was on the needs of my guests.

Suddenly, my friend Carol grabbed my arm to point out large clumps of white cookie crumbs under Tyler's feet.

"You better vacuum that up before it gets ground into your new carpeting," she warned, loud enough for everyone to hear. All eyes were on me and I felt for Shauntelle who was sitting nearby.

"Oh, I'll get to those later," I said, continuing to set up chairs for the guests filling up our lower level family room.

"There's a hand-vac in the linen closet," called my husband from across the room.

"Yes, go get it. You need to get them up right now, before they get ground into the carpeting!" Carol urged.

Reluctantly, I retrieved the hand-vacuum from the nearby closet. My cheeks flushed with embarrassment, even though it only took about thirty seconds to vacuum the crumbs up. There probably wasn't a single person in judgment of me for cleaning up the crumbs. But my heart convicted me for demonstrating more importance on the new carpeting than the value of our guest ministers or the dignity of a little guy, who had limited self-control.

After the crumbs were easily removed, Edward began to share information about their mission work in Kiev. Suddenly, for no apparent reason, Tyler began to cry out like a cat in heat. His mother simply ignored him, while the rest of us remained transfixed by this unusual experience with a handicapped child.

"Hey, Tyler!" I said with kindness. "Let's go see your friend!" I gently touched Tyler's head to get his attention then I led him by the hand across the room to my friend Katrina, who has a special way with kids. Tyler remained quiet for a few more minutes before the peculiar cries started up again. Just as I whispered to Katrina to take Tyler upstairs, his aggravated grandfather got up and stormed toward us. In frustration, the grandfather yanked Tyler up by the arm to march him outside for a scolding. Tyler is not able to speak or form a single word. Katrina rushed out to retrieve the handicapped child from a grandfather who was obviously at his wits-end. I doubt if anyone was judging him for being frustrated. Our Christian ministry time resumed in uncomfortable silence.

The Lord obviously grants Tyler's mother tremendous grace to cope with the challenges of her special needs child. This awkward dilemma made me appreciative of God's mercy. There was nothing in my heart that condemned this child, nor his grandfather. I'm certain that every Christian in that room felt the same compassion toward this family.

Later, Katrina came back downstairs to find me. She whispered that Tyler had urinated on the carpet in my husband's office. Apparently, he was not used to eating so many sugary goodies or drinking so much pop. I whispered back in her ear, explaining where the steam vacuum was located. One of my twin daughters took care of it for me.

So, here I was, the following morning, listening to my husband preaching on "the power of love." He gave the definition of a church, emphasizing that it is people, not the building that defines the true body of Christ. He clasped his hands together to demonstrate something we learned in Sunday school. "Here is the church, here is the steeple, open the door and see all the people." With that, Daryl flipped his hands over to wiggle fingers showing the congregation "the people."

The Lord began speaking to my heart, bringing to mind what had just happened the night before and another incident that morning as Katrina and I rushed into church. We were running late. We entered the building through the doors that connected the church with the new addition. Two door greeters, a man and a woman met us with official "welcome hugs."

When I inquired about a restroom, the man directed us to the ladies room located on the far side of the building, at least a four-minute walk around the entire building.

"Oh, yes, I know where it's located," I cheerfully replied. Church was getting ready to start, so we dashed down the very long corridor.

Thankfully, the lady quickly intercepted our unnecessary long walk by tapping me on the shoulder.

"Actually, we have another restroom over here," she said, in a hushed tone, pointing to the new ladies room a few feet away. By the sheepish look on her face, the other male greeter obviously didn't want us to use the new facility.

As I listened to my husband's sermon that morning, I realized why Pastor Ross had met with resistance over using the new community center. Events from our party the night before and what had happened that morning over the use of the new bathroom were keys to human behavior. It's part of human nature to be reluctant to use anything new— just ask my dogs! Taffy and Tawny are probably thankful that Tyler paved their way back into the family room by "christening" our brand-new carpeting with cookie crumbs.

My husband's excellent message on love, unity, and the importance of "accepting change" soon came to a close. Pastor Daryl looked in my direction to welcome a closing remark. He obviously sensed that I had something appropriate to say. I stepped forward to share the story of Tyler and the cookie crumbs on my new carpeting. It was a fitting exhortation about tolerance and not placing more importance on things than people. People *are* more important to God than fresh carpeting or a new facility that might get messed up from those less privileged in society.

God wants to stretch us. He desires to reach the poor and disadvantaged with genuine hospitality, whether it be in our homes or in our fine new church additions. As good stewards, we are certainly supposed to take care of our possessions. So, there is scotch guard for furniture, steam vacuums for spills, and fresh paint to cover smudges on walls. However, let us never place higher importance on "things" than the goal of winning the lost with the genuine love of Christ Jesus, our Lord.

Following service, I was eager to view the brand-new facility. Since I wasn't sure how to get there, I hailed a member before they exited the building.

"Excuse me," I asked. "Can you tell me how to get in to your new facility?"

"Do you mean The Community Life Center? It's right here," she said, proudly opening double doors into the carpeted basketball court. As I admired the spacious multi-purpose room, she responded to my compliments. "Yes, it *is very nice*, but we are waiting to spray the carpeting with stain protection before we use it."

I smiled to myself. The Lord obviously gave Pastor Ross *the solution* to all opposing concerns about "the carpeting getting soiled by careless strangers." And of course, Pastor Ross realized that after all the "newness" wore off, the center would be used just as the Lord intends.

For where your treasure is, there your heart will be also. Matthew 6:21 (New King James Version)

Discussion Questions

1. Have you opened your home to someone who needed a place to stay because of an emergency?
2. Do you actively have friends over for dinner to share the love of Jesus? If not why?

Chapter Twenty-Seven
In the Face of Death

It was to be just a routine physical exam with a new physician a friend had highly recommended. The year was 1997.

I was sitting on the exam table about to meet this female doctor when a young man knocked on the door before walking in to greet me.

"Hello, I am a resident doctor," he said. "Dr. Tallo will be coming in to continue after I do an initial exam, if that's okay with you."

He knocked my knees with a rubber hammer, checking my reflexes. Next, he had me cough while listening to my chest with a stethoscope. He felt my neck for enlarged lymph nodes and inspected my ears and throat with his battery-operated exam light. He turned every now and then to jot down notes on my clean white medical chart. Suddenly the door burst open and he respectfully stepped back as Diane Tallo whirled in to take over. Her magnetic presence filled the room as she took command, greeting me in an efficient and friendly manner.

The physical exam continued as Dr. Tallo, an endocrinologist, began probing my neck with the perceptive fingers of a gland specialist. She stood behind me, reaching around to the front of my throat, pressing here and there with tender pokes from her fingertips. She knew exactly how to explore for problems. I was a perfectly healthy human specimen coming in for a routine physical exam with a friendly new doctor.

Suddenly Dr. Tallo quickly filled a Dixie cup with water. "Here drink this," she said with a strange tone. As I swallowed, she pressed into my throat with those amazing fingers. Looking at the young intern, she pronounced with sternness, "She has a lump!" Ever the teacher, she instructed the young man to feel the place at the base of my neck, which he had missed in his initial exam.

My body stiffened. Within a split second she was directly in front of me about two inches from my face.

"Now, don't be alarmed," she cautioned, while peering intently into my frightened eyes. "I'm going to have this lump on your thyroid biopsied under ultrasound. So, even if it is cancerous, there is a 90-percent success rate for this kind. You can live a perfectly normal life on synthetic thyroid medicine in the event and . . ." I don't remember a thing from that point on because I was in mild shock. *Cancer* is all I heard.

I don't remember driving home that day. I regretted changing doctors, but that was a form of denial. I dreaded the thought of becoming a thyroid-disease victim like my husband who, for the last thirty-eight years, has been a virtual prisoner to thyroid medication three times a day. *No thanks . . .* I thought, also having trepidation about the aspect of another surgery in my life. I did not want to live out my remaining years dependent on drugs because I was highly sensitive to medication. Aspirin made my ears ring. When I had gall-bladder surgery I stopped breathing on the operating table. I was not looking forward to having my throat slit open to remove a cancerous growth.

The unknown is always more stressful than having to deal with the plain, simple facts spelled out. Uncertainty produces anxious and dreadful thoughts. I had been blessed with a vivid imagination, but the down side of a creative mind is the tendency to jump to wrong conclusions or imagine the worst possible scenario.

My faith wavered. I was afraid. Fear struck hard and left me motionless. This was not going to be easy. *I had a lump.*

Fear is tormenting. The scripture verse "Fear hath torment, but perfect love casts out fear," had not become a reality in my heart. At that point in time, perfect love was not in the main frame of my thinking while worrying about cancer.

After discovering a lump on my thyroid, I realized that God knew if I had cancer or not. However, I was afraid to ask Him. After two days of fretting, I sought Him in earnest prayer. I prostrated myself across the bed with my face buried on the comforter. I listened intently for the fateful answer. What I actually heard changed my life forever.

This has nothing to do with your thyroid, but it has everything to do with your ministry. You do not have cancer. This lump is nothing but tissue. You are afraid of success. You are afraid of failure. You are afraid of moving forward with me because you are afraid of jealousy. You are afraid of rejection. When you find out that what I said to you is true, you will have the faith to confront all your fears.

Naturally, I shared this exhortation from the Lord with my husband. Afterward, I also told an elder of the church and his wife.

It was a week before I could get in for an appointment at Riverside Hospital for the biopsy exam. Daryl was at my side. It was a somber situation, so neither of us said much in the waiting room. On the stainless-steel exam table, the young technician couldn't locate the infamous lump. Her ultra-sound wand was hooked up to a television monitor. She said, "I need to locate the physician who will be doing your biopsy." They returned moments later. The doctor poked and pushed my neck. He probed for several minutes. "How did Dr. Tallo locate this lump? I can't seem to find it . . ." He sounded nervous.

I explained how she stood behind me and wrapped her arm around my neck. So, the doctor had me sit up to perform the same exam as Dr. Tallo.

Looking very relieved, he said, "Oh, here it is, I found the lump." Looking at the technician, he said, "Put the wand right where my finger is on her neck." I froze with anticipation.

He looked at the monitor to examine the lump. "Oh, that's just *tissue*. I don't need to put you through the pain of a biopsy. You can get dressed and go home."

The scripture verse where Peter and John went "walking and leaping and praising God" had new meaning. Fueled faith to move forward with God was ignited. With invigorated faith, my next missionary destination was West Africa. I traveled to Lagos, Nigeria with an evangelistic team from our music department. Our church's music minister, Beth Emery, had frequently traveled to Nigeria as a guest of Dr. Chris Tunde Joda, MD. Our team of women felt confident to travel with Beth, who is a trouper. It was another mission trip that had great impact upon my life. I returned home with a soaring heart from being with so many dedicated and loving Christians in Nigeria. The quality of their lives is so inferior compared to the standards in America, but these precious Nigerians are very rich in faith. This trip caused me to become more determined to meet the needs of the poor and disadvantaged in my own sphere of influence.

The faithful men in our church were not idle during these years. Daryl organized and sponsored numerous teams to attend Promise Keepers founded by Coach Bill McCartney, a long-time friend of his. Promise Keepers has had a powerful impact on millions of men around the world by strengthening core Christian values and establishing greater integrity in marriages.

Thankfully, in Christ Jesus, there's always room to grow and improve relationships. We develop deeper compassion for the less fortunate through enrichment seminars and missionary journeys.

In God, whose word I praise, in the LORD, whose word I praise- in God I trust; I will not be afraid. What can man do to me? Psalm 56:10-11 (New International Version)

Discussion Question

1. Has fear ever kept you from traveling to an unknown place to share the Lord?
2. Do you believe that the fear of rejection often stops a person of venturing out to be used of the Lord?

Chapter Twenty-Eight

Take Me to the Nations

An astonishing revelation came to me one day while sitting at my kitchen counter talking with my husband, as he munched on a sandwich. It was a Saturday afternoon sometime in September 1991.

At this time, Bo, age 17, was attending a private Christian school and so were the twins. Elisa and Leanne were ten-years-old and completely caught up academically and socially for their age level. My two stepchildren, Tammie and Scott were both married by then. Daryl was a senior pastor of our busy, productive, mission-minded congregation. As his wife, our lives were consumed with tremendous ministry demands. We committed to be there forever, sold out to Jesus. But out of nowhere, the Lord threw us a curve ball, which catapulted our lives from the neighborhood ballpark to the Majar leagues.

For months, I had been singing or humming "Take Me to the Nations, as an Ambassador for Christ," which was the theme song from our church summer youth program that previous June.

While sitting on a kitchen stool, facing my husband, I made a seemingly presumptuous statement.

"The Lord is going to send me to Russia," I declared with uncanny certainty. This must have been a prophetic revelation coming from deep within my soul. "Oh, but you'll have to come too," I added, ignoring the "yeah-right" expression on Daryl's face. "You'll need to go with me because you know the Bible so well, and the Russians will have lots of questions." Daryl rolled his eyes because I did sound like Queen Elizabeth announcing to Parliament her next goodwill mission. My husband probably thought: *Now why on earth would God be sending my wife to Russia?* The poor guy – life with a visionary hasn't been easy for someone with his analytical mind. We balance each other and we've lived in harmony for more than 38 years. Through the contrast in our temperaments we complement one another by embracing our differences. We've learned to honor one another in marriage and support each other in ministry.

God didn't spring that Russian mission trip on me. He gave me several months to pray about Russia. Earlier that year, a lavender paperback Russian New Testament was left on my kitchen desk by my brother, David, and his wife Lorraine, while visiting us from Michigan.

Sometime that summer, I had watched my nephew and three nieces while Dave and Lorraine attended a home-schooling seminar in Tennessee. Lorraine informed me that the Russian New Testament translation was a token give-away gift from host Bill Gothard to remind his conferees to "pray for Russia." So, I did. Each time I passed that Russian Bible on my desk, I prayed for "missionaries to be sent to Russia." Remember what Dr. Myles Munro said about praying for missionaries? He said, "Don't pray for missionaries unless you're willing to go." I should have considered that the Lord might be preparing me to go.

The reason I never consider going is because I had such negative feelings toward all Soviet bloc countries, with good reason. The Lord needed to change my heart.

During a business trip to Germany in 1973, Daryl and I passed through the inspection at "Checkpoint Charlie," a sector in West Berlin, to enter East Berlin before the Cold War ended and the Iron Curtain was torn down. The burly agent yelled at me to close the door just as I entered the building. The woman was employed by the Russian KGB and acted like it, as she rifled through our stuff. My husband's newspaper was promptly confiscated from his briefcase. After being ill-treated by the rude and demanding communist inspection agent, we were finally allowed to exit without further ado. After going through the outlandish drill, we re-entered our taxicab to cross over the border. High-powered rifles pointed at our vehicle from a looming high tower in front of us. The communist guards acted like dictators. After riding past the Wall into East Berlin, we were stopped on the communist side. At that point, we had to step out of the car while the militant KGB used mirrors to inspect beneath the car, opened the trunk and yanked the automobile seats apart looking for contraband. On the return, they did the same thing, but this time they were searching for hidden East Berliners trying to escape to freedom.

Our driver informed us that the guards would confiscate my camera if I took pictures of the Wall. The stern armed officials shouted instead of speaking in a normal tone. It was just like in the movies. When we drove over to a nice hotel for lunch we entered the expansive, marble floored lobby. Instead of the hustle and bustle of a busy hotel, it was so deathly quiet that you could have heard a pin drop. Several people were standing around or sitting and I noticed how oppressed the East Berliners seemed with their downcast faces. I refused to stay for lunch. I couldn't wait to get back to freedom. I also vowed *never* to visit a communist bloc country again.

However, more than twenty-years later, I learned that Bill Gothard was featured on television in St. Petersburg, teaching life principles. I changed my tune. I thought: *Boy, Russia really must be desperate to know about God because Bill Gothard isn't on American television.*

A few days after the kitchen counter proclamation about going to Russia, Daryl and I attended a James Robison Crusade held in Columbus. Following the meeting we greeted one of our dearest friends, Marcus Vegh. Marcus was an extremely talented and bright young man, the son of Pastor Moses and Bette Vegh, our close friends. Marcus was the television producer for James Robison at the time.

With a headset on and a wire microphone coming out of his ear, Marcus joyfully embraced us with a hug. Years earlier, Marcus had been an early pioneer television producer for *Breakthrough* with his dear friend, Rod Parsley.

"How are your mom and dad doing?" I asked after giving him a kiss on the cheek.

"My dad just came back from Moscow in an evangelistic meeting with more than 10,000 students from all over Russia!" said Marcus with a huge grin, resembling his handsome look-alike, Hungarian father.

"Well, the Lord is sending me to Russia, too!" I announced with confidence.

"Wow! That's great! James Robison is traveling to Russia next month. Why don't you come along with us?"

The man listening to us was an extravagant gift-giver from of our church. Looking at me, he said, "If you have a passport, I'll pay your way, but just you, Barbara. I can't pay for Daryl's ticket, too."

I teased Pastor Daryl because he needed to raise money to *accompany me* to Moscow, a few months later. We didn't go with James Robison. Instead, we traveled on the coattails of Pastor Moses Vegh in what turned out to be a whirlwind introduction to Russia.

During the five-day Moscow conference, we met Pastors Pavik and Marina Savelev, the faithful leaders of the dynamic "Dew" ("ROSA") Church. During the terrifying communist regime, this unregistered church met "underground" to avoid persecution. Marina was a Jewish-Christian who led worship during most of the evening services. Thousands of high school and college students jammed into the expansive, but dimly lit, auditorium that offered only a center aisle. Each row was about fifty-seats wide.

Dozens of colorful flags displayed on wooden poles lined the back of the platform. Throughout the services enthusiastic students rushed to retrieve a flag, lifting up certain countries to wave. The responsive roar from thousands of young Christians reminded the enemy that Jesus Christ rules every nation and the victories are already won! Each time a country was high and lifted up for

Jesus, my heart soared.

During the evening praise services, I competed for a lone, dilapidated tambourine with missing cymbals. Kostya, one of the few church leaders who spoke English, was frequently pulled off the platform to interpret. Whenever Kostya set down his beat-up tambourine, I snatched it up to play. I looked forward to his departures since I hadn't brought my tambourine from home. He'd return moments later and make me give it back. This amusing tambourine tug-of-war went on every night. In the former Communist rule and reign, the auditorium was almost always filled with atheists. Playing a tambourine for Jesus on a platform where the Communist Party once stood was unimaginable.

"Kostya, when I come back to Moscow, I'm bringing you twelve white tambourines with colorful ribbons down on each side!"

In his husky voice with a thick Russian accent, Kostya declared, "And don't forget the ribbons!" He was a spunky member of the Dew church and ribbons matched his personality.

As a ministry team, in a large sauna tub of a nearby hotel, Pastor Daryl and Pastor Pavik water-baptized nearly a thousand students during the next four-days. What made it interesting is that Pavol spoke no English and Daryl spoke no Russian. What a team!

Hundreds of young adults from all over Russia were packed in the pool area like American teenagers lined up to buy rock star concert tickets. However, these youth were lined up to identify with the death, burial, and resurrection of Jesus Christ their Savior. It was a sobering sight.

Daryl scheduled a second trip to Russia with Pastor Moses Vegh in March 1992. This time they were going without me. However, the Lord had use for me on that upcoming trip, even though I was unaware of His plans.

After returning home from Moscow it seemed as if I was running into Russians living in Columbus every time I turned around! I used to be a live radio talk show hostess and I invited a young Russian fellow to be on the show to interview with the representative who helped him get out of the country because of religious persecution. The morning of the interview I slipped in the bathroom breaking my leg and spraining my ankle. I did the show and went to lunch with a girlfriend afterward. I have a high pain tolerance. At three o'clock that afternoon an x-ray of only my ankle missed the fracture in my leg. Two weeks later, after an additional x-ray, the doctor issued a cane because the bone had started to heal.

A few weeks before Pastor Daryl's trip back to Moscow, I was limping around in a fabric store with my cane, minding my own business. I had a designated church check to buy fabric to make an extra-long tablecloth to serve the deaconesses dinner the night before our next ladies' retreat. I still planned to cook and honor our women in service with an elegant sit-down dinner in spite of the fact that I was hobbling around on a broken leg using a cane. For the ladies' sit-down dinner, I planned to spend about $35.00 on white fabric to make a 20-foot long tablecloth to cover two 8-foot utility tables end-to-end.

While I was in the fabric store, the Holy Spirit spoke to my heart. "Buy enough white fabric to make six dance garments to send with your husband." Having sewn beautiful garments for our church dance team, I knew exactly what to purchase. I spent $238.00 on double circle skirt fabric, angel blouses, elastic, and pins. While hobbling to my car, loaded down with two heavy bags, the Lord said, "They don't own sewing machines, so I need *you* to sew these dance dresses." I froze in my tracks. *You tricked me Lord!* Daryl was departing for Moscow in 10 days.

I was tossing and turning all night – I had spent way too much money and sewing all those dresses in time for the upcoming trip was impossible! The next morning the Lord reassured me. *"Do not fret my daughter, you did the right thing. The Russian dancers will dance in the streets of Moscow to dispel the vast darkness over that city."*

That Sunday morning, I made an impromptu announcement without looking at my husband's face. Thankfully, several dedicated church ladies came to the rescue for this enormous sewing project. However, as I was cutting out the first skirt pattern, the devil whispered in my ear. "You're going to make a *fool* out of your husband when he arrives with *dance attire*. That church doesn't even believe in dancing!" At the first conference I had not seen any dancers, so I froze with doubt and fear. Therefore, that afternoon I called Moscow for confirmation. I dialed the number and got right through to Marina.

"Marina, will you have dancers in your conference next week?" I held my breath. It felt like my salvation hinged on her answer.

"Yes, yes. I will have some dancers at the conference."

When I mentioned this phone call to Marina, my husband exclaimed, "How on earth did you get through to Russia on one try? The church office has been trying to call Moscow for two weeks! All we get is a busy signal."

The Lord knew I needed the truth. Marina's response became like the fray check I was applying to ends of cut ribbon for the 12 white tambourines. Kostya was going to be thrilled to see those ribbons!

However, my husband was *not* thrilled about carrying a huge suitcase stuffed with dance attire, yards of satin fabrics, and colored sequins to make banners also. During the final moments of packing, I tugged Lora Allison's *Celebration* book out of the clutched hands of my dear friend

Marion to squeeze in a bulging suitcase. This instructional book featured beautiful pictures of Lora's banners.

When Pastor Daryl returned home he brought back a thank you note from the dance team. In the letter the lead dancer explained that she had been agonizing for months, praying for "dresses" for the dance team. Finally, the Lord rebuked her nagging, "You of little faith, I already have your dresses on the way." According to the dates mentioned in her gracious thank you letter, her answer from the Lord coincided with my divine moment of inspiration at the fabric store. Thank you, Jesus!

Daryl and I returned to another Moscow conference in September 1992. During an afternoon praise service, I was seated next to Marina, enjoying the six beautiful ballerinas as they ministered (all part Jewish) to Russian praise music in their new dance garments. Leaning toward my ear Marina said, "We had a *March for Jesus* this past summer . . . the dancers were in front, leading about 2,000 people marching in the streets." She hesitated before continuing, "Umm, how to say this in English? The dancers were the 'hit of the parade.'"

Grabbing her arm, I gushed, "Marina! How did you know about *March for Jesus*?"

"I read about it in *Charisma Magazine*, so I organized one here. We also made seven beautiful banners to carry from all the nice satin fabrics you sent us."

The Lord was true to His word about the dancers in the streets to *dispel darkness over Moscow*. My heart was overwhelmed by the Lord's faithfulness to perform His prophetic word.

In an upcoming month the *March for Jesus* organizers sent out a documentary, highlighting film clips of the participating cities worldwide. Daryl was at an organization meeting with several local pastors, planning the second Jesus march in Columbus. The video was moving along, showing brightly dressed Christians marching in Hong Kong, Japan, Korea, Australia, Great Britain, Switzerland, France, Italy, and Germany . . . then the colorful moving images stopped abruptly with a jarring black and white snapshot from Moscow. Pastor Daryl yelled out, "Wait! Stop the video, rewind to that picture from Moscow again." When the black and white reappeared on the screen, the still-frame featured six triumphant dancers leading their Moscow Jesus march. My husband exclaimed, "My wife sewed the dresses all those dancers are wearing!"

Hearing about my husband gush was solace for all the grief I took when it was time for him to lug that huge orange vinyl suitcase to those dancers in Russia!

A few years later, author/evangelist Lora Allison was ministering at a citywide Christian conference in Moscow. Lora told me that Marina quickly recognized her as the author of *Celebration* and introduced herself. Lora returned to Marina's church to view all the magnificent banners made from the fabric we had sent and from Lora's book that we'd also included.

Prior to his third return to Russia, Daryl had a prophetic dream of a large seaport filled with massive ships. The vision turned out to be Odessa, Ukraine, a beautiful seaport located on the Black Sea. Odessa is considered the "Riviera of the Black Sea" with its crossroads of cultures, languages, trade, and the Black Sea's largest port. Many Russians come to Odessa to vacation because of its Majar cultural hub with an opera and ballet theatre, philharmonic orchestra, and museums.

During that return trip to Moscow two male students were commissioned to Odessa "to scout out the land." We wouldn't have allowed them to go if we'd known how far they had to travel. Sending them from Moscow to Odessa was like a trip from Maine to Oregon by train.

We learned of "a new start-up Charismatic church," so our nine-member American team embarked to Odessa in faith. We traveled two-days by train with Alexander, our reserved, but mature high school student interpreter from Estonia. He called his parents to gain permission to travel with us an extra six days. On the long train ride, whenever Alexander heard a new word from us, he jotted it down in his handy pocket notebook. By the end of the train ride Alexander had more than 150 American slang terms on his list! Expressions such as *hang on a minute, let's roll,* or *catch ya later.*

On Sunday morning our ministry team visited the Odessa congregation unannounced. The former Pentecostal-turned-Charismatic Pastor was astonished to have nine Americans arrive and he honored us accordingly. Many of his church leaders were mature Christians and serious college students from Africa. The University of Odessa offered an affordable education for them. I fell in love with Africa through these devoted Christians, representing six or seven different nations. I bequeathed my lone tambourine to a somber-faced West African on the praise team. With a coy smile, she accepted my gift knowing why I had picked her from all the rest.

In Odessa that Sunday morning our team was asked to greet the friendly congregation. Pastor Ike from Lagos, Nigeria interpreted our words. When I was invited to take the microphone, I could barely speak to the wide-eyed congregation because the spirit of the Lord overwhelmed me. It seemed more natural to close my eyes, lift up my arms and sing in my Heavenly prayer language. Spontaneously, the fresh-faced, young congregation joined in one-accord, singing sweetly in various unknown tongues.

Years later when I ministered in Nigeria, I reunited with our dear friend "Pastor Ike," whom we had first met in Odessa. I emptied my pockets and gave him every American dollar I brought intended for souvenirs. He had been without a job for several months, so his brief reunion with me was a divine connection. It is in times like that when I wish I had millions of dollars to give to young ministers attempting to build the church of Christ in third-world countries.

During our first Sunday morning in Odessa, Daryl and I encouraged the church "musicians and singers" to come forward to be released in worship. Our team prayed for about twenty-five students who responded to the call.

The Lord gave me a prophetic word for this church, which I read from my journal. "I am showing the world Odessa by putting it 'on the map.' First the natural, now the spiritual – Christians in Odessa will become a light to the world as a result of this sign."

Olympic figure skater Viktor Petrenko had already won the gold medal that previous February. A worldwide television network highlighted Viktor's hometown of Odessa, Ukraine. Four years later 16-year-old Oksana Bauil, also from Odessa, won another gold medal. This certainly put Odessa on the map for the entire world to see!

However, God was painting a much bigger picture yet to be revealed.

During that weeklong visit Pastor Daryl was graciously introduced to other Odessa city leaders, including the number-two Bishop of the United Pentecostal Church district in Ukraine, Bishop Peter Serdichenko. Through this divine connection Daryl was eventually linked to the entire UPC network of leaders throughout Ukraine in the next few years.

The following summer we returned to Odessa with another evangelistic team from our church. We were wide-eyed with wonder at all the Lord was doing in our midst. But it was not without moments of frustration. One Sunday afternoon our five-member team walked about three miles from the church service. We arrived at our hotel, hot, dusty, thirsty, and tired. We piled onto the elevator to be lifted up to the fourth floor. However, the elevator stopped short on the second floor and the door would not open. We were trapped.

Thankfully, Alexander was able to shout for help in Russian. The lady at the desk shouted back in Russian. Alexander had recently moved to America with a host family from our church. He returned as our official interpreter. I joked that we might be trapped for hours before a maintenance man was summoned via the public transport system. My husband barked at me. He did not consider this a laughing matter. A temperamental team member became offended. She left the church over "the tiff" my husband and I had while being trapped in an elevator. The team toughed it out for a few more suffocating moments and the doors miraculously opened on their own. The Lord has ways of weeding out the weak-kneed or those not mature enough to handle ministry mishaps in the lives of pastors expressing frustration trapped in an elevator.

One morning I marveled at the over-sized, golden-yoked eggs on my breakfast plate. Marion, whose hands I had pried open to gain Lora Allison's book bound for Russia, was eating across the room with other team members. Marion chuckled, "I don't have the heart to tell Barbara that's she's eating duck eggs for breakfast."

The following year from our generous, mission-minded local church, the Lord planted Edward and Linda McPherson and their three-year old son, Ryan, in Odessa as full-time missionaries. Linda is a prophetic and gifted musician, originally from Hope Temple, Pastor Moses Vegh's former church in Findlay, Ohio.

After learning the Russian language, Linda trained key musicians and numerous choir members from the Charismatic church and several citywide United Pentecostal churches. Although most of the older UPC choir members frowned on Linda's short hair, earrings, and slacks, her music was well received. The prophetic anointing on Linda's life was vivid. Those humble Christians were dry sponges soaking up a fresh Holy Spirit spring of refreshment from the Lord. The youth especially gravitated to Linda's glorious music.

During a subsequent trip to the Ukraine, Edward and Linda organized a nation-wide Worship Conference in Odessa. From America, we brought a dance troupe and other anointed musicians.

Marion and I personally constructed three beautiful banners with words in Russian. Linda had a praise team ready with several singers and musicians from Odessa. During the conference some of the Pentecostal men pointed at my tambourine and snickered. But the Lord had the last laugh. In the years to come, numerous white tambourines were being played in countless Pentecostal meetings throughout Odessa. The Lord provided and multiplied!

For the Odessa worship conference, I arrived with another large suitcase, bulging with donated dance-garments, tights, ballet slippers, and white, long sleeved leotards to give away. I prayerfully sought the Lord for direction to the "right person" to bestow this extravagant gift upon. Later a church deacon informed my husband that I picked the perfect recipient – a mother and her 15-year-old daughter, who traveled *five-days* by train to attend our Worship Conference! Their hometown was the *only Communist-ruled city left in all of Ukraine!* Months later I received a thank you letter and photographs from this mother and daughter dance team. The black and white pictures featured dancers twirling among several worshippers in a "March for Jesus" processional, which demonstrated the light of Christ in a very dark, atheist-governed city.

During the Communist rule and reign, Christians prayed in hushed tones for fear of being deported to remote places like Siberia.

One evening our ministry team dined at Bishop Peter Serdichenko's lovely home.

"Who is that pretty woman?" I asked Peter's wife, pointing to the faded photograph on top of the piano.

"That's my sister. The Communists arrested her because she is a Christian. I haven't seen her in eighteen years," said Kateanna, quietly, with regret forever etched in her crystal blue eyes. "We still keep a suitcase packed . . . just in case they come to arrest us in the middle of the night."

For several years Linda and Edward continued to work tirelessly among the UPC network. Our generous local church supported them. Their young son, Ryan, also spoke fluent Russian.

One afternoon in Odessa, Daryl and I entered a smelly, urine-stained elevator with little Ryan who was then about four years old. A man also stepped on, not realizing we were Americans. The burly man nodded, then gruffly spoke Russian to us with a tone of disgust. Ryan said something in Russian to the man. Little Ryan looked up at us to explain, "He says, 'It smells like a pig pen in here.'" The man looked stunned when he heard Ryan also speak to us in perfect English.

Songs of praise were birthed and sung, in spite of deplorable living conditions – no running hot water during the summer and little or no heat in the winter. But worst of all, the McPherson's battled oppressive spiritual opposition during this challenging time period. Through intercessory prayer the Lord gave Linda more than 100 prophetic songs in the Russian language. The spiritual war waged on, but Jesus was the Victor! The Lord surrounded us with songs of deliverance, which are still being sung throughout the Ukraine and in all the Russian-speaking churches in America.

Last Sunday, in our city of Columbus, I attended a contemporary Russian/Ukraine church service with Linda and Edward. A delightful praise team of young men and women sang worshipful songs in Russian. At one-point Linda leaned over and whispered in my ear. "I wrote this song ten years ago," she said with a smile.

Those years in the Ukraine were a blessing for everyone. God desired to release the Holy Spirit on rigid congregations that had not entered the glorious courts of praise and worship.

Two years after we first embarked to that beautiful city on the Black Sea, Daryl was invited to be the keynote speaker at a national UPC leadership conference. Several thousand people, including bishops and pastors from throughout the Ukraine, were in attendance those few days. Pastor Daryl taught on the subject of worship.

I sat next to Bishop Peter Serdichenko, his dear wife Kateanna, and their pretty, 20-year-old daughter, Valencia, who loudly clapped and sang during the music service with exuberance. I didn't dare bring my tambourine that night! Educated in England, Valencia was eager to move away from religious bondage of her Pentecostal forefathers.

Linda enthusiastically led the large choir of men and women onto the large platform. Our visiting musicians from America joined Russian orchestra members to enhance the large UPC choir with violins, flutes, and brass horns. By the end of the evening Bishop Peter and Sister Kateanna were also clapping with joyous, newfound freedom!

The choir was filled with men and women of all ages. Depending on their age, the women were adorned with a "head-covering," which consisted of a lacey headscarf, a headband, or a drab babushka. The choir swayed and clapped to all of Linda's up-beat original songs. It was a dramatic departure from fear to freedom of spontaneous, heartfelt expression of praise.

Afterward, a UPC Bishop embraced my husband in tears. In broken English he managed to say, "I lost my song ten years ago. Your message on worship returned singing to me . . . Thank you and God bless you!"

Pastor Daryl traveled to the Ukraine many more times in the years to follow. Alongside another UPC pastor, they water baptized countless Christians in the Black Sea during an outdoor summer ceremony with Bishop Peter. It was documented that more than 10,000 Russian/Ukrainians accepted Jesus Christ as Savior during those few years of revival. Many other Christian organizations began flooding in through this great open door during the time when it was very affordable to travel in this vast country.

About eight years ago Edward and Linda came back to America on what seemed liked like a permanent furlough. In February 1998, Daryl and I resigned. It was a painful departure, but God was in it.

Unfortunately, the new church administration did not honor our commitment to our vast missionary support. Therefore, with heavy hearts, Linda, Edward, and Ryan were forced to return to Columbus. I love "the death of the vision." As painful as it is to experience, God always "raises *His plans* from the dead" for a greater worldwide impact and anointing than we could ever wish for or imagine.

Daryl and I were dining at a local restaurant and bumped into the McPhersons. I invited Linda to hear Evangelist Mark Condon minister in music at his United Pentecostal Church (UPC) in Columbus. We went on the following Sunday evening, which was Easter. Linda wept through the entire praise service.

Mark Condon has a unique style of music and this gifted songwriter has produced eight very anointed praise and worship music CDs. His songs are heard around the world. Following that anointed praise service, we went out for pizza with Mark and Carol Condon. On the way home, I suggested that Linda consider translating Mark's music into a Russian CD to take back for "the Lord's unfinished missionary service in the Ukraine."

The next morning through previous church related connections, I recruited a group of young

UPC Russian musicians, who embraced Linda with open arms. In fact, this group had been praying for Russian contemporary style praise music.

Within a few weeks, Linda and I began meeting on a weekly basis. They were eager to learn new praise music. Linda also taught them prophetic singing. By the following Easter, Mark Condon's *House of Praise* was translated and recorded by Russian singers in a professional music studio.

With Mark's Russian CD in hand, Edward and Linda returned to the Ukraine in 2003 to help with a new School of Worship and the Arts in the Kiev, the Capital of Ukraine.

Mark Condon's UPC church, along with Pastor Paul Cook, helped pave the McPherson's way back home. Back in the Ukraine, Linda trained gifted Russian musicians to flow in the prophetic. She also was able to link up with several global outreach ministries located in Kiev, including The Hillsong Church.

In 2005 Daryl was invited back to preach in Russia. This time he traveled to Vorkuta, located inside the Arctic Circle. He visited tents of the Komi Tribe out on the Tundra at temperatures of 50 degrees below zero!

He had quite an adventure, too. While going on a mineshaft tour with fellow workers, the train went out of control and wrecked about a mile below the surface. Thankfully no one was seriously injured, but it was the most frightening experience of my husband's life. It was a true adventure while sharing Christ in a remote part of the earth. The scripture came to him, "Ask of me and I will give you the heathen for an inheritance and the utter most parts of the earth as a possession…." (Psalm 2:8).

The chorus verse, "Take me to the Nations," was in my heart to sing all summer when the Lord first spoke to me about going to Russia. Our spiritual songs become tiny seedlings, nurtured by fellow Christians in fertile foreign soil. Someday, we'll see the Lord, in all His glory, and our worship will unite every tongue through love. We'll be planted together, singing for all eternity. We've seen glimmers of light among the nations to know that's true.

Daryl just returned from a Russian church conference in Seattle, WA. He was the keynote speaker as the guest of Senior Pastor Peter Cherbotov, who planned the event. Daryl met him in the Ukraine many years ago and had a powerful prophecy for him that came true. Therefore, at the conference, Pastor Peter introduced him as "his father in the faith."

However, two weeks prior to this important Seattle leadership conference Daryl underwent emergency knee surgery for a severe infection following knee-replacement in his left knee last August. A week later, after a culture identified the exact bacteria invading his knee, the infectious disease doctor put him on an antibiotic I.V. drip to combat the infection and he was transferred to a nursing home. Daryl was mandated to stay in the nursing home for another five weeks! Disappointed and feeling defeated, he canceled the Seattle trip and found a substitute preacher willing to take his place.

However, four days before the conference, the nursing staff came in and took out the I.V. drip from his arm. The doctor had changed his treatment to an oral antibiotic and his surgeon released him to travel. Daryl instantly felt a surge of faith to make the trip to Seattle after all.

His friend, Bert Lindsay, a successful automobile dealer in Columbus, accompanied my husband as his nurse – pushing his wheelchair through the airport and helping Daryl dress throughout the conference. Daryl was unable to bend his knee at that point in time, so Bert's assistance was certainly needed.

The blessing of this testimony is that many years ago, Bert helped finance that first Ukraine worship conference without being able to attend. After learning of Daryl's physical dilemma, he volunteered to be his traveling companion. This host Russian-speaking church, which originated in the Ukraine, has grown into a fruitful vine in America. Had it not been for the knee infection, Bert would have missed out experiencing the fruit of the seeds he planted all those years ago. In addition, Lord used Bert at the Seattle conference to extend helpful wisdom to the businessmen.

Daryl later said, "I couldn't have gone to the conference without Bert's help. The miracle of me being released from the hospital in time became a testimony for increased trust. The devil meant it for evil, but the Lord was ultimately glorified in my secondary infection. My knee became the focal point of a bona fide miracle. Thus, my knee enhanced the atmosphere for an intensified anointing in each service. The Lord took all of us in the conference to a deeper level of faith each time we met throughout the three-days.

Linda McPherson also attended to the conference to work with the musicians. I asked her to recap some highlights of the conference since I was not able to attend.

With joy she said, "Daryl was fantastic. His Bible teachings were rich and powerful as usual. But I got the biggest charge watching Bert in action. Each time he got up to introduce Daryl he'd give a timely exhortation to the church. He'd make a great preacher. You could tell he was loving every moment."

It's those kinds of unexpected blessings that make volunteer service so rewarding.

In fact, all our memories traveling to the Ukraine with teams of Christians are joyful. We have maintained wonderful friendships with our Russian and Ukrainian sisters and brothers in the Lord.

We're very grateful to Pastor Moses Vegh who accompanied us on our first few trips to Russia and the Ukraine. And in special memory of his beloved son, Marcus, who tragically passed away in October 2007 after a courageous battle with throat cancer.

I'm looking forward to a great and glorious reunion with Marcus in Heaven someday. He was one of our dearest friends. Well done, my good friend and kingdom warrior!

For Christ's love compels us, because we are convinced that one died for all, and therefore all died. And he died for all, that those who live should no longer live for themselves but for him who died for them and was raised again. 2 Corinthians 5:14-15 (NIV)

Discussion Questions

1. Have you ever considered signing up for a short-term mission trip with your church or a Christian agency such as Youth with a Mission?

2. Have you ever allowed your teenagers to travel on missions? Grandchildren?

Chapter Twenty-Nine
Perfecting Godly Character

Most teenagers flourish under pressure. Their resilience and flexibility make them perfect candidates for short-term mission jaunts to exotic places on the planet. A teen's sense of adventure makes it exciting and a pleasure to pack them off each summer.

As a teenager, our daughter Tammie spent a few summers working at a Christian horse camp for youth. Her war stories were horrendous, but she hung in there for the duration, in spite of the long hours and primitive living conditions. As a camp counselor by day, Tammie slept in a converted chicken coup with her assigned group of little girls, 8 to 10 years of age. One night, when a mouse darted across the ledge near Tammie's head, she let out a terrifying scream that set off an explosion of shrieks from the smaller squadron.

The following summer, Tammie recruited her Michigan cousin Sherri to work with her at this interdenominational Christian camp, retreat facility, and riding stable committed to providing wholesome farm fun for all ages.

After a few days, Sherri called me in tears. She begged me to come rescue her. But both teens stuck it out and laughed at their "hardships," by the end of the summer. Cousin Sherri was often stuck on "potato peel" duty in the afternoon while the young campers were off riding horses on trails. Sherri groaned that she peeled an actual ton of potatoes during her summer long work detail. The worst part was touching any rotten potato covered with maggots to toss out. Sherri remarked, "I never thought I would make it, but it ended up being the most rewarding time of my life. God did so much in my heart. I can't even explain it."

At 17, Tammie spent a subsequent summer in Mexico at a mission post our local church helped to build. Given a choice of doing domestic duties indoors or pouring cement roofs, Tammy's previous horse farm-boot camp experience led her outdoors with the guys. She loved it. She returned home brimming with the joy of the Lord.

"What I loved most about that trip was gathering with the Mexicans to sing each night,"

Tammie exclaimed. "We usually only sing three or four verses at our church. But not those Christians – if they liked a chorus, they sang it over and over, thirty or forty times!"

One summer, in college, Tammie and a few other Spirit Life dormitory directors from Oral Roberts University ventured off to Calcutta on a mission trip led by her friend Melody, the team leader. These brave, young women spent their summer helping out in one of Mother Theresa's orphanages. Melody did not put up with wimps. She expected everyone to live among the inhabitants. Therefore, the young ladies traveled through India by train in third class cars along with the peasants and suffered in ways I didn't want to hear about. On one such all-night train ride, Tammie rested on a rickety metal upper luggage rack praying for a feeble old woman lying on the filthy floor below, who moaned and groaned for hours. The lady was dead by morning and they had several more hours to travel while accompanying a dead body.

In their meager sleeping quarters at the Calcutta orphanage, a rat visited their room nightly. At first the girls were startled awake to hear the rodent gnawing on the wooden dresser with teeth marks in the wood as evidence. They started calling him "Ben," after the friendly rat in the sequel to "Willard," the Walt Disney movie. Even though "Ben" continued visiting, the women slept blissfully without fear.

As parents we nixed the scheme they cooked up for the following summer. Melody and Tammie wanted to travel down the Amazon River to work at medical mission posts along the way. Somehow the idea of two blondes, riding on a boat, in the midst of jungle rebels, didn't sound like such a good idea to either set of parents.

As the first woman to graduate with honors from Wheaton College with double master's degrees in 1984, Melody taught Christian principles at a Bible college in South Africa for the next several years. She eventually met the man of her dreams who happened to be in her village on a weeklong medical assignment. As a fellow American, Melody was elected to be his official tour guide. She married this handsome Harvard graduate, an infectious disease doctor. They now reside with their children in Atlanta, Georgia.

After graduating from college with honors, Tammie married the man of her dreams, too. Barry Farah is a successful entrepreneur who comes from a long line of committed Christian ministers. His father, the late Dr. Charles Farah was a professor of theology at ORU. Most of the extended Farah family members serve in full-time church ministry because their grandparents met Jesus in Syria, through an American missionary, more than 100 years ago! Barry spent most of his youth doing mission work with his dedicated parents. Three years ago, Pastor Barry and Tamra Farah used their resources, strength of character, community influence, and mutual love of Jesus to start an outstanding church in Colorado Springs where they reside with their two children, Allison and David are now grown. David is married to a nice gal, Judee.

David graduated from Pepperdine University in Malibu overlooking the Pacific Ocean. In high school he spent a few summers with "Teen Mania Ministries" in Costa Rica with other teens from around the nation as evangelistic outreach. Teen Mania's mission is to provoke a young generation to passionately pursue Jesus Christ and to take His life-giving message to the ends of the earth. Our grandson completed a year's study at Pepperdine in London, England to further his education in international business.

During high school, our tall and beautiful ballet dancer, Allison, "Alli" traveled with members of her youth group to Baja, Mexico as an outreach from church. The teens faced language barrier, hot climate and exhaustion while giving of their time, love and resources. Evangelism activities for the outreach included open-air preaching, house-to-house evangelism, and mime and puppet outreaches in the poor villages, where the majority of homes are dilapidated makeshift shelters.

Our son, Scott, spent a year working hard on a Kibbutz located on the Gaza strip following his junior year at Bryan Christian College. A Kibbutz originated as a collective gathering of families in Israel for the purpose of agriculture. Christians often served alongside the natives to show the love of Christ through good works because Israeli law strictly forbids evangelism.

One summer, Scott's teen daughter, Caroline Sanders, traveled to Australia with a program called "People-to-People." Their mission is to bridge cultural and political borders through education and exchange, making the world a better place for future generations. Our beautiful blonde blue-eyed granddaughter was the only one from Columbus to sign up for the program. However, in the pre-planning meetings she met many nice friends from other parts of Ohio. Their team of Ohioans became student ambassadors to a few impoverished schools in the Philippines. Caroline loved it.

When our twin daughters turned 13 they left for a six-week jaunt with a Christian program called "Get Dirty for God." They went through a weeklong rigorous jungle experience on an island in Florida. Elisa wrote "I've got 38 mosquito bites on one arm." After boot camp they traveled by bus and train to an Indian Reservation in Arizona. To help the poor and disadvantaged, the team stopped off in Chicago for a week to clean inner city, roach infested apartments for several elderly residents. At the Indian reservation they lugged large stones to clear the land for improvements. They definitely got dirty for God! I'll never forget the joy on their faces when they got off the plane. summer of 1996, Elisa and Leanne went off with "Youth with a Mission," which is an international, inter-denominational, non-profit Christian missionary organization. Founded by

Loren Cunningham in 1960, YWAM's stated purpose is to "know God and to make Him known." The twins were part of 4,500 YWAM volunteers at the 1996 Atlanta summer Olympics. Thousands of Christians from around the world traveled to Atlanta to help share the gospel during the Summer Olympics. Sixty-three countries were represented among the teams recruited for YWAM's wide-ranging games outreach, which continued as planned despite the Centennial Park bombing. While many groups presented the gospel to visitors through open-air music and performing arts, others turned their attention to Atlanta residents. Volunteers ran youth sports clinics for would-be future Olympians, and helped local ministries working among the city's homeless.

Our twin daughters have also gone on a teen mission trip to the Ukraine, which was sponsored by our former church.

Brother Bo was not exempt from doing community service, either. In high school, Bo spent a few weeks in Mexico with his church youth group building church pews. For two summers, Bo, along with a team of his college buddies, went door-to-door by bicycle, to promote educational materials sponsored by a national company. The hardships he endured by working long, strenuous hours in the severe heat of Alabama definitely gave our privileged son a greater appreciation for his nice air-conditioned bedroom back home.

Through dedication and willing sacrifice, God builds sound character in us. We develop genuine gratitude by observing how the less fortunate live and extending a hand of God's mercy to them. Thankfully, hard work pays off and the toughest lessons in life have eternal rewards whenever our good works bring glory to Jesus Christ.

As a proud American, I'm eternally grateful for our country's Christian heritage. I'm also extremely thankful for America's Founding Fathers. As a teenager, my own father fought in World War II as a courageous Marine in the South Pacific. God bless all the dedicated past and present soldiers that sacrifice dearly for our precious freedoms. Having traveled the world, I'm convinced that America is still the greatest place on earth.

My solemn prayer is that by sharing these inspirational stories, you are now stirred to reach out to those less fortunate. May you look at the poor and disadvantaged with the attitude, *there go I, but by the grace of God.* Motivating you is my utmost desire and a noble purpose that surely pleases the Lord. May you have a fruitful and prosperous journey fulfilling *The Great Commission* and extending God's many facets of wondrous love to those in need of our precious Lord and Savior.

Let your light shine. The laborers are few…the Lord has need of you.

But when Jesus saw the multitudes, He was moved with compassion for them, because they were weary and scattered, like sheep having no shepherd. Then He said to His disciples,
  "The harvest truly is plentiful," but the laborers are few. Therefore, pray the Lord of the harvest to send out laborers into His harvest. Matthew 9:36-39 (NKJV)

Discussion Questions

1. Have you ever considered being a chaperon on a church outing or summer camp outing?

2. Have you ever thought of traveling with a group of teens to help in a mission of helps?

3. How important do you think it is for teens to experience "hardship" by traveling to third-world countries?

Notes

Chapter Thirty

Faith is a Journey Forward

In the beginning of my faith journey with the Lord, I needed to grasp the heart of God in many areas of my life. Changes were needed in my life. Actually, a complete overhaul was more like it. Without Majar renovation I could not move forward. Eventually, I followed Pastor Anderson's advice and began seriously studying the Word of God and His promises. "Faith comes from hearing, and hearing by the Word of God," according to Romans 10:17. The Word of God challenged me and brought needed transformation in my life. It's difficult to write about faith without a deep understanding of why it's vital in the life of every Christian. Without faith it is impossible to please God.

In church I learned, through scripture, that Abraham is the "father of faith." Throughout the New Testament, Abraham is referred to as the "Patriarch of Faith." It is possible to gain wisdom from Abraham's life. Like Abraham, trusting the Lord for every step-in life helped me comprehend God's love for me. His love has helped me impact others with the love of Christ by unwavering belief in times of difficulty. It is possible to expand in faith, so let me guide you through some insights I gleaned from my study of Abraham.

The faith journey that changed the world began with a relationship between an obedient man named Abram and Jehovah, the self-existent, eternal God. Abram, whose name later became Abraham, was a man born a few generations after the great flood. God's wrath had destroyed an entire wicked civilization, except the family members of a righteous, blameless man named Noah. God told this obedient man to build an ark to save his family even though it had never rained before! Noah built in faith. Abraham followed in faith. "Do not be afraid, Abraham. I am your shield, your very great reward," (Genesis 15:1(NIV).

Abraham, the patriarch of ancient Israel, intimately knew God; the Bible tells us that He listened and *obeyed the voice of God.* God made a covenant with Noah and his sons. God directed them to "be fruitful and multiply, and fill the earth," (Genesis 9:1 NKJV). After the flood and

God's extensive discourse with Noah, the Lord didn't speak directly to anyone until Abraham and later, Moses.

Our ability to move forward with God began with Abraham's step of faith – *a result of hearing the voice of God.* God established glorious plans for *our* future. The Lord needed an obedient servant to accomplish His ultimate goal, which was Jesus Christ, the Savior of the world. He found His man, Abraham, whose name means, "exalted father of many."

God commanded Abraham to leave his father's house, his extended family, friends, and motherland to travel to an unknown country. The Lord said to Abraham, ""I will make you a great nation and bless you, and make your name great; and you shall be a blessing. I will bless those who bless you, and I will curse him who curses you, and in you all the families of the earth will be blessed. (Genesis 12:1-3 NKJV)

Abraham was a righteous man. His faith in God qualified him as a trustworthy servant to carry out this important assignment. God planned to make Abraham "a great nation," yet it's doubtful that's the motive why Abraham chose to follow God's commission. It is admirable that Abraham left everything to follow the Lord's commandments. *Abraham obeyed because he was loved and accepted by God.*

If we are ever to move forward with victory over darkness, we must be in right relationship with God. From the depths of our soul, Jesus Christ must be our Lord and the Master over every area in life. Through the power of the Holy Spirit, *we must hear God's voice* and allow Him to guide us. God is looking for obedient hearts to accomplish His purposes in this generation. To go forward with God requires courage and a willing heart to obey His every command. Jesus needs to be the captain of the ship – the commander-in-chief of every move for a collision-free journey.

We cannot expect the Lord to lead us to higher ground if we aren't prepared for the journey. Our motives must be pure, expecting nothing in return for our willingness to follow the Lord. Jesus is our reward. If we are in proper relationship, *His love is all we will ever desire in life.* Nothing satisfies our longings like Him. As we sojourn through life, His love can be compared to nothing else.

It is this wondrous love that compels us to obey. Abraham had flaws. He had doubts, fears, and setbacks. This journey with God was not without the same bumps we face in the road ahead. Abraham experienced detours, but with each test God made Himself known in *another faith dimension* by revealing more of His character. This is how Abraham's faith grew – through tests. Through each failure Abraham came to a place of repentance for character growth and stronger faith.

By accepting His divine love, I began to trust Him enough to expose my character flaws.

Without fear of rejection, I allowed God to magnify the stagnant and unproductive places of my heart with the lens of the Holy Spirit. As we submit to the process, He has ways to bring correction and discipline in to our lives.

His ultimate goal is to prepare us for the ongoing journey.

Abraham was *willing* to cross through desert plains in pitched tents. Abraham led a caravan of livestock, servants and their children, his wife, Sarah, and his nephew, Lot. It was an extreme hardship, requiring sacrifice. But the Lord faithfully appeared along the way to encourage Abraham during his demonstration of obedience.

"To your descendants I will give this land," (Genesis 12:7). Abraham responded to this tremendous future promise with an act of worship by building an altar to the Lord, who had appeared to him. Abraham could not have understood the dynamics of that promise since Sarah was barren, and *he had no descendants.* This altar was a display of Abraham's genuine love and honor for God – a place of total surrender.

Not my will, Lord; but Yours – the ultimate act of obedience to God.

There is nothing mystical or magical about faith. It is very practical. Faith is measured by our *acts of obedience* to the clear or complex commands from God. It is that simple. Every responsible act of obedience comes from our will. We must *choose to obey.* When we do, obedience produces joy that *motivates us to keep on trusting God.*

In my sincerest desire to please God, I don't always obey His commands because I am weak and easily tempted to avoid sacrifice, hardship, or inconvenience. It is my loss when I fail His expectations and standards of excellence for my life. Too often I fall short, but that does not affect the way the Lord feels about me. I may feel guilty for failing to obey, but I can freely ask for forgiveness, knowing that His mercy is extended to me. I learn from my mistakes. Therefore, I humbly ask for grace to follow more quickly the next time another opportunity for obedience comes my way. Through the years the Lord has asked me to fast from food for a certain situation or to simply fast for no known reason all. Skipping a single meal or several requires obedience. However, fasting is not something I have swiftly submitted to in the past. Sometimes it may take days or weeks to finally obey the Lord in this matter. But if I choose not to fast, I know that God still loves me. Fasting is for my benefit, not His.

Disobedience to God delays His overall perfecting process for my life.

He is perfecting all that concerns me. There is a master blueprint for my life, and the speed at which I fulfill His plans depends upon my obedience. God will love me *even if I never get there,* or ever attain what it is that He wants for my life. That's the mystery about this walk of faith. God accepts me, even if I fail miserably. He is a compassionate and merciful God. His love is unconditional.

His ultimate desire is that we succeed and achieve our fullest potential. He desires that we live productively, developing all of our God-given talents to the fullest potential. He wants to advance His Kingdom through a united army. A good soldier is disciplined and ready for battle at a moment's call.

God wants us to go forward in faith.

For many of us that requires getting unstuck from bondage, which is usually rooted in *fear*. To follow God in our own strength and natural abilities, we may become timid and reluctant to trust God completely. Failing to understand and accept God's *unconditional love* may happen because we might be afraid to let Him have *complete control* of our lives. Many Christians remain stuck in neutral, playing it safe, enjoying all the benefits of God and sensing a peace about going to Heaven. There are many sincere Christians leading godly lives, busy doing things for the Lord, serving in church work, but not spending time listening to Him for a *higher purpose. His Kingdom is at hand.*

For many years I played it safe by being busy, but I was in neutral and not moving forward with the Lord. A deeper, more intimate journey with God requires scripture meditation and daily prayer. Moving forward with God in faith also requires courage to face the unknown. If we remain in a comfort zone, we will miss the joys of the difficult journey. The Lord God Almighty has much more for our lives if we trust Him to take the controls. Learn to respond to the Lord's direction without a moment's hesitation.

So, what have we learned about faith from the life of Abraham? How do we come to trust in God completely? Is there a simple formula for faith? Do we have to cross the desert in pup tents to demonstrate genuine faith? What is the secret of success by great men and women of God who have accomplished mighty deeds for God? How do we move mountains with faith the size of a mustard seed? It is God who moves the mountains, but faith must be present to do so. Jesus said, "If you have faith as small as a mustard seed, you can say to this mountain move from here to there and it will move, and nothing will be impossible for you," (Matthew 17:20-21 NKJV).

Jesus responded with the "mustard seed illustration" after his disciples cried out in exasperation for *"more faith"* when they couldn't muster up enough love to forgive seven times in a day. They mistakenly thought that extending forgiveness required "more faith."

If your brother sins, rebuke him, and if he repents, forgive him. If he sins against you seven times in a day, and seven times comes back to you and says, 'I repent,' forgive him.
The apostles said to the Lord, 'Increase our faith!' He replied, 'If you have faith as small as

a mustard seed, you can say to this mulberry tree, 'Be uprooted and planted in the sea,' and it will obey you. 'Suppose one of you had a servant plowing or looking after the sheep. Would he say to the servant when he comes in from the field, 'Come along now and sit down to eat'? Would he not rather say, 'Prepare my supper, get yourself ready and wait on me while I eat and drink; after that you may eat and drink'? Would he thank the servant because he did what he was told to do? So, you also, when you have done everything you were told to do, should say, 'We are unworthy servants; we have only done our duty.' (Luke 17:3-10(NIV)

Through these two illustrations Jesus instructed his disciples that they didn't need "increased faith." What they needed was obedience to act responsibly – *obedience* to forgive, *obedience* to fast and pray, *obedience* to repent of pride, and *obedience* to express genuine love toward others.

The Lord wants us ready for the journey with frequent rest stops (prayer) along the way to refuel in spirit, mind, and body. Prayer cultivates an obedient heart.

The disciples cried out for more faith, but what they needed was *simple obedience.* Isn't that usually the case with us? We might bypass the elements of virtue and godly character development to demonstrate "faith through works." It might be exhilarating to lead a group of teenagers to repentance at a summer camp meeting. But if it is done with a prideful attitude of "see how spiritual I am," it misses the mark of Christianity. Being zealous in doing good deeds is prideful if the motive is to be seen by men. What we end up with is *dead works,* a boost to our egos, and the probability of a haughty and religious spirit.

Almost fifty years after God bade Abraham to follow Him, the Lord appeared to Abraham. He was ninety-nine years old. God told him the promised child would come into fulfillment by that time the next year. Sarah was listening nearby as the Lord spoke of this baby. She laughed at the prospect of having sex, let alone conceiving a child at their age! "I've grown old, shall I have pleasure, my lord being old also?" (Genesis 18:12 KJV) Sarah had already demonstrated doubt and disbelief years earlier by offering her handmaiden, Hagar, to bear Abraham's promised child. A child named Ishmael was conceived, but he was not the child of the Promise. Since Abraham was a willing participant, he must have been operating in unbelief as well.

A year after the Lord spoke Sarah and Abraham conceived a child and named this promised son Isaac, whose name means "laughter." Isaac was cherished by his parents and grew into a strong young lad. The Lord tested Abraham once again, but this was the ultimate *test of obedience* that changed the course of history forever.

God required Abraham to sacrifice his only son as a burnt offering on a mountain in the land of Moriah. What sort of God would test a man's faith with such a horrible request? It seems incredible that God would tell Abraham to *"take your son, your only son Isaac, whom you love,"* and offer him up as a sacrifice. The sacrifice seemed to go against God's promise of an heir, yet

Abraham knew God would still fulfill His Word, even if it required Him to raise Isaac from the dead (Romans 4:17). Isaac was in the hands of God; He was a gift from God. Isaac belonged to God. The ultimate test of obedience came when Isaac was a near teenager. The Lord presented Abraham with the ultimate test of obedience. God asked, "Are you willing to kill the very promise I gave you?"

In obedience to the Lord's direction, Abraham and his son, Isaac, took a three-day journey to the place on the mountain. They gathered wood for the burnt offering, but Isaac did not know he was meant to be the sacrifice that day.

Isaac said, "Look, the fire and the wood, but where is the lamb for the burnt offering?'

And Abraham said, "My son, God will provide for Himself the lamb for the burnt offering." So, the two continued walking together up the mountain path.

They came to the place where God had sent them. Abraham began building the altar for sacrifice and placed the wood down. He then bound Isaac, his beloved son and laid him on the altar, upon the wood. Abraham stretched out his hand and took the knife to slay his son. Suddenly the Angel of the Lord appeared from Heaven and said, "Abraham, Abraham! Do not lay a hand on the lad, or do anything to him, for now I know that you fear God, since you have not withheld your son, your only son, from Me."

Abraham lifted his eyes and looked, and there behind him was a ram caught in a thicket by its horns. Abraham took the ram and offered it up for a burnt offering instead of his son. The Angel of the Lord called to Abraham a second time from Heaven, and declared, "By myself I have sworn, says the Lord, because you have done this thing, and have not withheld your son, your only son—blessing I will bless you, and multiplying I will multiply your descendants as the stars of the heavens and as the sand which is on the seashore; and your descendants shall possess the gate of the enemies. In your seed all the nations of the earth shall be blessed, because you have obeyed My Voice," (Genesis 22:2-18).

Abraham's demonstration of trust and belief paved the way for future believers to come into covenant with God. God's promises made to Abraham have become our inheritance. Through Abraham's obedience came Jesus Christ, the Son of God, who died for our sins. Through His sacrifice, we come into a loving and eternal relationship with God the Father. Abraham's journey opened the gate for us to follow, allowing us to partake in the blessings of God.

Genuine faith comes from a relationship with God the Father, through Jesus Christ His Son.

Faith becomes the demonstration of heartfelt obedience to His voice as experienced by ancient fathers in the Bible.

Now faith is being sure of what we hope for and certain of what we do not see. This is what the ancients were commended for.

By faith we understand that the universe was formed at God's command, so that what is seen was not made out of what was visible. By faith Abel offered God a better sacrifice than Cain did. By faith he was commended as a righteous man, when God spoke well of his offerings. And by faith he still speaks, even though he is dead.

By faith Enoch was taken from this life, so that he did not experience death; he could not be found, because God had taken him away. For before he was taken, he was commended as one who pleased God. And without faith it is impossible to please God, because anyone who comes to him must believe that he exists and that he rewards those who earnestly seek him.

By faith Noah, when warned about things not yet seen, in holy fear built an ark to save his family. By his faith he condemned the world and became heir of the righteousness that comes by faith.

By faith Abraham, when called to go to a place he would later receive as his inheritance, obeyed and went, even though he did not know where he was going. By faith he made his home in the Promised Land like a stranger in a foreign country; he lived in tents, as did Isaac and Jacob, who were heirs with him of the same promise. For he was looking forward to the city with foundations, whose architect and builder is God.

By faith Abraham, even though he was past age—and Sarah herself was barren—was enabled to become a father because he considered him faithful who had made the promise. And so, from this one man, and he as good as dead, came descendants as numerous as the stars in the sky and as countless as the sand on the seashore. Hebrews 11:1-12 (NIV)

Discussion Questions

1. Abraham had an intimate relationship with God and he was motivated to obey by the love he felt from the Lord. Do you feel that love and acceptance from God?

2. Do you ever feel that you fail God by not obeying something He has directed you to accomplish?

3. Have you ever not apologized to someone for hurting their feelings?

4. How important do you think obeying God is?

5. Do you think your ministry or effectiveness as a Christian is related to your obedience?

Identifying Your Motivation Gifts to Serve in Church

Every Christian has unique and important roles to serve in church through recognizing and embracing our specific motivational gifts as explained in scripture.

*For by the grace given me I say to every one of you: Do not think of yourself more highly than you ought, but rather think of yourself with sober judgment, in accordance with the faith God has distributed to each of you. For just as each of us has one body with many members, and these members do not all have the same function, so in Christ we, though many, form one body, and each member belongs to all the others. We have different gifts, according to the grace given to each of us. If your gift is **prophesying**, then prophesy in accordance with your faith; if it is **serving**, then serve; if it is **teaching**, then teach; if it is to **encourage**, then give encouragement; if it is **giving**, then give generously; if it is to **lead**, do it diligently; if it is to show **mercy**, do it cheerfully.*
Romans 12:3-8 NIV

It's important to identify our God-given gifts because comparison is the root of insecurity and the frequent cause of jealousy. Understanding how gifts function and operate in unity will help us to remain humble and joyful through our divine purpose for kingdom living.

I love the way writer Mary Fairchild "pictures" these motivational gifts in operation within the body of Christ:

- Prophecy becomes the **eyes** in the body of Christ.
- Service becomes the **hands** in the body of Christ.
- Teaching becomes the **mind** in the body of Christ.
- Giving becomes the **arms** in the body of Christ.
- Exhortation becomes the **mouth** in the body of Christ.
- Administration becomes the **head** in the body of Christ.
- Mercy becomes the **heart** in the body of Christ.

The motivational gifts serve to reveal the personality of God. Let's look at them in detail as you try to pick out your gift(s).

Prophecy - Believers with the motivational gift of prophecy are the "seers" or "eyes" of the body. They have insight, foresight, and act like watch dogs in the church. They warn of sin or reveal sin.

They are usually very verbal and may come across as judgmental and impersonal; they are serious, dedicated, and loyal to truth even over friendship.

Ministering/Serving/Helps - Those with the motivational gift of serving are the "hands" of the body. They are concerned with meeting needs; they are highly motivated, doers. They may tend to over commit, but find joy in serving and meeting short-term goals.

Teaching - Those with the motivational gift of teaching are the "mind" of the body. They realize their gift is foundational; they emphasize accuracy of words and love to study; they delight in research to validate truth.

Giving - Those with the motivational gift of giving are the "arms" of the body. They truly enjoy reaching out in giving. They are excited by the prospect of blessing others; they desire to give quietly, in secret, but will also motivate others to give. They are alert to people's needs; they give cheerfully and always give the best that they can.

Exhortation/Encouragement - Those with the motivational gift of encouragement are the "mouth" of the body. Like cheerleaders, they encourage other believers and are motivated by a desire to see people grow and mature in the Lord. They are practical and positive and they seek positive responses.

Administration/Leadership - Those with the motivational gift of leadership are the "head" of the body. They have the ability to see the overall picture and set long-term goals; they are good organizers and find efficient ways of getting work done. Although they may not seek leadership, they will assume it when no leader is available. They receive fulfillment when others come together to complete a task.

Mercy - Those with the motivational gift of mercy are the "heart" of the body. They easily sense the joy or distress in other people and are sensitive to feelings and needs. They are attracted to and patient with people in need, motivated by a desire to see people healed of hurts. They are truly meek in nature and avoid firmness.

There is in-depth research available on motivational gifts in print by various authors, as well various tests to accurately identify your strongest attributes.

The Institute in Basic Life Principles offers a motivation-gift survey that is worth considering now. Check off each trait that applies to your personality. You may have a few checks in *every* category, but the majority-check of certain traits indicates an accurate result. Usually there are *three* motivation gifts that ring truest per test score. U

Person Number One

- Making sure that statements are totally accurate and true is important to you.
- You really love to learn and want to gain as much knowledge as you can.
- You react negatively to people who make unfounded statements.
- You tend to check the credentials of your instructors and teachers.

- When made aware of a debated issue, you tend to react by mentally analyzing the facts and drawing conclusions of your own, based on hard facts.
- Doing research is enjoyable to you.
- When asked to explain something, you tend to give more explanation than is necessary.
- You are attentive to details.
- You tend to be silent about matters until you have searched diligently for pertinent information and gathered the facts.
- You have good study habits and research skills.
- You prefer to solve a problem by studying it thoroughly rather than brainstorming about possible solutions or "jumping in" to fix the problem.
- You take particular delight in uncovering facts or details that have been overlooked by others.
- Others would describe you as a sincere and steadfast person.
- You would rather learn how to do something than actually do it.
- Most of your close acquaintances would say you tend not to be enthusiastic about most *things*.

Person Number Two

- You can confidently visualize a final, completed task before even the initial steps have been taken.
- You enjoy coordinating the efforts of a team to reach a common goal.
- You find it a simple task to break down a significant assignment into achievable goals and responsibilities.
- You are able to delegate assignments to others well.
- You see people as resources that can be used to get a job done efficiently.
- You are quite willing to endure resistance or criticism in order to accomplish a task.
- As a leader, you expect and require loyalty from those under your supervision.
- You tend to "rise above" petty issues to focus on reaching the final goal.
- You are good at encouraging your team members and inspiring them to action.
- Once a project is completed, you don't waste any time moving on to a new project. In fact, before the initial project is completed, you often are visualizing the next mountain that needs to be conquered.
- When made aware of a need, you tend to analyze it rather than jumping right in and starting to work on it.
- You tend to evaluate accomplishment on the basis of doing the best job with the fewest resources in the shortest amount of time.
- Although not opposed to expressing emotion, you tend to regard emotional expressions—positive or negative—as a waste of time.
- You usually make decisions based on what is best for the sake of a project, not on what is most convenient or enjoyable for the laborers.
- Because of your focus on the tasks at hand, sometimes others think you are uninterested or aloof.

Person Number Three

- You judge most actions as being either right or wrong—black or white, not gray.
- You tend to react strongly to people who are not what they appear to be.
- You especially enjoy people who are willing to be completely honest with you—even if the truth hurts.
- Before you sell an item in your garage sale, you would like to explain to the potential buyer exactly what is wrong with that item or why you don't want to keep it.
- When you observe someone doing wrong, you feel it's your responsibility to correct that person or bring it to the attention of his authority.
- You can quickly discern the true character of an individual, even when he tries hard to conceal his poor character or the wicked motives of his heart.
- You separate yourself from those who refuse to repent of evil.
- You are not hesitant to share your opinion, especially if you think obvious wickedness has been overlooked or ignored.
- When you fail, you are quick to judge yourself.
- Your employees who have bad attitudes are sources of irritation to you.
- In your opinion, compromise is *never* the best solution.
- When you observe or discern sin, to say nothing about it is, of itself, sinful.
- It is not difficult for you to accept absolutes.
- You are not easily swayed by emotions—your own or those of others—when a decision has to be made.
- You have a deep capacity to trust God.
- Sometimes others tell you to "cheer up and look on the bright side" because you tend to look on the not-so-bright side of things.
- You are committed to doing what is right and true, even if it means that you must suffer for it.

Person Number Four

- When you observe insensitivity or harshness in others, you tend to respond with anger toward the harsh or insensitive person.
- You are sensitive to the hurts of others, even when they do not express that hurt verbally or directly.
- When others express genuine love, your heart responds with joy and gratitude.
- If given a choice, you would prefer to have a few close friendships rather than a great number of shallow relationships.
- People who have problems seem to seek you out, so that they can tell you about their woes.
- Being firm with individuals who need to be corrected or exhorted is something you tend to avoid.
- It is difficult for you to be decisive in some circumstances.
- You need quality time to explain how you feel about things.
- When you see someone, who is hurting—physically or emotionally—you want to offer help and remove the source of the pain.
- You want to remove people who inflict hurt on others.
- You often wonder why God allows people to suffer.

- If a close friend or family member is offended, you find yourself being tempted to take up that offense too.
- You tend to cry easily when you see or hear something sad or touching.
- You sincerely and enthusiastically rejoice with those who rejoice!
- You enjoy being needed by others.
- You do not judge sin lightly—your own or anyone else's.
- You desire to pray faithfully and fervently.
- Sometimes the people you're with don't understand why you seem to be drawn to "down-and-outers," individuals whom others usually try to avoid altogether.

Person Number Five

- When you meet someone, you tend to visualize his or her potential.
- You like to give counsel to others.
- You can usually discern a believer's level of spiritual maturity pretty easily.
- Because you enjoy helping people grow spiritually, you like to encourage them by proposing projects for them to carry out, which you hope will result in spiritual growth.
- You motivate people to become what you "see" they could become.
- Sometimes you unintentionally make others think they will see results a lot faster than they actually will see those results, especially in relation to spiritual growth.
- You don't see much use for teaching that doesn't give practical instruction.
- When you counsel others, you prefer to observe their facial responses rather than to correspond with them remotely, such as with a letter.
- If someone comes to you with a need for counsel, you quickly make yourself available to him or her, even if it means sacrificing family time or other activities you had planned to do.
- It gives you special delight to relate examples of success or to use illustrations of failure as effective teaching tools.
- Finishing a project is not nearly as exciting as starting a project.
- You tend to identify with people "where they are" in order to counsel them effectively.
- Enthusiasm is something that you tend to exhibit regularly.
- Your confidence in the loving sovereignty of God tends to make you a hopeful, positive person.
- You see trials as opportunities to grow spiritually rather than as reasons to despair.
- As you study God's Word, you often discern principles and patterns that should be followed.
- When someone is facing a hard situation, you are eager to support and encourage him, to come alongside him as needed.
- In your eagerness to bless someone with encouragement, sometimes you find yourself oversimplifying a solution in order to help the needy person get over his or her reluctance to embrace your counsel and give it a try.

Person Number Six

- When others have practical needs, you tend to notice them before everyone else does.

- It gives you pleasure to help others, especially if your assistance with a practical need will free him or her to carry out more important responsibilities.
- You are willing to neglect your own work in order to help others.
- As a particularly diligent person, sometimes you foolishly go beyond your physical limits and suffer for it.
- You seem to have a special ability to remember what people like and dislike, and you enjoy using this knowledge to bless them.
- You wonder why other people don't respond to needs that are so obvious to you.
- To get a job done, you are willing not only to invest your time and energy, but you are often willing to invest your resources as well.
- It's hard for you to say no when someone asks you for help.
- You enjoy putting "extra touches" on things you do for others.
- You are dependable and hardworking.
- You don't mind doing a job by yourself, but a slothful person disgusts you.
- You don't seek out public recognition for your efforts, but you do enjoy being appreciated.
- You'd rather get busy than stand around talking about it.
- Sometimes time limits frustrate you.
- You'd much rather do a job yourself than delegate it to an unreliable helper.
- When volunteers are requested, you find yourself being one of the first to raise your hand.

Person Number Seven

- When you learn about a Godly ministry, you find yourself wanting to contribute to that ministry.
- You tend to stay out of the limelight.
- You are frugal, especially with your own resources.
- You have an uncanny ability to recognize opportunities to make money.
- When you give monetary gifts to others, you prefer to do so in secret rather than overtly.
- When you hear pressure appeals for money, you tend to react negatively.
- You want your gifts (time, money, resources, energy) to encourage others to give.
- You expect others, especially those in authority, to be frugal and accountable for all decisions, especially financial decisions.
- When you become aware of a need that others have overlooked or ignored, it gives you delight to help meet that need.
- You'd rather pay a little more to get excellent quality than save a small percentage and get the cheap version.
- Learning that your gift was an answer to prayer gives you particular satisfaction and joy.
- You rarely, if ever, incur debt, even in tough times.
- You tend to evaluate spirituality in terms of resources, accountability, and dependability.
- Saving money gives you almost as much pleasure as making money!
- When you give to a family, an individual, or a ministry, you frequently enjoy getting more personally involved with that family, individual, or ministry if the opportunity to do so arises.
- Sometimes others accuse you of being too focused on getting the best deal and taking too long to do that.
- Sometimes others accuse you of been stingy.

Which One Best Describes You?

Discerning which person above best describes you will help you identify your motivational gift. If you are most like:

- **Person Number One,** you probably have the motivational gift of **teaching**.
- **Person Number Two,** you probably have the motivational gift of **organizing**.
- **Person Number Three,** you probably have the motivational gift of **prophecy**.
- **Person Number Four,** you probably have the motivational gift of **mercy**.
- **Person Number Five,** you probably have the motivational gift of **exhortation**.
- **Person Number Six,** you probably have the motivational gift of **serving**.
- **Person Number Seven,** you probably have the motivational gift of **giving**.

Discovering and embracing your *prominent three or four* motivational gifts will help you grow in Godly-character to advance the Kingdom of God.

Carrying forth social reform by her Christian legacy

Harriet Beecher Stowe

[5]Within a decade of publishing *Uncle Tom's Cabin*, Stowe was greeted by President Lincoln at the White House in 1862. "Is this the little woman whose book started this great war?" Whether Lincoln uttered these specific words (or made any similar observation) is unknown. Yet, the anecdote does reveal the extent to which Stowe had already become a famous cultural spokesperson. She championed the American civil religion, articulated a conservative message of women's rights and motherhood, and envisioned a Christian America unified around a strong embrace of Scripture.

In short, Stowe gradually became a recognized cultural heavyweight with wide ranging political influence—one of the first American women to achieve that stature.

As great as her reputation was during her lifetime, *Uncle Tom's Cabin* began taking some critical hits with the advent of a new century. There arose a more modern temperament in literature that grimaced at the book's appeals to sentiment and faith. As a consequence, Stowe's masterpiece was relegated to the ash heap of literary history. But Stowe has been making a comeback…

---

[5] Koester, Nancy, author "Harriet Beecher Stowe on the Christian Life" Journal of Lutheran Ethics

Harriet Beecher Stowe

Historic Putnam located in Zanesville, Ohio

Harriet Beecher Stowe was a devout Christian and abolitionist. In 1852, she popularized the anti-slave movement with her best-selling novel, *Uncle Tom's Cabin.* She brought clarity to the harsh reality of slavery in an artistic way that greatly strengthened Northern abolitionism. The most influential novel ever written by an American, it was one of the contributing causes of the Civil War.

Stowe spent meaningful time with her brother, a noted abolitionist, Reverend William Beecher, the first minister of the Putnam Presbyterian Church, a stop on the Underground Railroad in Zanesville, Ohio.

The Wise Women Council advocacy desires to advance Stowe's legacy by birthing future writers and strengthening the Power of Voice for social justice and the peaceful resolution of racial tensions. Christian values are advanced through future writers and publications that promote the Kingdom of God and the charitable acts of mercy motivated by Christ Jesus.

This book cover features the statue of *Peace,* located on the north side of Capital Square at the Ohio State House in Columbus, Ohio. This winged angel, clad in flowing garments is holding an olive branch, the universal symbol of peace.

This statue was erected soon after the completion of the First World War. This monument honors those who served in the American Civil War.

The Woman's Relief Corps, the auxiliary of the largest and most influential Civil War veterans' organization, the Grand Army of the Republic, commissioned the statue from Bruce

Wilder Saville, a faculty member of The Ohio State University. The statue was unveiled in 1923, and in honoring service during the Civil War, recognized the contributions of the troops on the battle field and the women they left behind.

Last August 2020, with my newly acquired family inheritance, I purchased a house in Zanesville, Ohio for a spiritual daughter who had been homeless for a year. We co-own this historic home built in the late 1800's. It's been a work in progress since it was sold under-market value as a fixer-upper.

My novel, HIDDEN is historical fiction that takes place in Putnam, Ohio in 1851 before the American Civil War. My hope is that this story will become recommended reading for Black History Month.

This mystery/suspense adventure unfolds through the eyes of a precocious nine-year-old bi-racial child who yearns to find her missing mother. Treated as an indentured servant in a Savannah, Georgia home of a wicked woman (wearer of the bloodstone ring with alleged mystical powers) Lilly is unaware that she is the daughter of a white mother of royal society in England. Lilly is later sold into slavery to pay off gambling debts to a slave trader. Years earlier, her mother was told that her baby Lilly had died in route to America (to hide from high-brow English society).

To write Lilly's story that advances race reconciliation, I did vast research about this dark time in American history, reading actual slave narratives, biographies of abolitionists and brave Underground Railroad conductors like Harriet Tubman.

Of course, I read *Uncle Tom's Cabin* by Harriet Beecher Stowe. I was deeply moved by the fictional character, Uncle Tom, whose honorable life was based on Josiah Henson, a former slave who revealed his horrific life to Stowe. I wondered how "Uncle Tom" had developed into a racial slur by my lifetime.

Thankfully, the racial slur-mystery has been solved by Canadian author Jared Brock. Jay produced a riveting documentary entitled "Redeeming Uncle Tom: The Josiah Henson Story." Actor Danny Glover plays Uncle Tom. It is a film worth watching because Harriet's beloved Uncle Tom returns as the original and genuine hero who never lost his faith in Christ Jesus.

When I landed in Zanesville, I was extremely delighted to learn that Harriet Beecher Stowe had a spiritual history in this city through her brother, Reverend William Beecher, an abolitionist who pastored the Putnam Presbyterian Church. The Putnam Underground Railroad is located in the historic district of Zanesville.

While helping to restore my recently purchased historic home, I discovered a boarded-up mansion located on a prominent ridge overlooking downtown Zanesville. *What a perfect place for a cultural art center,* I imagined after passing it several times. I made inquiries and learned that this town is top-heavy with gifted artists, galleries and art classes. In fact, author Frank Rocco Satullo, publisher of *The Ohio Traveler* wrote a piece called "Ohio's Art Town."

As a writer and an advocate, my passion led back Harriet Beecher Stowe and her achievements in advancing social justice and fueling the Civil War effort to end slavery.

Thus, the vision for the future "Harriet Beecher Stowe Center for Creative Writing & Learning Language Arts," was birthed with encouragement from city leaders and fellow artists.

My most earnest prayer is to honor the *Christian* legacy of Harriet Beecher Stowe and her cry for social justice. By demonstrating our charitable acts of service among the poor and disadvantaged in our society, we become the Light of Christ to bring hope to others.

Midwest Book Review
HIDDEN
Scheduled for 2025 publication

In the 1840s, love between a white woman and any man of color is verboten. The result of the union of an English noblewoman, Lady Carmen, and Jamaican man Jake thus leads to a love child who is banished without knowledge of her heritage, leading to a series of events that involves young Lily in kidnapping, the slave trade, and a mysterious and powerful Baroness who wears a mysterious bloodstone ring with demonic powers.

The stage is set for high drama and tension, and in this story does not disappoint. HIDDEN provides a whirlwind of adventure laced with social inspection as Lily traverses her world, faces abandonment and danger, and embarks on a long road to find home, her roots, and the truth about her heritage.

Unexpectedly, the heart of *HIDDEN* is actually synthesized in its introductory paragraph: "*The ancient road crossed the entrance to her father's brewery, taking a sharp turn to the south once it passed the massive stone buildings that produced England's favorite ale. The road was well traveled. For centuries, neighboring Scotsmen used this trail since it was the easiest and shortest route to the mining town she was from. No one in Carmen Wright's family considered the history of this matter, nor did one consider that notables of the highest court also once traveled the same path.*"

Historical precedent, well-worn paths chosen without regard for or knowledge of their past, and easy routes which turn into complex entanglements all permeate a story line replete with satisfyingly thought-provoking stories as a young girl's destiny turns out to reflect the greater social and political changes of her times.

The ideal reader of *HIDDEN* will appreciate the history dashed with fantasy in a rollicking read that features abolitionists, private detectives, Dutch slave traders, racial and social issues, Christian sentiment and spiritual determination, and more. Many candid, raw emotional moments are presented as nine-year-old Lilly considers her world and its options, forging a path for survival against all odds and assessing the potential salvation of faith: "*Lilly wished she had their enthusiasm for God. It seemed so genuine. There wasn't anything fake about it because they seemed to have unfeigned faith in God. She sensed they loved Jesus with all their heart and soul. She admired such demonstration of happiness even though she felt very sad inside.*"

The result is not a singular focus or production, but a wider-ranging, sweeping blend of history, religion, and social issues in a coming of age story especially recommended for historical and religious fiction readers who like their novels complex, enlightening, and absorbing.

D. Donovan, Sr. Reviewer
Midwest Book Review

A special exhortation from Barbara...

My sincerest prayer in life is to advance the Kingdom of God by inspiring volunteerism and community involvement to encourage race relations. The following agencies offer help to the downtrodden who cross your path or enter your church seeking help.

Through prayer, please do all you can to offer assistance. Our beautiful country has countless agencies that help the poor and disadvantaged. God will reward your good works to help humanity. They also offer volunteer opportunities!

God has chosen the poor of this world who are rich in faith—Salvation is gained by keeping the whole law—Faith without works is dead. James 2:14-26

I pray you become a participant in the *Wise Women Council* movement to advance the Gospel of Jesus Christ through acts of charity and goodwill. It begins with a decision to make a difference with the God-given gifts and talents you possess!

You can recruit other Titus 2 women in your congregation. Round up a team of dedicated ladies to pray for open doors. God will give creative ways to reach the lost with the Light of Christ Jesus.

"*Let your light so shine before men, that they may see your good works and glorify your Father who is in heaven*" Matthew 5:16 KJV

Thank you for reading these stories that I have collected over the years. I trust you have been encouraged and inspired to get involved in your church or community to be a light for Jesus!

If you are seeking a meaningful relationship with the Lord Jesus Christ, please confess the following prayer with an honest heart to make Him Lord of your life.

Dearest Heavenly Father,

Thank you for dying on the Cross for my sins. I confess that I am a sinner. I accept Jesus Christ as my personal savior because I need saving from my destructive path.

I pray my life pleases you by my love for others. Teach me to lovingly consider those in need as your special children. Help me have a heart of mercy to help those you place in my path by divine connections.

Teach me Your ways to follow in Your divine path of righteousness. Thank you for grace to obey when you lead me through difficult situations.

Please increase my faith as I extend love to those less lovely. Please remind me to pray

for those crossing my path at every intersection in life.

I love you Lord. I am so grateful for your love and acceptance of me.

Teach me to sing new songs of deliverance whenever life seems hard. Help me always be an example of Your Light and Love. That is my heart's desire.

I pray this book and these stories will encourage others to be faithful to You and to sacrifice time and resources for the sake of others. And bless them when they do, Lord. This world needs Your love.

You are the true source of any goodness we extend on Your behalf. Thank you for helping us see the beauty in others because we are fearfully and wonderfully made and marvelous are the works of Your Hands.

"For I know the plans I have for you," declares the Lord, "plans to prosper you and not harm you, plans to give you hope and a future." Jeremiah 29:11.

For those interested in becoming part of the *Wise Women Council* community outreach, I encourage you to start-out with a home Bible study to include neighbors and friends.

Please contact *Stonecroft Ministries*, which is an excellent resource for guidance with countless published Bible studies and also offering community outreach programs.

Stonecroft has been in successful operation for over 80-years!

Fifty-years ago, I accepted the Lord Jesus into my heart at a *Stonecroft* neighborhood bible study and my life was forever changed. I am eternally grateful for this excellent nationwide ministry. There is also a monthly luncheon in most cities where Stonecroft ministries is represented.

For further information please visit their website at www.stonecroft.org

Stonecroft Ministries

P.O. Box 8900
Kansas City, MO 64114

800-525-8627
Email: connections@stonecroft.org

National Directory of Agency Help

The *Wise Women Council* salutes the following national agencies that help men, women and families achieve assistance.

The United States of America offers protective aid to every human need through faith-based and government agencies. Most Christians desire to help the poor and disadvantaged, but they might not know where to seek available support. Volunteer advocate and author, Barbara Taylor Sanders spent a lifetime learning to network with agencies for fund-raising and raising social consciousness to the needs of the impoverished. This scripture-based discussion guide is a tool for wise, mature women to become Titus 2 mentors to younger women. These inspiring and motivating testimonies have advanced the Kingdom of God through sacrificial acts of charity and goodwill. These human stories are a close glimpse into the lives of those once struggling to exist and finding refuge and healing in Christ Jesus by dedicated Christians lighting the way to freedom.

This author now resides in Florida, so these agencies are mostly located accordingly. However, these national websites extend help in all U.S. cities and states.

Economic Stability

Florida Department of Children & Families
www.MyFLFamilies.com
Applications taken for public assistance and caseworker assignment

Lutheran Services Florida Case Management Organization
Https://www.Lsfnet.org

Employment and Transitional Services for Ex-Felons

The purpose of ex-offender reentry programs is to mitigate these problems to allow the offender to concentrate on adjusting to life on the outside. Many of the following programs offer short term house, job assistance and often have other spiritual and therapy aspects in the program.

Prison Fellowship-Advocating for Justice
www.prisonfellowship.org/

Prison Fellowship is the world's largest Christian nonprofit organization for prisoners, former prisoners, and their families, and a leading advocate for justice reform. We have programs in prisons around the world that re prove to restore prisoners, help their families, and integrate them back into the community—for good!

2nd Chance
www.americanhoperesources.com/
Mental Health Center, Substance Abuse

Haven of Hope
http://havenofhopehc.org/

One Way Out Ministries
http://onewayout.org

Florida Employment Directory for the Benefit of Ex-Felons and the Homeless provided by Order of Malta, American Association
https://orderofmaltaamerican.org

Programs for ex-felons in Florida
www.felonopportunities.com
Remar USA
www.remarusa.org
Rehab Ministry located in Clewiston, Miami and Lakeland
They provide housing, food and Christian ministry

Work Force Central Florida (WCF)
www.greatnonprofits.org
Job training
Project 180
www.project180reentry.org
Reentry program for male prisoners

Florida Reentry Programs and Assistance
www.dc.state.fl.us
FDOC Reentry Resources Directory

Housing

Florida Housing Coalition
www.flhousing.org

Public Housing
www.PublicHousing.com
Affordable rental housing. Most property listings are Section 8 and HUD subsidized.

Senior Low-Income Housing
www.After55.com

Homeless Shelters
www.homelessshelterdirectory.com

Food Assistance

Electric Benefits Transfer (EBT)
www.myfamilies.com
http://www.fns.usda.gov
Apply for Supplemental Nutrition Assistance Program (SNAP). Eligibility is based on income.

Women Infants and Children (WIC)
www.floridahealth.gov
Child rearing programs offered, along with baby formula, milk, fruit, and other free nutritious food items at participating grocery's.

The Emergency Food Assistance Program (TEFAP)
www.feedamerica.org
Harry Chapin Food Bank
www.harrychapinfoodbank.org

Finding a Food Pantry
www.PantryNet.org

Food for Shut-Ins and the Elderly

Meals on Wheels
MOW@communitycooperative.com

Seniors, the disabled or chronically ill adults (under sixty) can receive a daily meal delivered by volunteers.

F.I.S.H "Friends in Serving Humanity"
www.fishcharity.org
Community volunteer run emergency food service delivered to those shut-in due to surgery recovery, short-term medical need or the elderly.

Education

Florida—GED
www.ged.com
High School Equivalency Diploma Program—General Educational Development

Early Childhood Education and Development
https://www.cdc.gov

Head Start
www.flheadstart.org

Florida Literacy Coalition
www.floridaliteracy.org

Florida Department of Education
www.fldoe.org

Federal Pell Grant
www.pell-grants.org
Open to any citizen with extreme financial need.

Federal Supplemental Educational Opportunity Grant (FSEOG)
www.fseog.com

Open to incarcerated felons:
Grants through State and Federal assistance is available to qualifying ex-offenders through the agencies listed under transitional services.

U.S. Department of Labor
www.DOL.gov.home
The DOL offers employment, training programs and other services for dislocated workers, Indian and Native American programs, Job Corps, migrant and seasonal farmworkers, people with disabilities.

Crisis Pregnancy Agencies
www.prolifeacrossamerica.org
www.guardlifenow.com

Free pregnancy test, ultrasound, counseling, prenatal vitamins, baby layettes, diaper bags, formula & bottles with additional guidance after baby is born.

Childcare Assistance

Government programs helping pay for childcare
www.Childcare.gov

Health and Mental Health Care

Poison Control Center:
(800) 222-1222
Available 24 hours every day

National Suicide Prevention Lifeline:
800-273-8255
Counselors available 24 hours every day
www.suicidepreventionlifeline.org

National Domestic Violence Hotline
1-800-799-SAFE (7233)
www.thehotline.org

Substance Abuse and Mental Health Services Administration (SMAHSA)
http://www.samhsa.gov

National Institute on Drug Abuse (NIDA)
http://www.drugabuse.gov

Abuse Counseling and Treatment, Inc. (ACT)
ACT serves victims of domestic violence and their children and survivors of sexual assault.
Ft. Myers, FL (239) 939-2553
Most major cities offer similar programs

Alcoholics Anonymous
www.aa.org

National Council on Problem Gambling
http://www.ncpgambling.org

Normal, Problematic and Compulsive Consumption of Sexually Explicit Media
http://www.ncbi.nih.gov

Society for the Advancement of Sexual Health
www.SASH.net

Teen Challenge

www.teenchallengeusa.org

A national Christian residential treatment program for substance abuse. A six to nine-month commitment for adult men or women (of all ages) with a proven 70 percent success rate for those who finish the program.

The website for each agency represents the national organization. The website will direct you to state assistance and other important information offering assistance.

Agencies for Ministry Opportunities:

Bridge of Hope

Founder: Pastor Rod Parsley
World Harvest Church
4595 Gender Road
Canal Winchester, OH 43110
Phone (614) 837-1990
Email: customerservice@rodparsley.com

Cook International

4050 Lee Vance View
Colorado Springs, CO 80918
Telephone: (719) 536-0100
Email: suzanne.ralston@cookinternational.org

Life Reach International

Founder: James Robison
P.O. Box 982000
Fort Worth, TX 76182-8000
Phone: 1-800-947-LIFE (5433)

Promise Keepers

Founder: Bill McCartney
P.O. Box 11798
Denver, CO 80211-0798
1-866-PROMISE (1-866-776-6473)

Samaritan's Purse

Founder: Franklin Graham
P.O. Box 3000
Boone, NC 28607
Phone (828) 262-1980

Teen Mania

Founder: Ron Luce
P.O. Box 2000,
Garden Valley, TX 75771
Contact Us: 1.800.229.8336

Youth with a Mission (YWAM)

Founder: Loren & Darlene Cunningham
75-5851 Kuakini Hwy
Kailua-Kona, HI 96740
USA
Phone: 1-808-326-7228

Support for Pregnant Women and Children:

Feminists for Life of America

P.O Box 320667
Alexandria, VA 22320
www.feministsforlife.org
www.KidsOnAShoestring.com

National Right to Life Committee

512 10th St. NW
Washington, DC 20004(202) 626-8800
NRLC@nrlc.org

North American Council on Adoptable Children (NACAC)

970 Raymond Avenue, Suite 106
St. Paul, MN 55114
Phone: 651-644-3036
Email: info@nacac.org

Help for Families in Crisis

Alcoholics Anonymous (A.A. Chapters)

A.A. World Services, Inc.,
11th Floor 475 Riverside Drive at West 120th St.
New York, NY 10115
(212) 870-3400

National Coalitions Against Domestic Violence (NCADV)

1120 Lincoln Street, Suite #1603
Denver, CO 80203
Phone: (303) 839-1852
TTY: (303) 839-8459

Email: mainoffice@ncadv.org

Teen Challenge

Founder: David Wilkerson
Teen Challenge International, USA
5250 N Towne Centre Dr
Ozark, MO 65721
(417) 581-2181 phone
(417) 581-2195 fax
Email: info@teenchallengeusa.com

Suicide Prevention Resource Center (SPRC)

1-800-TALK-8255
55 Chapel Street, Newton, MA 02458
877- 438-7772
Email: info@sprc.org

About Barbara Taylor Sanders
Author/Advocate/Artist

Barbara is a versatile writer of literary fiction and inspirational non-fiction books.

As a lifelong advocate residing in Columbus, Ohio, she spent years of volunteer service in *Children's Hospital* and *Scioto Village Correctional Institute.*

Along with her husband, Daryl, they pioneered *Zion Christian Fellowship* in 1985. During those thirteen-years of pastoral leadership, they organized numerous goodwill and evangelistic trips to China, Africa, Russia and the Ukraine.

Current affiliations are memberships with *Christian Women in Media & Speaker's Bureau and National League of American Pen Women.* One of her oil canvases earned the first-place award in the annual May Flowers contest at the Cape Coral Arts Studio in 2014.

While living in Columbus for over 35-years, Barbara served on the trustee board of *Teen Challenge* while being actively involved with *Women in Philanthropy, Action for Children,* and the *Association of Fundraising Professionals.*

As the past president of the *Columbus Christian Writers Association* for over ten-years, she has also taught creative writing at the Cape Coral Art Studio.

Producing a talk-show program on a local Christian radio station gave her an opportunity to interview executive directors of non-profits to promote volunteerism. Her monthly television show was called *The Good Book Review,* featuring authors of Christian publications.

Both Daryl and Barbara both served on the executive board of *The 1993 Billy Graham Crusade* and she was also co-chair of the women's committee, recruiting 4,000 women volunteers from the one-thousand churches involved from every county in Ohio.

One Foundation was a philanthropic 501c3 charity organization they formed to provide economic support to financially struggling inner-city ministries working among the poor and disadvantaged. On April 3, 1993 Barbara was personal hostess to Mrs. Coretta Scott King in honor of the 25th anniversary of Dr. Martin Luther King, Jr.'s death. The event was sponsored by *One Foundation* for race reconciliation.

The *Wise Women Council* was birthed by Barbara's friend, the late Olivia Weatherly, who passed away in 2019 after life-long faithful Christian service. Olivia's brother, Ohio Senator Ray

Miller, had challenged his sister to advance the Kingdom of God by inspiring wise women to mentor younger women in the ways of the Lord. Ray's challenging words were like apples of gold in frames of silver.

Barbara has been married to Daryl Sanders for 52-years. They have five-children and four-grandchildren. As a graduate of Ohio State University, Daryl played offensive tackle in a Big Ten championship football game before being drafted as a number-one draft pick for the NFL. Daryl is a gifted teacher who has authored several in-depth scripture studies for the serious Bible student.

They have resided in Southwest Florida since 2010 and remain active in prophetic church ministry and evangelistic mission work to the nations.

Barbara's books are listed on this website: www.barbarataylorsanders.com
She can be reached by email: expressimagepublications@gmail.com

WISE WOMEN COUNCIL

EIN 88-3378470

The Corporation's charitable purpose includes relief of the poor, the distressed, or the underprivileged; advancement of religion; advancement of education or science; erecting or maintaining public buildings, monuments, or works; lessening the burdens of government; lessening neighborhood tensions; eliminating prejudice and discrimination; defending human and civil rights secured by law; and combating community deterioration.

In carrying out such exempt purposes within the meaning of Section 501(c)(3) of the Internal Revenue Code, the Corporation may engage in any lawful act, activity or business not contrary to and in which a nonprofit corporation may engage under Chapter 1702 of the Ohio Revised Code, including, but not limited to, the following:

1. (a) To carry forth as a human rights, social justice, and community-minded entity;

2. (b) To support and fund social agencies that offer solutions to end poverty-related problems such as illiteracy, domestic violence, drug and alcohol-related crime, hunger and homelessness;
3. (c) To advance efforts in the future downtown Zanesville river front development plans and protect the valuable historic anti-slavery Putnam district.

All tax-deductible financial donations to Wise Women Council are greatly appreciated. Mailing address is 1624 Emerald Cove Drive, Cape Coral, FL 33991.
For questions concerning this 501c3 foundation, please call 614-306-3637.

Filename: Wise Women Council BOOK.docx
Directory: /Users/owner/Documents
Template: /Users/owner/Library/Group Containers/UBF8T346G9.Office/User Content.localized/Templates.localized/Normal.dotm
Title:
Subject:
Author: Microsoft Office User
Keywords:
Comments:
Creation Date: 7/27/24 9:58:00 AM
Change Number: 3
Last Saved On: 7/27/24 9:59:00 AM
Last Saved By: Barbara Sanders
Total Editing Time: 2 Minutes
Last Printed On: 7/27/24 10:22:00 AM
As of Last Complete Printing
    Number of Pages: 214
    Number of Words: 68,120 (approx.)
    Number of Characters: 388,289 (approx.)

Made in the USA
Columbia, SC
03 August 2024

9e94e05f-a664-4aa9-a9ec-23c24bffedf4R01